HOW TO TURN
COMPUTER PROBLEMS
INTO
COMPETITIVE
ADVANTAGE

TOM INGRAM

Library of Congress Cataloging-in-Publication Data

Ingram, Tom.
    How to turn computer problems into competitive advantage / Tom
Ingram.
        p.   cm.
    Includes bibliographical references and index.
    ISBN: 1-880410-08-7 (pbk. : alk. paper)
    1. Client/server computing--Costs. 2. Industrial project
management. 3. Competition. I. Title.
QA76.9.C55I44 1998
004' .36' 068 – – dc21   98–22351
                                                                CIP

Published by: Project Management Institute Headquarters
                Four Campus Boulevard, Newtown Square, Pennsylvania 19073-3299 USA
                Phone: 610-356-4600 or Visit our website: www.pmi.org

ISBN: 1-880410-08-7

PMI Book Team
Editor-in-Chief, James S. Pennypacker
Editor, Toni D. Knott
Proofreader, Lisa M. Fisher
Graphic Designer, Michelle T. Owen
Graphic Designer, Allison S. Boone
Acquisitions Editor, Bobby R. Hensley
Production Coordinator, Mark S. Parker

PMI books are available at special quantity discounts to use as premiums and sales
promotions, or for use in corporate training programs. For more information, please
write to the Business Manager, PMI Publishing Division, Forty Colonial Square, Sylva,
NC 28779 USA. Or contact your local bookstore.

The paper used in this book complies with the Permanent Paper Standard issued by the
National Information Standards Organization (Z39.48—1984).

PMBOK™ is a trademark and PMP® is a registered certification mark of the
Project Management Institute.

10 9 8 7 6 5 4 3 2 1

DEDICATION

The fear of the Lord is the beginning of knowledge.

Proverbs 1:7

Thousands of years ago God inspired men to write down His Word, which became our modern-day Bible. Among these words we learn about loving our God, loving our neighbor, and redemption from our sin and failings through the risen Christ.

Among those truths, we also find instruction for conducting business. We learn that the Book of Proverbs was written so that we might "receive instruction in wise behavior, Righteousness, justice, and equity" (Proverbs 1:3).

The research conducted for this book shows that foolish, corrupt leadership is costing shareholders billions of dollars, just as the Bible predicts. We also see that the solution to those problems is based on returning to a Godly standard of leadership integrity. This book is dedicated to the Living God, whose Word, again, proves true.

> An excellent wife, who can find? For her worth is far above jewels. The heart of her husband trusts in her and he will have no lack of gain. Charm is deceitful and beauty is vain, but a woman who fears the Lord shall be praised.

Proverbs 31:10, 11, 30

Some twenty years ago the Lord blessed me with a beautiful wife who fears the Lord. This book is also dedicated to my wife, Jeanette, for her smile, her joy in life, and for standing by me through great testing and trial. Her skills at the *details* have made this book possible. I have found an excellent wife.

TABLE OF CONTENTS

Dedication   v

Forward   xi

Section 1: Some High-Level Conclusions   1
   1.1 The Impact of Bad Computer Projects: Quantifying the Cost   1
   1.2 Understanding the Four Forces That Consistently Damage Projects   4
   1.3 A Cross-Industry Benchmark: How the *75% Gang* Does It Right   8

Section 2: The Current and Future State of Client/Server Project Outcomes   15
   2.1 Good News First: What We Can Learn from the Success Stories   15
   2.2 The Client/Server *Cost of Quality* Findings   16
   2.3 Why Project Management Needs to Become a Core Competency:
       Additional Trends and Facts   29
   2.4 Additional Problems and Trends That Need to Be Addressed   30

Section 3: Key Lessons from Other Industries and the
          Project Management Institute   33
   3.1 PMI Key Lessons   33
   3.2 Some Good News and Rays of Hope   37
   3.3 Some Additional Lessons Learned   39
   3.4 Pulling It All Together: The Project Foundation   41

Section 4: To Investors: Awareness and Warning   43
   4.1 Recognize the Hole in Project Accounting   43
   4.2 Assessing the Immediate Exposure   44
   4.3 Understanding What to Do: A High-Level Flow Chart   48
   4.4 Weighing the Cost and Benefit of Action   48
   4.5 Consider Getting Personally Involved   50

Section 5: Eight Principles for Turning Weaknesses into
          Competitive Advantage   53
   Principle 1: Ownership Involvement and Third Party Monitoring   53
   Principle 2: Initial and Ongoing Cost of Quality Reviews   56
   Principle 3: Getting the Right Expertise on Your Team   57
   Principle 4: The Pilot: A Crucial Small Win   58
   Principle 5: Developing Project Accounting and Management Standards   59
   Principle 6: Grow, Train, and Certify Business Managers, Project Managers, and
           Executives   66
   Principle 7: Organize for a Solid Project Foundation   69
   Principle 8: Fads, Traps, and Dirty Tricks to Avoid   71
   A Summary: Turning Weakness to Competitive Advantage   78

Section 6: The Cases—Horror Stories, Success Stories, and Study Methods   81
   6.1 Horror Stories   81
   6.2 Success Stories   150
   6.3 Study Methodology and Cautions   185

Appendix A: A Summary of Current Research on Client/Server Project Outcomes   187

Appendix B: Glossary of Terms and Definitions   193

Appendix C: A Study of Symptoms   195

Appendix D: Literature Search Results   213

Appendix E: A Cost of Quality Questionnaire   215

Appendix F: Issues for Field Testing and Further Research   219

Appendix G: An Overview of the Differences between Mainframe and Client/Server Computer Systems   221

Appendix H: List of Reviewers and Contributors   225

Appendix I: About the Author   227

Appendix J: A Summary of Projects Studied by Industry   229

Notes   233

Index   235

LIST OF ILLUSTRATIONS

Figures

Figure 1. A Model of Four Forces That Consistently Cause Computer Project Blowups   4

Figure 2. Consolidated Model   6

Figure 3. Cross-Industry Success Rates for Complex Technical Projects   9

Figure 4. Sample Organization Chart for a Department of Defense Contractor (Avionics Subsystem for a Missile)   10

Figure 5. Sample Organization Chart for an Electric Utility Construction Project (Average Conventional Fuel Power Generation Plant)   11

Figure 6. Sample Organization Chart for an Oil Refinery Construction Project   12

Figure 7. The Root Issue Score Card   20

Figure 8. Kerzner's Project Triangle   35

Figure 9. Responsibility Map   41

Figure 10. A Horror Story in the Making? A Sample Earnings Forecast Analysis for Client/Server Exposure   47

Figure 11. What to Do to Turn Client/Server Project Weakness into Strength   49

Figure 12. The Project Foundation   60

Figure 13. Suggested Organization Model (Based on Research Findings)   69

Tables

Table 1. Earnings Improvement for Doing One Horror Story Project Right the First Time   3

Table 2. The Relationship between Original Budget and Total Cost of Quality for Client/Server Horror Stories   18

Table 3. The Correlation between Cost of Quality and Root Issues   21–23

Table 4. Behaviors Observed Where Self Is Put before the Good of the Shareholder   25

Table 5. Additional Questionable Behaviors That Were Observed but Not Cataloged   27

Table 6. Project Phases and Key Objectives   36

Table 7. Contrasts between Being a Project Manager and a *Project Manager*   38–39

Table 8. Horror Story Correlation to Stock Price   45

Table 9. A Sample Budget for Implementing These Recommendations for a $500 Million Manufacturer Over a Three-Year Period   51

Table 10. A Sample Cost of Quality Review   57

Table 11. Misery of Choice and Exponential Complexity   222

Table 12. A Summary of Projects Studied by Industry   230–231

Client/Server and Imaging: On Time, On Budget, As Promised!
Part I: The Client's Perspective   151
    Figure 1. Texas Instruments Client/Server-Imaging Accounts Receivable Project   152

Client/Server, Imaging, and Earned Value: A Success Story
Part II: The Consultant's Perspective   161
    Figure 1. Questioning the Surface Data   162
    Figure 2. Using Earned Value to Find the Answer   163
    Table 1. WBS and Budget-to-Actual Comparison   164

Managing Client/Server and Open Systems Projects:
A Ten-Year Study of Sixty-Two Mission-Critical Projects   196
    Figure 1. Project Outcomes for Forty-Seven Mission-Critical Open Systems Projects   197
    Figure 2. Project Outcome Correlation Ratings   198
    Figure 3. Project Outcome versus Technical Score   206
    Figure 4. Project Outcome versus Project Management Score   207
    Figure 5. Project Manager Skill Mix   208
    Figure 6. Uncertainty, Inadequate Planning, and Impact on Project Completion   209
    Figure 7. Uncertainty, Effective Planning, and Impact on Project Completion   210

FORWARD

Some Words for Those Who Know the Pain

The Beginning of Wisdom ... Not the End

I do not wish to set myself up as anyone special, but you probably want to know my background in order to judge the validity of these recommendations. If you have any interest, you can read more about my fourteen years in the client/server business in Appendix I.

Some Successes and Some Failures

To summarize, I have worked in nearly every role that exists in client/server, from technical to sales to management. I have been blessed with some spectacular successes and humbled by dismal failures. Thanks to my early experiences with Xerox and Sperry Univac, I came to client/server with two core beliefs:

1. Computer systems exist to improve business processes and business results.

2. The good of the customer and the interests of my employer must come before my personal interests.

In the process of standing up for these values I have been dismissed as project manager from a total of six projects. All but one of those projects have turned into Horror Stories.

A Word to Others Who Have Lost Their Jobs
While Trying to Do the Right Things

In 1986 I started my own system integration firm. I thought that I knew enough to deliver fixed-price programming projects on client/server computer systems. I could not have been more wrong. We tried everything to deliver on our promises to the customers, but case numbers 122, 123, and 125 show how badly we performed. My company ultimately went out of business.

My frustration at failing to perform as promised has been a driving factor behind this research. Along the way, I often wondered if I was the problem. *This research concludes that fixing the root problems of client/server projects requires both*:
- improvements in all areas of project management competence
- improved integrity among those in leadership positions.

If you are like me, you are not overly upset at failing because you didn't have necessary skills. We can learn those skills and do better next time. *Failing because someone above me is serving his own interests instead of the good of the project is another matter.* If you have any doubt that this happens, see Section 2.2.7.

One of my greatest personal revelations has been that this integrity issue is the primary cause of project problems, and not me personally. I have been criticized for personality clashes, *style* problems, and nearly every other *subjective* project problem, but it nearly always turned out that someone above was acting for her personal agenda instead of the good of the whole. *If you have stood up for the right things and been penalized, I salute you. You are not alone, and this research should help you understand that you probably were not at fault.*

Time to Take a Stand

I believe that it is time to stand up for leadership integrity in the workplace. Although it is difficult to do, we need to position ourselves so that we are not forced to submit to the whims of those above us, who place their own interests above the good of the shareholder.

Some two years ago, my wife and I decided that I would not accept any role or responsibility that might violate this principle. We have chosen to manage our financial situation in such a way that I could decline assignments if leadership integrity was not present. This has meant some sacrifices, but I wish I had done it ten years ago. It would have saved me a lot of pain.

Only a Beginning

Even with fourteen years in client/server projects, it would be the height of presumption for me to believe that I know it all. We must remember that we are dealing with forces that have toppled giants like IBM. If we accept that leadership integrity is at the heart of the matter, we need to realize that we are dealing with forces of human nature that have shaped history and project management since Rome began building roads.

This book is about fixing root problems. If you have something to contribute, challenge, or correct, contact me at:

Tom Ingram
c/o Project Management Institute
Publishing Division
Forty Colonial Square
Sylva, North Carolina 28779
bookauth@pmi.org

One of my greatest hopes is that we can share information and expertise in this area. Your input is appreciated and needed.

Pardon the Simplification

This book is written for investors and executives, as well as for project managers. Project management practitioners will notice that I have simplified some concepts severely. Academics and statisticians will note that the sample size is small and the statistical treatment is very simple. Technology professionals will probably cringe at the oversimplification of complex computer issues. I ask indulgence for three reasons:

1. My primary goal is to help investors, executives, and project managers recognize a significant set of root problems with computer projects. I am also trying to provide information that will assist in addressing the underlying root issues.

2. The first recommended step is an internal *cost of quality* review to see if a particular organization truly has the risk and expense that the research predicts. We are not asking firms to spend significant money or time based solely on this research.

3. The research and this book are not sponsored by any organization. This has been done to advance my personal ability to help my clients and to advance client/server project effectiveness as a whole. The conclusions are significant enough that I felt it was important to publish them immediately rather than take the time to improve the rigor of the study. I ask my learned colleagues to bear with some liberties taken for the cause of clarity (or help me find a better way to communicate the message)!

Non-Disclosure Issues

Unfortunately, most of the work I have done for clients has been covered by non-disclosure agreements of one form or another. In other cases, the people I interviewed would only speak on condition of anonymity. In this book I have attempted to convey the principles and lessons from these engagements without violating those agreements. Consequently, many company names have been omitted from the Horror Stories.

I intend no harm to any corporation or person. In the event that I have made some mistake and revealed information that should not have become public, I apologize and beg your indulgence for the greater cause of solving this industry-wide problem. In Section 2 we will see how over $2.5 billion has been wasted among these sixty Horror Story projects. While it is natural for any firm to want to suppress the *dirty laundry*, I believe it is time to speak openly of this nightmare and collectively work toward solving the root problems.

Some High-Level Conclusions

In this section we will examine some concepts that should appeal to the interests of high-level executives and investor/owners. In addition, this material can help the project management professional who wishes to present those executives with a case for change.

1.1 The Impact of Bad Computer Projects: Quantifying the Cost

In order to communicate the cost of not doing computer projects right the first time, the study team presents two thought processes: 1) rule of thumb, based on original project budget; and 2) estimating the impact on corporate earnings.

1.1.1 Rule of Thumb, Based on Original Project Budget

Appendix A presents summaries of seven different studies of client/server[1] and information systems projects. Section 2 describes the detailed findings of this research effort. In an attempt to combine the results of all the research and produce a useful rule of thumb, we present the following:

- A *Horror Story* is generally defined by the study team as a project where the direct project costs were ultimately more than twice the original budget.
- Approximately *50 percent of all the computer projects* in the seven studies ultimately cost more than twice their original budget in direct project costs and are, therefore, *classified as Horror Stories.*
- The sixty projects described in this research effort had an average cost of quality[2] (the total cost of not doing the project right the first time) of *between eight and ten times the original project budget.*

Conclusion. By integrating the above three statements, simple math predicts that *the average new computer project will ultimately have a total cost to the organization of between four and five times the original budget.*

1

(**Caution #1**: These are simple averages, and individual results will vary widely. Many projects will ultimately break-even or be mildly profitable. A few will be wildly successful, but many will become serious Horror Stories, costing eight or ten times the original budget. If a project is being contemplated, the reader is cautioned to review the cases in Section 6 and look for similar projects. The lessons of history are quite sobering.)

(**Caution #2**: These rules of thumb are the compilation of eight different studies. The studies varied considerably in approach, rigor, and other factors. The reader is cautioned to treat these rules of thumb as generally accurate but far from perfect in a rigorous, statistical, scientific sense.)

1.1.2 Estimating the Impact on Corporate Earnings

In an effort to further examine the impact of bad computer projects on an organization, the study team selected thirteen case studies for closer scrutiny. These were cases when the firm was publicly held, and we had access to financial statements for the years affected by the bad computer projects.

Recasting Earnings. Our objective was to *examine by how much earnings would have been improved* if these thirteen projects had been done correctly the first time. Since the projects were often multiple year, we allocated the impact over the years most affected. We used the cost of quality figures for each case, as shown in Section 6. Assumptions were made as to likely gross profit margins in the cases where the cost of quality included costs of unrealized sales. Table 1 summarizes the results.

Observations:

1. In these thirteen firms, one bad computer project damaged earnings by nearly 6 percent in a single year.

2. This impact is derived from only one bad project, but we know that 50 percent of new computer projects attain Horror Story status. It is likely that the impact is much greater.

3. Remember that while these firms are not a representative sample, this is the best available data showing the magnitude of impact.

4. Dr. Frank Toney and Ray Powers have researched the same problem with an *executive roundtable* approach. Their approach has presented similar questions to over sixty executive roundtables, looking for a consensus of executive opinion. During an interview with Toney in May 1997, he observed that his research indicated that "earnings for the average U.S. [United States] corporation are probably damaged between 10 and 20% per year by poor project management."[3]

Conclusion. While research methods differ slightly, and solid, representative data is difficult to come by, a finding is beginning to emerge: *It is very likely that the average U.S. corporation wastes between 5 and 20 percent of annual earnings on poor project management.* While industries and companies vary widely, it is likely that improvements in project management root problems hold the promise of improving earnings significantly.

Table 1. Earnings Improvement for Doing One Horror Story Project Right the First Time

Case Name	Case ID	Industry	Total Cost of Quality (COQ) (in $1,000)	Percentage Earnings Improvement
American Airlines (Confirm Project)	101	Airline	$460,000	19.11
Very Large Central United States Bank	107	Financial Services	$6,200	0.77
Greyhound	110	Transportation	$3,500	13.70
Diamond Shamrock	111	Energy	$3,000	2.75
CIGNA	112	Insurance	$4,000	0.57
American Management Systems	113	Computer Software and Services	$2,000	3.74
West Coast Savings and Loan	134	Financial Services	$1,500	0.40
Dallas-Based Telecommunications Manufacturer	137	Manufacturing	$11,500	0.83
Duke Power	153	Utility	$87,000	1.31
FoxMeyer Corp (Delta Project)	155	Medical Supplies	$25,000	5.27
Upper Midwest Steel Manufacturer	158	Manufacturing	$160,000	23.82
Large United States Service Firm	159	Services	$106,000	2.08
Independent Telephone Company	141*	Telecommunications	$875,000	2.27
Average			$134,208	5.89

* Case was too large for meaningful analysis. A COQ is roughly estimated here for order of magnitude impact.

Figure 1. A Model of Four Forces That Consistently Cause Computer Project Blowups

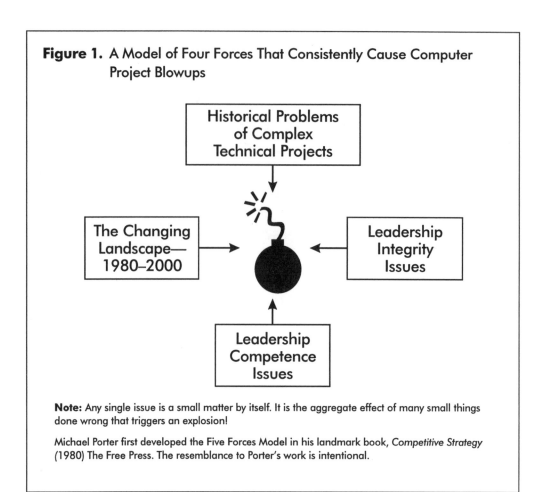

Note: Any single issue is a small matter by itself. It is the aggregate effect of many small things done wrong that triggers an explosion!

Michael Porter first developed the Five Forces Model in his landmark book, *Competitive Strategy* (1980) The Free Press. The resemblance to Porter's work is intentional.

1.2 Understanding the Four Forces That Consistently Damage Projects

1.2.1 The Four Forces Model

Figure 1 is presented to help the reader *think through* the strategic issues that often cause projects to be doomed before they begin. On the following pages a summary of the major aspects of each force is described.

Historical Problems of Complex Technical Projects. From a historical perspective, it might be said that the first complex technical projects were the roads and bridges of Rome, or the Pyramids. Since the beginning of organized human labor, complex technical projects have been fraught with waste, fraud, risk, and poor management. Following are some of the aspects of history that seem to affect computer projects the most.

- The hole in project accounting: General auditing and accounting practices are not able to prevent project disasters.

- Just plain hard to do right the first time: If we look at a new manufacturing process we see that it takes many iterations to achieve cost efficiency and consistent quality. How can we possibly expect to do a complex, intangible project right the first time? Is it reasonable to expect cost efficiency?
- Intangible nature of technical projects breeds corruption: Intangible, technical projects are generally hard to measure. The result is that those charged with using shareholder assets diligently cannot enforce accountability. Projects become skewed to personal interests and, potentially, outright corruption. This is particularly evidenced by the construction industry's history of corruption back as far as Rome building roads.
- The nature of bureaucracy: Any human endeavor, left uncontrolled, will tend to accumulate the self-perpetuating negative attributes of bureaucratic behavior.
- We have to use human beings as executives and managers: When a human being holds power, it is human nature to want to retain that power. Natural tendencies include maneuvering to retain and increase power as well as suppressing any negative information or challenge to that power (as well as the many other faults of human beings in organizations).

Leadership Integrity Issues. While hard to believe, in over 50 percent of the Horror Stories studied, executives were actually observed doing such things as:
- Attempting to personally benefit while actually damaging the project; examples include:
  — positioning scapegoats to take any blame while positioning themselves to receive credit for success
  — trying to draw budgets and personnel under their control (building the empire)
  — redirecting project objectives for personal political gain
  — resume building
  — focus on the appearance of progress rather than actual progress.
- Ego, arrogance, greed, power lust, preoccupation with appearances, and impatience were repeatedly observed. These attitudes often caused significant mistakes and a lack of due diligence.
- Avoiding accountability when things go wrong; introducing change (often large-scale change) to prevent accountability for original promises (as well as for other responsibility avoidance behaviors).
- Resisting recommendations of subordinates and proven best practices; nearly every Horror Story studied included suppression of attempts to improve the situation because the executive perceived a threat to her personal agenda.

Leadership Competence Issues. Executing a significant computer project is very different from running a line organization, yet many of us think we already know how to manage projects. The following issues repeatedly emerged as project management weaknesses (even though the people involved were otherwise quite capable):
- absence of effective project executive and project manager training or certification
- failed match of authority/responsibility/competence (The research repeatedly identified situations when the person that actually held the authority did not allocate the proper time to execute his responsibilities. Responsibility was often delegated to those perceived to have competence, but this repeatedly proved ineffective.)
- failure to separate technical issues from the business purpose of the project
- failure to effectively merge business process issues with computer project constraints

Figure 2. Consolidated Model

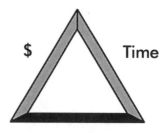

Deliverables

(Quantity, Quality, Technical Effectiveness)

ACCOUNTABILITY

Objectivity	Right People Right Motives Right Actions	Authority/ Responsibility Match

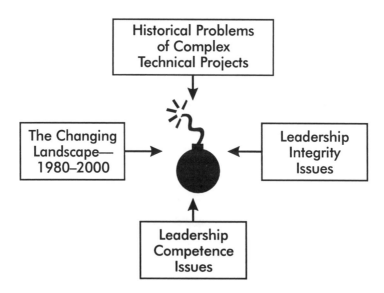

Historical Problems
of Complex
Technical Projects

The Changing
Landscape—
1980–2000

Leadership
Integrity
Issues

Leadership
Competence
Issues

- lack of objective decision-making, including:
  — the business justification for doing the project in the first place
  — effectively thinking through the balance between scope, cost, and deadlines
  — objective technical design.
- breakdown of accountability
- traditional business axioms that are counterproductive (Several standard business tactics are actually damaging to computer projects; these include the following.)
  — When in doubt, spend money, hire people, and look busy.
  — Charge ahead!
  — Always appear confident; never admit uncertainty.
  — Never admit a lack of personal skills.
- board of directors and executive compensation committee issues. Evidence is emerging to indicate that management may have some counterproductive incentives. The tangible and intangible reward systems in corporations tend to reward the following behaviors, even though they are damaging to project outcomes:
  — accumulating and retaining power
  — doing anything possible to accomplish quarterly gains
  — keeping your job/power/empire at all costs
  — Wall Street rewards anything that creates the perception of growth—take risks, no matter how big!

The Changing Landscape, 1980–2000. Many factors have arisen in the last twenty years that actually damage our ability to execute projects. These include the following:

- Downsizing has had several effects, including:
  — There is a reduction in the number of people with significant project management track records.
  — Profit gains from downsizing are largely gone; growth is now required. Profit gains from growth will be more difficult to attain and will result in an increasing number of projects.
- By and large, current project managers are:
  — under trained
  — under qualified
  — under resourced
  — fundamentally unable to deliver as expected for reasons not under their control.
- Project management does not attract talented people as a career option. This may be changing, but it is certainly a cause of great concern if our objective is to consistently improve project outcomes. For many of the reasons described throughout this text, many capable people are attracted to other career paths.
- Significantly more projects are now required. Several factors have caused the overall number of projects to rise dramatically, including the following:
  — Client/server is replacing the mainframe as the dominant computing environment.
  — Shorter product life cycles require more computer projects to support new products.
  — Shorter organization life cycles create more computer projects.
  — The information revolution has caused the execution of computer projects to increase in strategic importance.
- The year 2000 is looming; large numbers of additional projects will be required to convert existing computer systems to systems that can handle the date change to the year 2000.

1.2.2 A Consolidated Model for *Thinking through* Root Issues

The study team presents the *consolidated* model in Figure 2 to help understand the relationship between the *front-line* project work (the triangle), the root issues (the stool), and the four strategic forces. While many project management books will address issues at the front line, we can begin to see how a project may easily be doomed from the start because of root issue problems or strategic forces. We perhaps can begin to understand why 50 percent of all computer projects turn out to be Horror Stories. (See the above discussion of the four forces and Section 2 and Section 5 for checklists and suggestions for thinking through *your* root problems and strategic forces—and how to take steps to correct them!)

1.3 A Cross-Industry Benchmark: How the *75% Gang* Does It Right

1.3.1 The Single Most Important Finding

As we see in the studies of Appendix A, and as developed in the Section 2 conclusions, commercial computer projects currently perform very poorly.[4] They are on time, on budget, and as promised only about 30 to 35 percent of the time. This leads us to ask several questions:

1. Is this terrible level of performance a simple fact of life (as some would have us believe)?

2. Is there any reason to believe significant improvement is possible?

3. Are there any precedents from history or other industries that can help us improve?

For the last fifteen years, the Project Management Institute (PMI) has advocated a cross-industry, historical view of project management. We owe a great debt of thanks to PMI and its visionary people. PMI has made possible the compilation of the following cross-industry, historical benchmark: *To compare the success rates of complex, long-term technical projects from three other industries against the success rates of commercial computer projects.*

Project Success Definition. A project was considered successful if it was on time, on budget, and performed as promised. (**Note**: Due to difficulties in comparing vastly different projects, industries, and study data, the statistics presented in Figure 3 should be interpreted as generally accurate, plus or minus 5 percent, unless otherwise noted.)

The Single Most Important Finding of This Entire Body of Research. History and cross-industry precedents show that it is possible to improve the success rate of commercial computer projects by double or threefold! Stop for a moment and contemplate the implications. If your organization can raise the success rate for computer projects from 35 to 75 percent, the following things would probably happen:

1. Your firm would plug a leak that is probably costing 5 percent of earnings per year or more (almost certainly saving millions of dollars)!

2. Your firm would double or triple its ability to execute cost reduction and revenue enhancement projects.

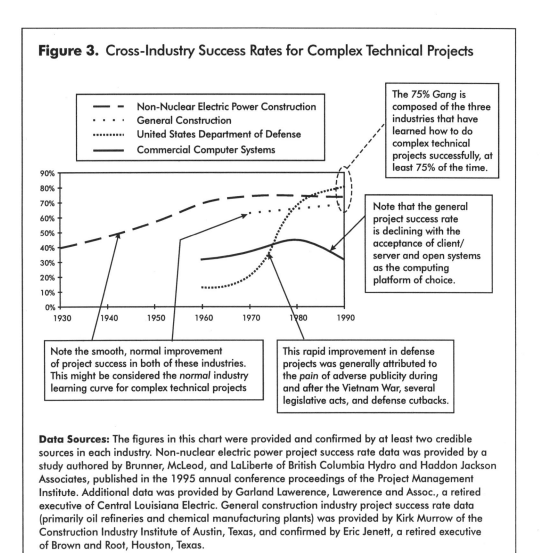

Figure 3. Cross-Industry Success Rates for Complex Technical Projects

Legend:
- — — Non-Nuclear Electric Power Construction
- · · · · General Construction
- ·········· United States Department of Defense
- —— Commercial Computer Systems

The *75% Gang* is composed of the three industries that have learned how to do complex technical projects successfully, at least 75% of the time.

Note that the general project success rate is declining with the acceptance of client/server and open systems as the computing platform of choice.

Note the smooth, normal improvement of project success in both of these industries. This might be considered the *normal* industry learning curve for complex technical projects

This rapid improvement in defense projects was generally attributed to the *pain* of adverse publicity during and after the Vietnam War, several legislative acts, and defense cutbacks.

Data Sources: The figures in this chart were provided and confirmed by at least two credible sources in each industry. Non-nuclear electric power project success rate data was provided by a study authored by Brunner, McLeod, and LaLiberte of British Columbia Hydro and Haddon Jackson Associates, published in the 1995 annual conference proceedings of the Project Management Institute. Additional data was provided by Garland Lawerence, Lawerence and Assoc., a retired executive of Central Louisiana Electric. General construction industry project success rate data (primarily oil refineries and chemical manufacturing plants) was provided by Kirk Murrow of the Construction Industry Institute of Austin, Texas, and confirmed by Eric Jenett, a retired executive of Brown and Root, Houston, Texas.

3. You would gain competitive advantage because your competitors would still be floundering with the status quo.

Additional Observations, Interpretations, and Conclusions.

1. You do not have to tolerate the current, abysmal success rate in computer projects.

2. Studying and adapting the lessons learned by these industries is the quickest way to shorten the learning curve.

3. Absent any substantial corrective action, the outcomes of commercial computer projects will probably improve gradually over the next twenty or thirty years. Those firms that can compress this natural industry learning curve will gain substantial competitive advantage.

4. The defense industry shows us that rapid improvement is possible.[5] (**Note on the credibility of the defense department data and techniques:** Many of us may hold negative views of the effectiveness of defense department management and

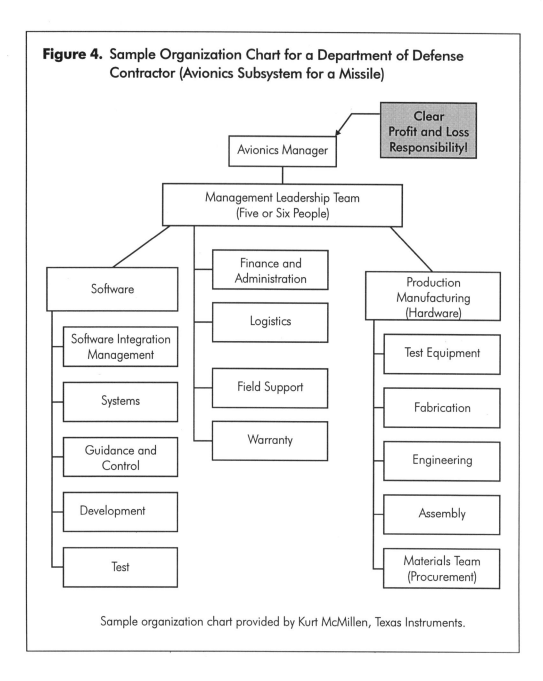

Figure 4. Sample Organization Chart for a Department of Defense Contractor (Avionics Subsystem for a Missile)

Clear Profit and Loss Responsibility!

Avionics Manager

Management Leadership Team (Five or Six People)

Software
- Software Integration Management
- Systems
- Guidance and Control
- Development
- Test

Finance and Administration
- Logistics
- Field Support
- Warranty

Production Manufacturing (Hardware)
- Test Equipment
- Fabrication
- Engineering
- Assembly
- Materials Team (Procurement)

Sample organization chart provided by Kurt McMillen, Texas Instruments.

techniques. We might also think that these success rates are inflated because the government and bureaucrats have a history of *self-justification* and other abuses. The study team attempted to compensate for these factors but makes no claim as to the absolute veracity of the defense department data. One fact is, however, undeniable. Since the Vietnam War, the defense department has made order-of-magnitude improvements in the results from its complex technical projects. I have personally applied several of its techniques (see Section 6.2.1) and have come to believe that we in the computer industry have a great deal to learn from the defense department and

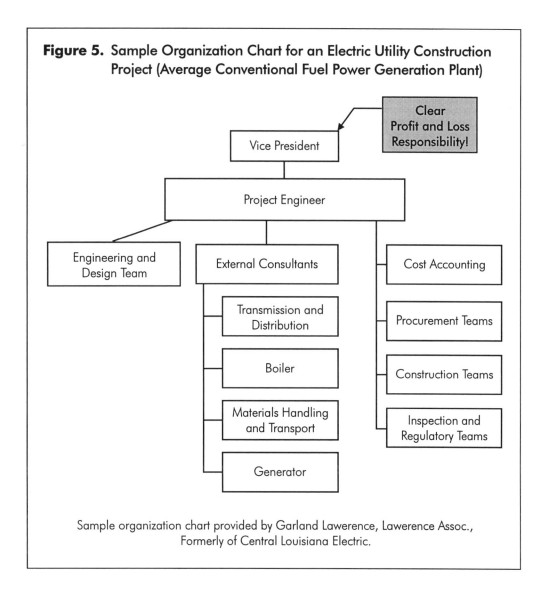

Figure 5. Sample Organization Chart for an Electric Utility Construction Project (Average Conventional Fuel Power Generation Plant)

Sample organization chart provided by Garland Lawerence, Lawerence Assoc., Formerly of Central Louisiana Electric.

its contractors. It is also worth noting that two other industries have attained the same general success rate as the defense department, further corroborating these claims. *Collectively, we call these three industries the 75% Gang because they have learned how to deliver complex, technical projects on time, on budget, and as promised at least 75 percent of the time.)*

1.3.2 Important Best Practices from the 75% Gang

Volumes have been written for each of these industries, and the reader is directed to the Project Management Institute and the Construction Industry Institute for further detailed information. *The following items emerged across all three industries and appear directly relevant to improving computer project outcomes.*

11

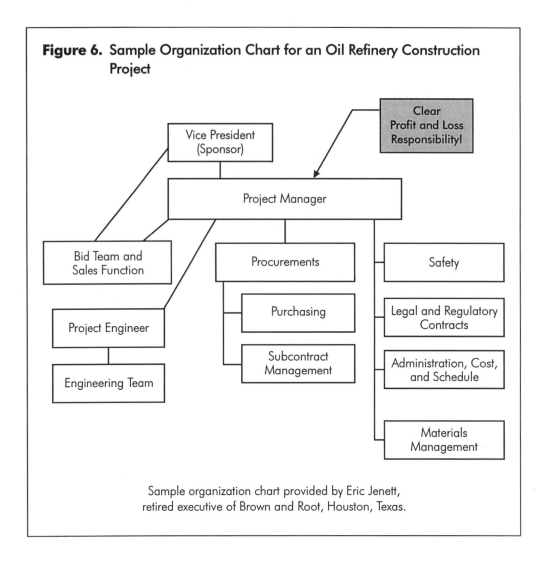

Figure 6. Sample Organization Chart for an Oil Refinery Construction Project

Sample organization chart provided by Eric Jenett,
retired executive of Brown and Root, Houston, Texas.

- Projects are defined in business terms (not technical): A project is regarded as an investment of capital and time, with a degree of risk. It is expected to produce a defined return on that investment. The project must be able to stand alone as a viable cost/benefit endeavor. *Technical issues are clearly separate and not allowed to compromise business results.*
- Measurement, command, and control systems: Mature, effective systems have evolved, which accomplish four key things:
  — effective early warning of projects at risk
  — tangible measurement of progress for intangible technical tasks
  — clear, visible, inescapable accountability for all concerned
  — measurements and incentives that are easily understood by executives, middle management, and those doing the work.
- Project officer/project manager competence requirements: By law (in the case of the Department of Defense) and long-standing practice in the other industries, a high level of competence is required for those holding project authority. A set of

rigorous hurdles must be overcome before project officers (or managers) are vested with the authority/responsibility of a multimillion dollar project. These hurdles are generally business experience driven, with technical experience a distant second.

- Executive, management, and worker compensation: Executive compensation is directly tied to delivering the defined business results as promised. Substantial bonuses are often available for performing better than promised, and real money is lost when performance is not up to par. The command, control, and measurement systems form the basis of the compensation system, and many organizations also have significant results-oriented incentives for middle- and lower-level people.
- Organization: The organization is defined from the business goal of the project as a *line organization*. The organization *is specifically not* a staff function supporting another line organization (e.g., a computer project to implement a new order processing system for the sales department). Figures 4, 5, and 6 present sample organization charts from each industry. Note how the projects are organized around the project's business outcome; this is a marked contrast to the organization of most computer projects as low-level entities supporting and subordinate to functional departments.

The Bottom Line among the 75% Gang. A single, competent person with authority matching responsibility is clearly accountable for delivering promised business results. Organization structures, measurements, and compensation systems support this person (rather than making the job more difficult).

The Results. Results enjoyed by the 75% Gang—which we should be able to emulate in computer projects—are complex, technical projects delivered on time, on budget, and as promised over 75 percent of the time!

SECTION 2

The Current and Future State of Client/Server Project Outcomes

2.1 Good News First:
What We Can Learn from the Success Stories

Section 6.2 is a collection of case examples featuring successes from which we can learn. My favorite success story is about Texas Commerce Bank (TCB). Using client/server technology, reengineering, and raw persistence, TCB managed *to reduce its consumer loan turnaround time from two weeks to less than three hours.* TCB saved hundreds of thousands of dollars in administrative expenses, but that is not what is really important. By improving customer service in a commodity business like bank loans, TCB totally reshaped the competitive playing field in the South Central United States. I do not have access to actual data, but I would speculate that TCB's loan volume increased by hundreds of millions of dollars.

This Case Helps Us See What Is Important. Even though the TCB project cost much more than originally anticipated, the outcome more than justified the expense. As you review both the Success Stories and the Horror Stories in this book, keep in mind that our goal is to improve the chances for these successes in a controlled fashion. Those who are proposing these projects generally don't have all of the facts (or they don't tell you if they do). I believe that shareholders are currently exposed to risks—of which they are not aware—with client/server.

The next time someone starts telling you of the anecdotal successes in client/server, take a long look at the Horror Story list. This book is about obtaining the benefits of the successes without subjecting shareholders to the risks that accompany these projects at present.

2.2 The Client/Server *Cost of Quality* Findings

The First Study—Symptoms. In June 1994 I published a study of sixty-two client/server projects that attempted to determine why these projects had so much trouble and what we could do about it. As a practicing consultant I had the opportunity to use these findings. While they were of some value (see Appendix C), it quickly became apparent to me that we were *addressing symptoms*, not the root problems.

The Second Study—Root Problems. Between 1994 and 1996 we initiated another study focusing on root issues and the *cost of quality*. Philip Crosby first defined this term in his 1979 book *Quality Is Free*.[1] We adopted his definition that the *cost of quality equals the total cost of not doing something right the first time*. The study team investigated sixty client/server Horror Story projects to search for root causes, total costs of quality, and what might be done to prevent these problems.

A Horror Story was generally defined as a project that was materially late, materially over budget, and/or failed to deliver some of the material business benefits that prompted investment in the project. In order to be consistent with the research shown in Appendix A, we are adopting a *hard* definition of a Horror Story as *a project that exceeded its original budget by approximately 100 percent or more*.

The study team was looking for overall trends and correlations rather than absolute statistical or research precision, so we would caution against any overly precise interpretations. The specifics of the study team participants, methods, and cautions are contained in Section 6.3.

2.2.1 Primary Conclusions

1. At least 50 percent of all client/server projects will turn into Horror Stories. Appendix A contains a summary of research published by Carnegie Mellon's Software Engineering Institute, The Software Productivity Research Center, The Standish Group, IBM, me (my original research), and several others. The conclusion is inescapable. According to the hard definition, at least 50 percent of client/server projects will become Horror Stories by costing twice their original budget in direct project costs.

If we also consider that projects are supposed to be completed on time and deliver their benefits as promised, the Horror Story rate is much higher than 50 percent. The reader is invited to review the research summaries in Appendix A to confirm this conclusion.

2. A client/server Horror Story project will have a cost of quality to the organization between eight and ten times the original project budget. After adjusting the averages due to some very large projects, we concluded that the average project studied had an original budget of about $2.5 million and a final project cost of about $10.5 million. While this type of overrun may seem horrible, the total cost to the organization of not doing this project right the first time is far higher. *By looking at lost incremental revenues, unrealized cost savings, and other costs, we determined that the average Horror Story project would cost a total of about $25 million!*

3. Two broad categories of root problems emerged; they are:
   - Competence issues: somewhat understandable due to the emergence of new technology and changes in the current business environment; training, infra-

structure, standards, and lessons learned from other industries can fill this vacuum relatively quickly.

- Leadership integrity: primarily observed as the tendency to put self before the good of the shareholder. It seems that a significant fraction of executives and managers view projects as opportunities for personal gain. We attempted to catalog this behavior and develop recommendations for mitigating its effect on project outcomes. *Approximately half of all Horror Stories exhibited specific behaviors when those in leadership put their own interests ahead of the good of the shareholder (or the good of the project).*

4. Four specific root issues were identified; they are:
- objectivity
- right people, right motives, and right actions
- authority to match responsibility
- accountability.

Together, these four seemed to form a foundation for the project. If these items were done well, the foundation was strong and the project tended to succeed. If any of these areas were noticeably weak, the project tended to suffer and experience a high cost of quality.

2.2.2 How the Cost of Quality Conclusions Were Developed

Section 6.1 contains a profile on each Horror Story, including budgets, actual totals, project objectives, root problems, and so on. Be aware that this is sensitive information and in many cases companies strongly preferred to suppress this bad news. In other cases, my confidentiality agreements with clients prevent me from disclosing company names and confidential information. As you review the cases, remember that the primary action recommended in this book is to conduct a cost of quality review for your organization. Whether these numbers are absolutely accurate is far less important than the cost of quality in your company.

Some Definitions. The total cost of not doing these projects right the first time was divided into two broad categories:

1. Direct project costs: These include wasted internal and external labor and wasted hardware/software investments. These costs were broken down as:
- original project budget
- total costs actually spent as of the day the interview was conducted
- wasted project costs. (We made the assumption that anything spent over the original budget was waste because the project should have been estimated correctly when originally approved. Also, some projects were completely canceled and the entire budget was attributed to waste.)

2. The cost of unrealized project objectives:[2] This cost category is designed to quantify *the benefits that the organization did not receive because the project did not meet its promises.* Most computer projects promise some level of increased sales and/or reduced operating costs in order to get approval. Some examples of these lost benefits would include late product introductions, missed market windows, lost customers due to poor service, labor cost reductions that didn't take place, premature divestitures, internal confusion, decline of morale, management time wasted trying to cover problems, and so on.

Table 2. The Relationship between Original Budget and Total Cost of Quality for Client/Server Horror Stories

Case ID	Original Direct Project Budget	Total Project Direct Costs Spent to Date	Overage	Overage Percentage	Total Estimated Cost of Quality	Cost of Quality as Percentage of Original Budget
159	$4,000,000	$10,000,000	$6,000,000	150%	$106,000,000	2650%
117	$25,000	$250,000	$225,000	900%	$475,000	1900%
147	$12,000,000	$120,000,000	$108,000,000	900%	$208,000,000	1733%
104	$5,000,000	$15,000,000	$10,000,000	200%	$40,000,000	
122	$25,000	$100,000	$75,000	300%	$175,000	700%
153	$13,000,000	$25,000,000	$12,000,000	92%	$87,000,000	669%
139	$2,000,000	$4,000,000	$2,000,000	100%	$12,000,000	
123	$25,000	$75,000	$50,000	200%	$150,000	
114	$100,000	$500,000	$400,000	400%	$600,000	
121	$25,000	$100,000	$75,000	300%	$125,000	
136	$7,000,000	$15,000,000	$8,000,000	114%	$28,000,000	400%
119	$100,000	$200,000	$100,000	100%	$300,000	
120	$175,000	$350,000	$175,000	100%	$525,000	
125	$25,000	$50,000	$25,000	100%	$75,000	
111	$1,000,000	$3,000,000	$2,000,000	200%	$3,000,000	
157	$700,000	$1,500,000	$800,000	114%	$1,800,000	
130	$200,000	$500,000	$300,000	150%	$500,000	
113	$1,000,000	$2,000,000	$1,000,000	100%	$2,000,000	
134	$1,000,000	$2,000,000	$1,000,000	100%	$1,500,000	
Average	$2,494,737	$10,506,579	$8,011,842	321%	$25,906,579	1038%
(Nineteen Projects Total)						

The *total cost of quality* was calculated by adding the wasted project costs and the cost of unrealized project objectives. This is, again, *the cost to the organization of not doing the project right the first time.*

The Data. In order to calculate a reliable cost of quality we needed to have all of the above data elements with a reasonable degree of accuracy. Twenty of the sixty projects had sufficiently accurate data and are displayed in Table 2, with one exception. Case 162 was a $500 million mega-project that severely skewed the averages, so it was omitted. Note that these projects all qualified for the formal, hard definition of Horror Story by exceeding their original budgets by approximately 100 percent.

2.2.3 The Relationship between Original Budget and Total Cost of Quality for Client/Server Horror Stories

Summary. For the nineteen projects depicted in Table 2, the average original direct project budget was $2,494,737. The average total cost of quality was $25,906,579, or *approximately ten times the original budget!*

Seven other projects were identified where data was complete, but the project was not officially a Horror Story based on the *hard* definition. As a cross check, we added these seven projects (case numbers 124, 112, 140, 155, 118, 137, and 107) to Table 2 and recomputed the average direct project costs and total cost of quality.

The result was that, for these twenty-six projects, the average original direct project budget was $2,478,846. The average total cost of quality was $20,785,577 or *approximately eight times the original budget.*

Overall Conclusion. In order to be conservative and in consideration of the small sample set of data, the study team chose to frame a conclusion in the following words: *A client/server Horror Story project will tend to have an average cost of quality to the organization between eight and ten times the original project budget.*

(**Caution**: The sample set in Table 2 is limited, and many factors could have either suppressed or inflated the total cost of quality figures. Absolute accuracy was never a significant objective of this research effort. A primary purpose of this book is to motivate project managers, shareholders, and executives to personally take action to see if these trends and dangers are present in their organizations.)

2.2.4 How the Root Issue Conclusions Were Developed

Root Issue Analysis. In the horror stories described in Section 6.1, you will find a Root Issue Scorecard for all the cases where we had sufficient data to make an assessment. As we interviewed people over the two years of the study, the root issues that emerged seemed to fall into the following natural groupings:

Objective decision-making:
- having a solid cost/benefit business case for doing the project in the first place
- having deadlines based on the scope of objectives instead of arbitrarily set
- having technical-solution designs based on solid thinking instead of personal agendas or happenstance
- having objectives and scope defined sufficiently so that changes can be controlled
- having budgets, deadlines, and the scope of objectives balanced before promises are made to secure funding.

All of the above are able to stand as sound decisions when reviewed by outside expert scrutiny.

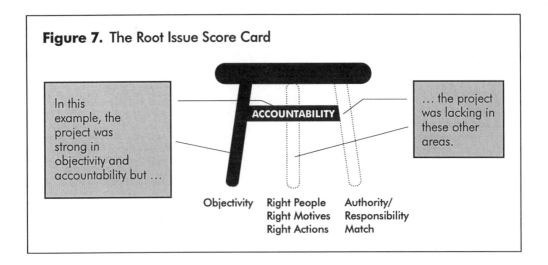

Figure 7. The Root Issue Score Card

In this example, the project was strong in objectivity and accountability but ...

ACCOUNTABILITY

... the project was lacking in these other areas.

Objectivity   Right People   Authority/
                Right Motives   Responsibility
                Right Actions   Match

Having the right people with the right motives taking the right actions: Examples of these questions include the following. Were the team members competent? Did the executive sponsor actively assist the project or maneuver to blame a scapegoat when things went wrong? (See Appendix E for more examples.)

The authority/responsibility match for the project manager: The project manager, who presumably knows the right things to do, should have the authority to do those right things. An example would be whether or not the project manager's sign-off is required before deadlines are set. Does the project manager really have the option to disagree? (**Note**: This is the most difficult topic we have to understand and resolve. See the questionnaire in Appendix E and the recommended project standards in Section 5, Principle 5, for more information.)

Accountability for all parties: Did everyone perform as promised or pay a price? Was the price paid sufficient to deter negative behavior? Appendix E has a sample questionnaire from the study and can provide additional detail on the actual questions asked. We used Figure 7 to graphically represent our assessment of the root issues. If a leg of the stool is unshaded, the project had problems in this area.

Table 3 shows all Horror Stories where we were able to identify cost of quality and root issue problems. Note that we have sorted it from the highest cost of quality to the lowest so you can see the correlation to root issues.

2.2.5 The Correlation between Cost of Quality and Root Issues

You will note that as the projects suffered from fewer root issue problems, the cost of quality tended to decrease. The study team arrived at the following general conclusion: *Total cost of quality is directly linked to the effective management of root issues.*

Projects that had little or no effective, observable management of root issues tended to have extremely high costs of quality. As more effective root issue management was observed, total cost of quality tended to decrease significantly. Table 3 demonstrates this correlation.

Table 3. The Correlation between Cost of Quality and Root Issues

Case ID	Industry	Original Direct Project Budget	Total Project Direct Costs Spent to Date	Total Estimated Cost of Quality	Root Issue Score Card
101	Transportation	n/a	n/a	$460,000,000	
109	Transportation	n/a	$244,000,000	$400,000,000	
162	n/a	$250,000,000	$500,000,000	$250,000,000	
147	Telecommunications	$12,000,000	$120,000,000	$208,000,000	
158	Manufacturing	$40,000,000	n/a	$160,000,000	
102	Manufacturing	n/a	$65,000,000	$130,000,000	
154	Financial	n/a	$40,000,000	$110,000,000	
159	Services	$4,000,000	$10,000,000	$106,000,000	
144	Manufacturing	$8,000,00	n/a	$100,000,000	
151	Government	n/a	$45,000,000	$95,000,000	
153	Energy	$13,000,000	$25,000,000	$87,000,000	
136	Government	$7,000,000	$15,000,000	$28,000,000	
155	Medical Supplies	$10,000,000	$15,000,000	$25,000,000	
145	Restaurant	n/a	$5,000,000	$15,000,000	
139	Insurance	$2,000,000	$4,000,000	$12,000,000	

Continued on next page

Table 3—*Continued*

Case ID	Industry	Original Direct Project Budget	Total Project Direct Costs Spent to Date	Total Estimated Cost of Quality	Root Issue Score Card
137	Manufacturing	$2,000,000	$3,500,000	$11,500,000	
138	Travel Agency	n/a	n/a	$10,000,000	
106	Medical Supplies	n/a	$5,000,000	$7,500,000	
107	Financial	$1,200,000	$2,200,000	$6,200,000	
110	Transportation	n/a	$2,000,000	$3,500,000	
108	Government	n/a	$2,000,000	$3,000,000	
157	Medical Services	$700,000	$1,500,000	$1,800,000	
134	Financial	$1,000,000	$2,000,000	$1,500,000	
118	Manufacturing	$250,000	$400,000	$1,150,000	
115	Financial	n/a	$500,000	$750,000	
114	Medical Supplies	$100,000	$500,000	$600,000	
117	Energy	$25,000	$250,000	$475,000	
142	Telecommunications	$400,000	n/a	$400,000	
119	Insurance	$100,000	$200,000	$300,000	
140	Government	$200,000	$300,000	$300,000	

Continued on next page

Table 3—*Continued*

Case ID	Industry	Original Direct Project Budget	Total Project Direct Costs Spent to Date	Total Estimated Cost of Quality	Root Issue Score Card
116	Energy	n/a	n/a	$250,000	(stool icon)
132	Medical Supplies	$400,000	n/a	$200,000	(stool icon)
135	Insurance	$600,000	n/a	$200,000	(stool icon)
122	Personnel Services	$25,000	$100,000	$175,000	(stool icon)
123	Manufacturing	$25,000	$75,000	$150,000	(stool icon)
121	Manufacturing	$25,000	$100,000	$125,000	(stool icon)
133	Energy	$400,000	n/a	$100,000	(stool icon)
125	Public Warehouse	$25,000	$50,000	$75,000	(stool icon)
143	Government	$40,000	n/a	$50,000	(stool icon)
124	Energy	$400,000	$400,000	$50,000	(stool icon)

2.2.6 How the Competence Issue Conclusions Were Developed

As mentioned above, we have broadly grouped these root issues into two categories: competence and leadership integrity. Addressing competence problems is relatively straightforward. Once it is acknowledged that a competence gap exists, training, education, and programs can be implemented to rectify the problem.
- The data and trends discussed throughout Section 2 should provide ample evidence that competence, in the area of project management root issues, needs to improve. Sections 3 and 5 contain a number of recommendations in the area of competence that most will find readily acceptable.

23

(**Caution**: It may be tempting to blame a set of individuals. We could decide that most project managers, business unit managers, and executive sponsors are incompetent and that they are the source of all problems. If you are tempted to think this way, please refer to the specifics of Sections 2.3 and 2.4. The competence issue I refer to is one of a changing business climate coupled with general understaffing and the Herculean task of learning how to manage projects.)

Taking myself as an example, I have had the luxury of doing little else but managing client/server projects for the last ten years. As it happens, my personal life allows some extra time to devote to professional development. I have benefited from some of the best project management training in the world. As a consultant I also have the benefit of being able to observe what works and what doesn't across hundreds of corporations. Even with all of these advantages, it has taken me over a decade to come to what I consider a *degree of maturity* in project management.

My personal definition of maturity for a project manager is when that project manager has enough knowledge, capability, and conviction to either:
- accept projects and deliver them as promised on a consistent basis, or
- refuse to accept the project assignment until the root issue conditions are such that the project can be successful.

As you read this book, ask yourself if it is reasonable to ask a middle manager or a project manager to have developed these necessary skills on his own.

Competence Is Only Part of the Answer. At the time of this writing, it seems that project management is the current fad. Software products, training classes, books, PMI membership, and project manager certifications are all experiencing a dramatic rise. All of these efforts are laudable and help to address the competence issue.

It will only be another fad, however, unless the leadership integrity issue is addressed, as well. We are starting to see some hard evidence that competence training alone cannot solve the problem. The Canadian Department of National Defense (DND) has found that project management tools have little positive effect on project outcomes (see Section 5, Principle 1.)

Horror Story #141 describes an independent telephone company that has attempted to standardize on PMI project management practices but is likely to ultimately incur costs of quality in the hundreds of millions of dollars. Another large telephone company has been one of the most ardent supporters of PMI's principles. Off the record, however, some of their people question the value of these efforts.

In the next section we will examine leadership integrity. Continue to ask yourself if competence training can have any real significant effect until the leadership problems are solved.

2.2.7 How the Leadership Integrity Conclusions Were Developed

As discussed earlier, the study team observed a tendency for executives and managers involved in projects to put their own interests ahead of their responsibilities to the shareholders. Like most of us, I look for the inherent good in people first. To be faced with significant evidence to the contrary is troubling, but I can find no basis for disregarding this conclusion.

The Political Model Prevailing over the Rational Model. Professor Al Lederer of the University of Oakland in Rochester, Michigan (United States), has advanced a theory that many recurring project problems can be better understood if we examine a "political" (or self-interest) model[3]. He contends that we are taught

Table 4. Behaviors Observed Where Self Is Put before the Good of the Shareholder (For ease of communication, these behaviors are expressed as the thoughts and motives of the person involved.)

Behavior Category	Observed Behavior	Number of Horror Stories Where Observed or Strongly Suspected	Some Consequences
Grabbing for Control at Project Startup	"Get control of dollars, headcount, and projects whenever possible so I can build my power, control, career, and ability to help the organization." "These opportunities don't come along that often. I need to grab control now."	27	Executive sponsor will be more interested in self-promotion than in project. Executive will not make enough time for project. Executive will abandon project when things get tough, jeopardizing the entire project due to lack of committed sponsorship. Empire building may lead to project control but not buy-in from other departments/areas. Cross-functional efforts will be at risk.
Combining Separate Phases into One Large Project at Project Startup	"I want to be in charge of big dollar, exciting, high visibility projects. These are the best opportunities for advancement."	27	Encourages lumping all phases into one pot, preventing due diligence.
Attempting Too Much with Too Little	"We can do this. We will look good. Nobody will believe what we've accomplished."	32	Shortcuts objective thinking. Anyone voicing concern is "not a team player."
Resume Building	"Technical projects are great because they always help my resume, and no one will ever prove that I'm wrong."	46	Encourages technically driven project approach.
The Appearance of Progress	"To make sure I look busy and in control I will: • spend money • hire people • produce lots of detail (and) • talk up the great progress we are making."	33	Often causes work to be done in unproductive directions, putting project so far behind it can never catch up.
Survive at All Costs	"I will deliver some good for the organization if I can, but it is more important that I look good and survive."	28	Tends to leave project direction-less. Often results in leadership vacuums. When this behavior starts, project is almost certainly doomed.
Scapegoating	"I'm going to keep control, but the project manager will handle the details. Between the project manager and the vendor, there is no way I can be blamed if things go wrong." "Always make sure there is a project manager, vendor, or somebody to take the blame instead of me."	35	Destroys the project team's belief that working for the good of the project will benefit the team members personally. Creates extreme waste of everyone's attention and energy in attempts to place blame.
Change Prevents Accountability	"Keep 'em off balance. Change helps keep others in the loop and sharing the blame. Shuffle the executive sponsorship, add some new things, take the project in a new direction." "I can tell them that we've discovered this is a lot bigger than we thought, and that's why the changes are necessary."	29	Results in projects that have nebulous, ever-changing objectives. These types of projects seldom accomplish much of value.
Just Deliver Something	"Just get something in by the end of the quarter."	30	Pushes back important features to later releases (or never). Creates large amounts of overtime and stress.

that projects proceed on a "rational" model of cost, benefit, and the good of the shareholder, but real life doesn't work that way. He suggests that we examine the self-interest behaviors of executives, managers, users, and outsiders associated with the project.

I have great respect for Lederer's work. This is because he is both a practitioner and an academic, and his recommendations have worked in my personal consulting practice. My passion for uncovering root issues has been greatly aided by his efforts.

It seems that a significant fraction of executives and managers view projects as opportunities for personal gain. They seem to be willing to pursue that gain even at shareholder expense. I believe that this is wrong and a significant abuse of trust. Part of this research is intended to help project managers, executives, and shareholders understand how much it costs to tolerate these behaviors. Table 4 lists the behaviors observed, the cases, and the consequences.

General Conclusion on Management Behaviors Where Self Is Put Before the Good of the Shareholder. Though this is a *soft* area and subject to much potential debate, the study team framed the following general conclusion as a starting point: *At least half of all Horror Stories included behaviors (either observed or strongly suspected) where managers and executives were seen putting their own interests ahead of their responsibilities to shareholders.*

While we do not have hard evidence to conclude that these behaviors caused the Horror Stories, it seems highly likely. Table 4 shows repeated negative consequences that tend to accompany these behaviors.

The Multiplying Effect: $2.5 Billion Wasted. When taken separately, either competence problems or leadership integrity problems are bad enough. When we consider their combined effect, we begin to see why client/server projects are so problematic. The sixty projects in this study had a total cost of quality of $2.5 billion. Clearly, action is called for. The next section examines trends that could cause the situation to get even worse.

2.2.8 The Correlation between Horror Stories and Stock Price

General Conclusions on the Horror Story Correlation to Stock Price. Fifteen Horror Stories were from public firms, and sufficient information existed for relevant examination. (See Section 4.2.1 for the full data set and cautions.) The study team draws the following general conclusions:

1. Of those fifteen firms, it appears likely or very likely that seven firms had their stock prices adversely affected by the Horror Stories.

2. Those seven firms appear to have lost an average of 59 percent of their stock value during the time that the projects were under way.

(**Note**: Remember that the expectations of a large new project might initially inflate stock price, and bad news made public will tend to deflate stock prices. We did not have the information necessary to determine if stock prices remained depressed after the project.)

Table 5. Additional Questionable Behaviors That Were Observed but Not Cataloged

Behavior Category	Observed Behavior
Justify Decisions and Actions	"I'll have the project team scramble to document all the benefits and good things about the project."
Promises Forgotten	"I'll just act as though everyone will forget the promises, see the good things, and write if off as the way the business works."
Outsource to Cover Problems	"Maybe now is the time to outsource this whole thing. That way, no one will ever be able to prove how bad it is."
Cronyism	"I'll see that my pal gets this project. It will help his career." (If project in trouble) "It looks like my pal is in trouble. I better get her out of there before she pays the price."
Arrogance and Presumption	"I know all that I need to know. I can run this project."
Can't Admit Lack of Skills	"If I admit that I don't know how to do this, I could be out of a job!"
Getting Further Behind as You Go	"We may be behind, but we can make it up in the next phase." "Now that we got the project started, I can coast a little. Nothing big is due for three months."
Getting the Toe in the Door	"If we look too closely at what this will really cost, they may not apporve it."

2.2.9 Some Additional Observations and Conclusions

The following items were observed and noteworthy. Although they should not be considered *proven* in a strict sense, they are consistent with the many sources of information that make up the overall set of recommendations in this book.

More Information Systems Projects Are Being Driven by Business Units. In the last ten years we have seen client/server overtake the mainframe as the business computing platform of choice. This has reduced the power and authority of centralized information systems (IS) departments and transferred much of that power to business units. The business unit-driven projects now far exceed IS-driven projects among my clients and those studied in this research.

The Good News. Client/server has lowered the cost of systems dramatically, so business units can more readily forge ahead under their own power.

The Bad News. Unfortunately, this means that more projects will be initiated and controlled by people with limited project management experience or training. We must consider that the extreme cost of quality experienced by the Horror Stories can be significantly attributed to the lack of experience of the project's decision-makers. (**Lesson**: The management of all types of projects needs to become a core competency of the entire organization, including both business units and information systems departments.)

Project Authority and Responsibility Are Inherently Mismatched in Most Organizations. As we have seen in the *Leadership Integrity Issue,* there appears to be a tendency to desire control and authority but delegate or avoid responsibility. When executives want to hold onto control but manage at a high level, the authority/responsibility is mismatched. We repeatedly observed that those who were close enough to the work to *know* what needs to be done almost never had the authority to affect such things as scope, budget, and deadlines.

Looking at it another way, consider the relative newness of client/server. It is quite unlikely that someone close enough to the work to really understand it has risen to the authority level of signing off on multi-million-dollar project issues. Again, this authority/responsibility root problem has proven the most difficult problem to understand in the study. Refer to the Cost of Quality Questionnaire in Appendix E and Principle 5, Developing Project Accounting and Management Standards, Section 5, for more information.

Accountability for Project Outcomes Is Lacking in Many Organizations. Consider all of the excuses that might be brought to bear when a project is in trouble. As the executive sponsor for a project in trouble, I might say:

- The vendor lied to us.
- The project manager messed up.
- We had six different vendors all pointing fingers at each other.
- The user couldn't tell us what he wanted.
- The objective keeps changing.
- The woman that estimated the project didn't know what she was doing.
- Sales said we had to have this change.

The list goes on. The present state of project management does not sort through these excuses to affix responsibility. Unfortunately, the personal interests or resume of the individual often benefits even though the project is a failure. Improvement in accountability is certainly called for.

Some Managers Are Attracted by a Lack of Accountability. Professor Paul Strauss, Ph.D., with some twenty-five years of personality research and measurement experience, describes the situation:

At least nine bodies of research exist on basic human personality attributes. One of the items nearly all agree on is that some people inherently dislike accountability. These people are often attractive, engaging, and persuasive. They manage images very well.

A situation such as the executive responsibilities of a large Client/Server computer project holds some distinct attractions for them. The issues are so new, technical, and complex that the top boss doesn't have time to fully understand, so he/she will tend to rely on impressions and image.

The newness and technical complexity will diffuse accountability, so this type of person can often find ways to look good even though things are in trouble. Unfortunately, this personality type is more focused on how he or she looks than getting projects accomplished.

A significant portion of the recommendations in Section 5 are directed toward fixing this accountability problem.

2.3 Why Project Management Needs to Become a Core Competency: Additional Trends and Facts

Profit gains from downsizing are gone. Companies now must grow revenues and profits to remain in the top half of their industries.

On July 5, 1996, *The Wall Street Journal* published results of a study of 800 major United States companies by Mercer Management. Of the 800, 145 companies had achieved earnings above industry average through cost cutting as of the late eighties. However, only thirty-four of the 145 were able to switch to a growth strategy and attain above average revenue growth by 1995. Clearly, cost cutting and growth are different strategies calling for different sets of expertise. *My conclusion is that growth requires a much higher level of project skills from the average manager. The management of all types of projects needs to become a core competency of the organization.*

More Projects (of All Types) Will Be Initiated as the Pace of Change Continues to Increase. Most would agree that, as compared to twenty years ago, product life cycles are shorter, merger and acquisition activities remain high, and organizational life cycles are shorter as startup and divestiture activities have increased. This level of change will continue to create more client/server projects, product development projects, reengineering projects, and so on. *The management of all types of projects needs to become a core competency of the organization.*

Project Management Excellence Appears Linked to Revenue and Profit Growth. On August 16, 1993, *Business Week* ran a significant article on product development. In that article, Thomas Hustad, editor of the *Journal of Product Innovation Management,* quotes study results concluding that "companies that lead their industries in profitability and sales growth get 49 percent of their revenues from products developed in the last five years. The least successful get only 11 percent of sales from products developed in the last five years."

Product development and the client/server computer systems that will support these new products go hand in hand. One of the key lessons of the Project Management Institute is the similarity of these two types of projects. It stands to reason that the leading companies described by Hustad must have been able to develop the new products *and the systems to support them*. A side benefit is that excellence in one of these areas tends to encourage excellence in the other. (Unfortunately, the reverse is also true.) This study comprises some of the most compelling, direct evidence that we have that shows again that *project management needs to become a core competency of the organization*.

2.4 Additional Problems and Trends That Need to Be Addressed

As troubling as the above conclusions are, we need to keep in mind that client/server represents an enormous overall change to the business community, and we will eventually adapt. Our competitive, free enterprise system will tend to help solve these client/server problems. In fact, history shows one particular lesson.

An Example of Technology Changing Faster Than Tactics (a Military Lesson). The Civil War had the highest casualty rate in United States military history (over 30 percent). One reason was that weapons technology had accelerated far beyond the tactics for using that technology. Repeating firearms, Gatling guns, improved gunpowder, and other improvements rendered tactics obsolete and led to bloody slaughters. Eventually, the tactics (or management, if you prefer) of these technologies caught up.

I believe that we are in such a period and that client/server has leapt ahead of most firms' abilities to manage their effective business use. While we will eventually adapt, *we must consider also the following trends and factors that could serve to worsen the situation*.

Mainframe Projects Are Still in Trouble 40 to 50 Percent of the Time. If you will again refer to Appendix A, A Summary of Current Research on Client/Server Project Outcomes, you will note some references to mainframe project outcomes. The mainframe project studies were cited as a *control* against which to measure client/server outcomes. We've noted that between 50 and 80 percent of client/server projects fail to perform as promised. In the research conducted by KPMG Peat Marwick and Al Lederer of the University of Oakland, we see that mainframe projects fail to perform as promised between 40 and 50 percent of the time.

It is understandable that a new technology such as client/server would have a much higher failure rate than a stable technology such as mainframe computers. The troubling aspect is that we have had thirty years to practice mainframe projects, yet we are still in trouble over half of the time! *Thirty years from now, will client/server still have a 50 percent failure rate?*

Technology is not the problem. *I believe that this points to a fundamental problem in our ability to manage computer projects effectively*. The balance of this book is centered on how to address that underlying set of problems.

A Symptom: Project Management Is Not Attracting Talent. The study did not specifically address the relative talent level of the project manager, but many of my clients and those interviewed have commented on the lack of able project managers. Several people have observed that it seems typical to promote technical people to project management when their technology skills are no longer current or the organization simply needs a place to put them.

When we look beyond this symptom to the root issues discussed above we begin to see that, in many cases, project management is a *no-win* job. Also consider that many people have a choice between a technical career track and a management career track. Most students of management would agree that American business as a whole is overly focused on technology. If you had a choice between a coveted, respected technical job, where you get to play with the *new toys*, and a project management job (with all the warts we've discussed), what would you do? I personally know a number of very capable people who have tried the management track and returned to technology for these reasons. *When it becomes the norm for project decisions to be objective, for authority to match responsibility, and for those above the project manager to be held accountable, I believe we will see information systems project management attract talent.* This seems to be confirmed by my contact with project managers in other industries. Although I have not studied the issue in detail, it seems clear that there are many industries where project management is an attractive career path.

Downsizing Consequences. *Downsizing has left most managers severely under-equipped for project management.* Downsizing has reduced the ranks of middle management considerably. Unfortunately, this is where much of the organization's project expertise resided. Projects are unique events that require managerial attention and expertise to create something from nothing. We now often find that those charged with managing a project face a number of constraints, including:
- very limited time for proactive measures
- little relevant experience in project management
- no project management training (or marginal training at best)
- fear or desire for self-promotion may lead managers to accept project responsibilities when they should not.

Additionally, we are coming to realize that effective project management in the current climate requires an enormous body of knowledge. For example, note that this book is intended as an *overview* of the issues. Substantial additional knowledge is required beneath each major topic to actually do a project effectively.

A Word on Organization. Dealing with these constraints and realities certainly involves developing the right organizational structure. Since we have not had the opportunity to study a large number of successful client/server projects, it would be premature to suggest a definitive model. I suspect that each organization will need to evolve on its own. The Project Management Institute does recommend investigation of the *project office* concept. This is primarily a staff function to help would-be project managers have access to the vast body of expertise needed. Typically headed by someone with significant project experience, the project office also can provide advice, counsel, warning, and administrative assistance. See the discussion on organization in Section 5, Principle 7, for further information.

The In-Built Positive Bias plus Lack of Accountability Leads to Disaster. I would like to again reference the work of Al Lederer of the University of Oakland as discussed previously (see the Leadership Integrity section subheading, The Political Model Prevailing over The Rational Model). Recalling his theory that projects are driven by the personal interests of those involved, let's examine the bigger picture.

Nearly everyone wants to have successful client/server experience on his resume, regardless of his level. A mainframe programmer that acquires client/server experience adds $10,000 to $20,000 to his annual salary (to say nothing of the increased chances of remaining employed). In one of the Texas Instruments success stories described in Section 6.2, the accounts payable manager, Hal Finley, successfully led his department to substantially improved performance through the use of client/server technology. He is now probably worth $20,000 to $35,000 more per year than an equivalent manager who has not done this.

As most senior executives will readily admit, information going up the chain of command tends to have a distinct positive spin. Speaking good news to those in power is a pleasure. Bringing bad news is, at best, unpleasant and traumatic. Now let's add the outside influence of vendors and consultants wanting to sell something. I call the combined effect the in-built positive bias toward going ahead with the project.

If we add the additional factor of the lack of accountability, we see a prescription for trouble and begin to see why the client/server Horror Stories got into so much difficulty. *The project foundation standards and accountability that we recommend in Section 5 are largely aimed at controlling these combined effects.*

Year 2000 Risks—Understanding the Millennium Problem. Unfortunately, many computer systems and components were never designed to handle the date change from December 31, 1999, to January 1, 2000. On January 1 of the year 2000, every computer system will be at risk. This includes not only your systems, but those of your customers, suppliers, partners, and even the United States government. Identifying and preventing these problems will initiate a large number of projects in a short period of time.

Consider that simply fixing this date problem creates an expense with no real benefit to the organization (other than avoiding disaster). I have already talked to a number of firms that plan to completely convert from mainframes to client/server in order to accomplish something positive at the same time. While this sounds great on paper, remember the project outcomes we've discussed above. *With 50 percent of client/server projects costing eight to ten times their original budgets, caution is certainly called for. Organizations clearly need to implement the type of controls discussed in Section 5 if authorizing a large number of new client/server projects.*

Tough Questions for the Chief Executive Officer (CEO). Roger Lowenstein has taken the risks associated with the year 2000 problem to the investment community.[4] He advocates that investors ask the CEO some tough questions, such as:
- "How much is it going to cost to fix this problem?"
- "Why hasn't this number been disclosed?"

Caution and due diligence are called for in considering any approach to the year 2000 problem.

Key Lessons from Other Industries and the Project Management Institute

One of my personal criticisms of the information systems industry is that it tends to be inwardly focused. The best people move around among the various vendors, consultants, and end-customer jobs. We talk to each other in techno-babble. We advertise and sell to each other. We survey each other to see what we're doing, and what is going wrong.

The Project Management Institute (PMI) stands as a significant exception to this *inbreeding*. Twenty-five years ago PMI was founded as a non-profit professional association to promote excellence in the management of construction projects. About ten years ago PMI saw that the same concepts applied across many industries and functional areas, including information systems, product development, defense contractors, electric utilities, and organizational transformation projects (reengineering, quality initiatives, and so on).

- For ten years PMI has been expanding its ability to assist industries other than construction. PMI now has specific interest groups for most of the above disciplines and has expanded its books, annual conferences, periodicals, and certification to encompass the broader needs of project management.

3.1 PMI Key Lessons

Definition of Project Success: Performing as Promised! Conforming to specifications (or performing as promised) is the definition of quality put forward by Philip Crosby in *Quality Is Free*.[1] There are some softer definitions of *quality* and project success that center around customer happiness and satisfaction. While these definitions have merit, I want to strongly urge the use of *performing as promised/conforming to specifications* in measuring client/server project success.

As we have seen in the above findings, client/server project outcomes are in a state of crisis and subject to being damaged by personal agendas. One of the most significant root problems is that of charging ahead without a clear definition of what is to be accomplished. In several of these Horror Stories I have observed people working very hard to find a way to call a failed project a success. The current lack of accountability seems to have created an atmosphere where people are not too concerned about promises made in order to secure funding. *At the present time, we need to send a clear message that it is the responsibility of those proposing the project to define it well enough that performance against that set of promises can be objectively measured.*

Two Different Types of Projects. It is important to understand PMI's general definition of a project. A project is a complex, unique, one-time event. It is executed by a unique organization that usually exists only for the duration of that project. Projects consume resources and time to produce an output. For our purposes here, let's broadly group projects into two main types by the outputs they produce:

- Stand-alone output: An output that has a stand-alone, commercial value (a bridge, a house, an oil drilling platform, a nuclear submarine, and so on). *Generally speaking, these projects lend themselves to effective subcontracting and can readily stand alone on a profit and loss basis.* I call these *stand-alone projects.*
- Supporting output: An output that fundamentally supports another process within the organization (e.g., a computer project to support the sales process, a product development project to support the sales and manufacturing process, a reengineering project to redesign the purchasing process, and so on). *Generally speaking, these projects are difficult to subcontract because their value is based on how well they support another internal process. They generally have great difficulty standing alone on a profit and loss basis.*

To summarize, we can generally group all projects as either *stand-alone projects or supporting projects.* It is important to note that the organizations that perform stand-alone projects have had to learn to do them on a clear and visible profit and loss basis. On the other hand, the *effectiveness of supporting projects is often masked by the profitability of the larger organization.*

The Most Important Lessons. The Project Management Institute (PMI) brings some key lessons, such as the following, to the client/server and information systems industries:

1. Other industries have been managing projects for significantly longer than we have.

2. Those industries have had to develop strong project techniques and controls in order to survive.

3. Many of those techniques are directly applicable to client/server and can dramatically improve project outcomes.

Once we accept the notion that we need to learn the lessons of other industries we are on the road to significantly improved project outcomes. Section 6.2 contains a success story write-up on a project at Texas Instruments when we used several of these concepts, notably the earned value method of project accounting and management. In this case, the PMI concepts prevented a late and possibly over-budget delivery.

Attributes of Industries Where Projects Are Generally Successful. As we examine stand-alone projects and supporting projects further we see that they fall into two primary industry groups:

- Project-driven industries tend to conduct stand-alone projects because this is how the organizations derive their primary profits. Examples would include construction, oil and gas drilling, defense contractors, electric utilities, and so on.

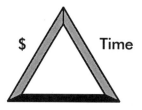

Figure 8. Kerzner's Project Triangle

$ Time

Deliverables

(Quantity, Quality, Technical Effectiveness)

Project Management, 6th ed., Harold Kerzner, Van Nostrand Reinhold, 1998.

- Operations-driven industries tend to conduct supporting projects because their primary purpose for doing projects is to improve the repetitive operations of the business. Examples of these industries would include manufacturing, services, wholesale distribution, retail, and so forth. The types of projects they conduct the most are information systems, product development, reengineering, quality initiatives, and so on.

To be sure, there are exceptions to this broad grouping, but the point is that *project-driven industries have had to become good at accomplishing profitable, effective projects.* As we try to extract the lessons that we might apply toward effective client/server projects, let's examine some of the key, visible attributes of project-driven industries and the organizations in them. Project-driven organizations generally have:

- Project managers (regardless of title) that know the work to be done, have the authority to match their responsibilities, and have very clear accountability.
- Strong but flexible project controls that ensure objective decision-making. These controls also require that a certain set of key tasks must take place prior to the expenditure of large amounts of money or time.
- Project managers and other team members generally must have significant training, experience, or certifications before they are given responsibilities.
- Often there is a visible, public accounting of the project's performance. The records are often made public and are subject to regulatory controls that have taken decades to develop.

No industry is perfect. We certainly would not want to impose the regulatory nightmare of the defense industry on client/server projects. We do, however, have a unique opportunity to take advantage of decades of project management expertise, extract the useful components, and substantially improve project outcomes without waiting to learn all of these lessons ourselves.

I find the model shown in Figure 8 very useful in helping people understand why projects are so expensive and take so long. The work to be done to deliver a project creates a fixed amount of work, shown by the fixed area in the triangle. It doesn't matter how badly we want to do more for less, or how short the budget dollars are; it will simply take a certain amount of time and money to accomplish a specific set of project objectives (or deliverables).

Table 6. Project Phases and Key Objectives

Phase	Approximate Percent of Project Budget	Key Objective
Concept	5%	Define an order of magnitude cost-benefit business case for the project.
Development	20%	Refine the order of magnitude findings into defined requirements, scope, budgets, deadlines, and resource requirements to the point where the project can be predicted and controlled.
Execution	70%	Execute the actual project according to the approved items from the development phase, including change control.
Finish	5%	Evaluate the project and close out contracts.

The project triangle also shows some of the tradeoffs we have available. If dollars are tight, it may be possible to reduce the scope of deliverables or increase the amount of time allotted. If time is the constraint, we might be able to shorten that leg by increasing the dollars or decreasing the scope of deliverables.

In Section 5, Principle 8, we will examine some traps that the Horror Story projects fell into. One of the biggest (I call it a mega-trap) is the *root-of-all-evil* trap. This trap is encountered when a project charges ahead, spending money, hiring people, and making promises *without balancing the triangle first*.

Basic Project Structure: C/D/E/F. Another of the most significant standards recommended by PMI is the adoption of a *standard project structure*. The use of the alphabetical sequence of C/D/E/F is intended to make it easy to remember. Table 6 shows these key phases and their purposes.

(**Note on *development* term used**: In PMI standard language, the development phase refers to expanding and refining the findings from the concept phase into a project definition that can be effectively executed and controlled. *It does not refer to software development or programming.*)

I cannot overstate the importance of adopting this standard. Refer to Section 5, Principle 8, Fads, Traps, and Dirty Tricks to Avoid. The *root-of-all-evil* mega-trap is avoided by the application of this one standard. The single biggest mistake among the Horror Stories was charging ahead with the execution phase before due diligence was completed in the development phase. The Horror Story projects would buy hardware, start writing software, and think up additional features to add without ever fully defining the project.

The purpose of the development phase is to define the project so that it can be reasonably executed and controlled. This would have saved hundreds of millions of dollars among the Horror Story projects.

3.2 Some Good News and Rays of Hope

Ninety Percent of Electric Utility Industry Projects Come in on Time and on Budget. As a ray of hope for our industry, I want to cite a study authored by Brunner, McLeod, and LaLiberte of British Columbia Hydro and Haddon Jackson Associates. It was published in the 1995 annual conference proceedings of the Project Management Institute. The study covered over 200 projects spanning more than ten years. (For purposes here, on time/on budget is defined by meeting original targets plus or minus 20 percent.)

As we think about why the electric utility industry is so much more successful than the information systems industry at delivering on time and on budget, we may be tempted to conclude that it is too different to be applicable. Certainly there are differences between building an electric power plant or substation and creating a computer system that must interact with humans and an ever-changing business process. I have even argued the point myself. I was told, quite bluntly, by my PMI colleagues that I needed to try it before I could judge.

My PMI peers were right, and I was wrong. The principles do apply across industries, and the Texas Instruments success stories in Section 6.2 are my personal testimony to that fact. *In Section 5, Principle 3, we recommend that you put someone on your team with cross-industry project training and experience.* It will be her task to help your organization sort through what is most applicable to your specific needs.

The Department of Defense and the United States Air Force Can Accurately Predict Project Overruns by the Time the Project Is 20 Percent Complete. Fleming and Kopplemen presented these research findings.[2] Their article discusses the results of over 600 defense-related projects. The earned value method of project accounting and management has evolved largely through the defense industry. Fleming and Kopplemen cite very strong evidence that the earned value methods can accurately predict and prevent unacceptable overruns by defense contractors before the project is 20 percent complete.

One of the primary recommendations of this study is the adoption of these earned value methods to prevent the client/server Horror Story overruns that shareholders have been paying for. See Section 5, Principle 5, Developing Project Accounting and Management Standards, for more information.

The Project Management Body of Knowledge and Project Management Professional Certification. The Project Management Institute (PMI) has developed and continually refines a document called *A Guide to the Project Management Body of Knowledge (PMBOK Guide).* PMI has also developed a project management certification process called the project management professional (PMP). The certification requires some practical experience, education, and a test on the *PMBOK Guide.*

In Section 5, Principle 3, we recommend some expertise that needs to be on your team. Being a certified project management professional myself, I have some vested interest in this recommendation, so I will stop short of insisting that you must have a PMP on your team. I will say, however, that I know of no other way to garner the same cross-industry expertise at a relatively low cost. There are now over 5,000 certified PMPs, so it should be possible for you to gain access to this expertise fairly easily.

Table 7. Contrasts between Being a Project Manager and a *Project Manager*

Area	Attributes of the type of project management role found in most of the Horror Stories	Attributes of the type of project management role found in project-driven industries where projects are usually successful
	Project Manager Attributes	***Project Manager* Attributes**
Budget, Scope, Deadline Authority	Very little authority. He is a recommender at best.	His sign-off is required for the project to proceed.
Change Control Authority	Very little authority. Saying no or insisting that additional money or time be provided may label her as *not a team player*. Recommendations are often overridden by the personal agendas of those above.	Her sign-off is required for the project to proceed. Politics and personal agendas still exist, but project controls help prevent major damage.
Team Authority	Generally cannot hire/fire/assign team members according to his best judgment.	Generally has control of who is on the project.
Upper Management Support	Very little face-to-face time, visibility, or support from upper management. May be blamed for things beyond his control while those above evade accountability.	Clearly a part of the middle-upper management team. Management supports him or removes him.
Truly Operate for the Good of the Project	If conduct above her is threatening the greater good of the project, she cannot escalate the project above that level. Either short-term or long-term reprisals would certainly occur.	Much greater latitude to escalate.
Technical Solution Authority	Technical solutions are frequently mandated. Project manager is often not free to press for objective decision-making.	If a better solution exists, he is expected to make the case for it.
Career Risk/Reward for Doing the Right Things	Project manager's job and future is at risk if she speaks too loudly about correcting underlying problems. She often does not perceive a clear link between diligently doing the right things for the organization and career progression. Other, more political types seem to be progressing faster.	Results and profit/loss accountability are very visible. If she delivers the results, progression is usually forthcoming.

Continued on next page

Table 7—*Continued*

	Attributes of the type of project management role found in most of the Horror Stories	Attributes of the type of project management role found in project-driven industries where projects are usually successful
Area	**Project Manager Attributes**	*Project Manager* **Attributes**
Training, Qualifications, and Talent	He has probably had no project management training of substance. The experience he does have will have come at a high price. The role often does not attract top talent. In the case of technical people being promoted to project manager, business sense is often lacking.	Often has a relevant degree and some significant project management experience. The role attracts top talent. Generally has a much more mature business sense, though engineering and technical backgrounds still can sway people into unproductive digressions.
Capacity to Hold Others Responsible for Promises	Generally very helpless in this regard.	Generally has a significant accounting and control infrastructure to see that everyone performs as promised.
Internal Standards and Processes Supporting the Project	Processes tend to be either too loose and inconsistent or are so overly rigid and bureaucratic that progress is inhibited.	Generally has an effective set of internal standards and processes.
Available Time	She will generally be severely pressed for time by other responsibilities.	Her primary job will be the management of one project.

3.3 Some Additional Lessons Learned

Difference between a Project Manager and a *Project Manager*. One of the most notable, measurable differences between industries where projects are consistently successful and of most client/server projects is the authority, status, capability, and responsibility of the project manager. I call this the (regular type) Project Manager versus the (italics) *Project Manager* trap. Table 7 is a summary of some of the items discussed relative to these two roles.

Treating Symptoms Isn't Working. As we've discussed, this book is about root issues. I spent several years addressing symptoms with only marginal results. This is a complex, emerging topic, and several factors will tempt us to believe that we are addressing the real problems when we are not. Following are some typical activities that organizations are taking to improve project management. Though people look busy and immersed in detail with these activities, I want to offer some cautions.

Project management software is advertised as the cure for all ills. Unfortunately, many people seem to believe this. While project management software has its role, it operates on the assumption that the root issues are fundamentally in place. There is also a *black-box* quality to most project management software. I have seen several disastrous situations arise because the project team did not understand what was happening to the information that was entered and could not rely on it. At least one study has concluded that project management tools (including software) have relatively little impact on positive project outcomes. (See Section 5, Principle 1, under The Roles and Duties of the Independent Third Party.)

I inevitably end up using a spreadsheet that I have built myself and exporting the data to a project management program for scheduling and printing graphics. This is particularly important with earned value concepts. The project manager must understand what is going on. While some of the higher-end project management packages have great value, it is essential that the new project manager understand what is important first. I believe you have to do it yourself with a spreadsheet the first few times.

Project management training is of great benefit, but if the root issues of a project are weak, the project has no chance for success. The student tries to use what has been taught but finds out that it doesn't help as expected because, for example, senior management has mandated a date that simply cannot be met. Often the courses focus far too much on quantification and numbers and far too little on how to cope with real root issues.

The PMP certification process is a pleasant exception. We begin to learn about root issues and how large the PMBOK really is. Unfortunately, those that have the time to pursue certification seldom have the authority to mandate the needed changes. Over time, these people will rise in the organizations and ultimately have that authority. At present, even the best project management training can make little immediate impact without resolution of the underlying root issues.

The Military Model and Strategic Lessons of History. Another research project that we have under way is that of comparing projects to military engagements to see what we might learn. Although further study is needed, two items already emerged as directly applicable:

- Strategy is more important than tactics: Even the most brilliant battlefield tactics can only win, at best, one battle at a time. If the strategy is flawed and, for example, the troops run out of supplies, the war is lost. The newness of client/server and it's intriguing technology have caused us to be focused tactically. The price for that failure is certainly evident in the Horror Stories. *It is time for us to address the underlying, root strategic issues of client/server and stop being distracted by tactical aspects and technology.*
- Control the initiative; be proactive: From Genghis Khan to Napoleon, from Sun Tzu to Angelo Dundee (boxing trainer for Mohammed Ali and Sugar Ray Leonard), one maxim is clearly above all others: You must act rather than react. The client/server Horror Stories underestimated the need to be proactive, often causing a need to react to an extended series of problems. A large price was paid for this failure. *It is time to be proactive in dealing with client/server root issues, rather than reacting to the symptoms.*

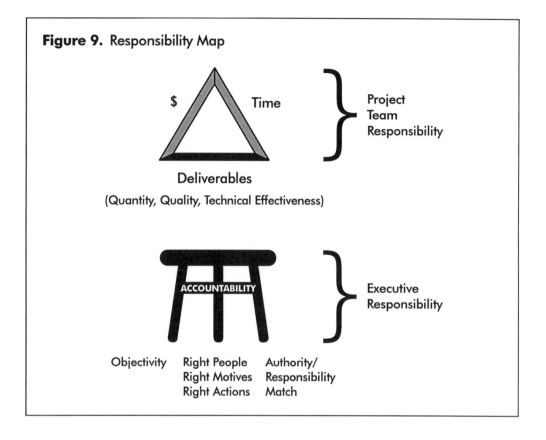

Figure 9. Responsibility Map

As we try to bring some clarity and direction to this complex subject, I'd like to present Figure 9 to remind us *who* is responsible for *what*. As can be seen, everything rests on the project foundation. The project team alone cannot deliver a successful outcome when one (or more) of the legs is missing. The project will *crash to the floor* as we have seen over and over in the Horror Stories. *If we want improved client/server project outcomes, the executives must proactively put a solid foundation in place.*

3.4 Pulling It All Together: The Project Foundation

As we try to bring some clarity and direction to this complex subject, I'd like to present Figure 9 to remind us *who* is responsible for *what*. As can be seen, everything rests on the project foundation. The project team alone cannot deliver a successful outcome when one (or more) of the legs is missing. The project will *crash to the floor* as we have seen over and over in the Horror Stories. *If we want improved client/server project outcomes, the executives must proactively put a solid foundation in place.*

To Investors: Awareness and Warning

You will probably agree that the evidence presented earlier calls for action, but you may be wondering:

* If this is all true, why has no one told me about it before now?
* How do I know if this is happening in my firm, and what is my exposure?
* What is it worth to solve these problems?
* In broad terms, what do we need to do?
* Do I really have to get personally involved, or can I hand this off?
* If I am a member of the board of directors, do I have any personal liability or SEC exposure for not taking action?

Following is my attempt to recommend some steps for thinking through these issues from an investor's perspective.

4.1 Recognize the Hole in Project Accounting

Simply put, the current accounting and auditing processes are not adequate for preventing the type of Horror Stories we have been examining. The evidence is quite clear: well over half of the sixty Horror Stories were multi-year projects, yet they were not prevented by the standard safeguards.

Why No One Has Told You This Before. Recall the in-built positive bias above. The basic conclusion is that nearly everyone in the organization has much to gain from doing the project and little to lose due to the current lack of accountability. We have also raised the issue of leadership integrity. It is clear that we cannot assume that today's business executives and managers will put the good of the organization before their own.

There is another factor involved when a project is in trouble. All of the human factors we've discussed tend to cause people to conceal bad news and hope that they can keep it under control.

Why the Auditors Don't Catch These Problems. In April 1996 I met with Joe Miller, retired auditor from EDS. We reviewed the earned value method of project accounting and discussed other project and accounting control issues. When I asked Joe why auditors don't catch these problems, he replied:

> Auditors are not trained to think about the value that a project has promised to create. Our training and regulations are primarily centered around seeing that money is spent according to the rules and procedures. In the Horror Story projects you've shown me, I would expect that the labor and materials purchased were probably accounted for according to the audit rules. The fact that they did not produce the value that they were supposed to is outside the auditor's scope.

Miller then commented on earned value:

> What you've shown me about this method of project accounting seems to have merit. There has always been a large separation between those who do the work and those who account for the work. This method closes that gap and could help see that the money spent produces the value it was intended to produce.

A final comment from Miller caught my attention:

> An auditor cannot smell a client/server project that is in trouble. This area is just too new. In the old days, an auditor might sense a mainframe project that was in trouble but would still be hesitant to speak up. Remember that auditing focuses on clear rules violations, and these problems do not fit into any of the standard rules. Also keep in mind that outside auditors don't want to take a chance on escalating a problem that is less than clear. Auditing is a commodity business that allows accounting firms to bill young accountants for $70 plus per hour for a lot of hours. They will tend to not jeopardize that revenue stream.

I have had two informal conversations with other auditors who echo Joe Miller's comments. It is clear that we cannot count on the audit process to catch this problem.

4.2 Assessing the Immediate Exposure

4.2.1 The Correlation between Share Price and Horror Stories

Table 8 looks at the relationship of Horror Stories to stock price. *While it appears that several stocks lost value due to client/server Horror Stories, we must be careful about drawing conclusions from this limited sample.* Stocks can fluctuate for any number of reasons. (Appendix F lists several areas where further research is called for, and I consider this topic one of the areas for further research.) We need a much more controlled setting before we can firmly conclude that stock price can be significantly affected by computer projects.

General Conclusions on the Horror Story Correlation to Stock Price. Fifteen Horror Stories were public firms, and sufficient information existed for relevant examination. Given the above cautions, the study team draws two general conclusions. 1) Of those fifteen firms, it appears likely or very likely that *seven firms had their stock prices adversely affected by the Horror Stories*, and 2) *those seven firms appear to have lost an average of 59 percent of their stock value during the time that the projects were under way.*

Table 8. Horror Story Correlation to Stock Price

Case Profile Name	Case ID #	Stock Price High (in early stages of project)	Stock Price Low (during or shortly after project)	Percent Change	Any Significant Stock Price Movement That Might Be Correlated to Project Problems?
Greyhound Lines, Inc.	110	23	2	91%	Hoover's handbook identifies significant computer problems as well as other problems.
Large United States Service Firm	159	84	66	21%	Very likely—stock price fell 21 points at same time as project's first missed deadline.
American Airlines (The Confirm Project)	101	72	48	33%	Very likely—project problems were public knowledge.
FoxMeyer Corp. (Delta Project)	155	30	7	76%	Very likely—project problems were public knowledge.
West Coast Savings and Loan	134	26	12	53%	Likely.
Independent Telephone Company	141	50	30	40%	Likely.
Upper Midwest Steel Manufacturer	158	18	12	40%	Likely.
Very Large Central United States Bank	107	43	32	25%	Possible—distinct price dip during largest project problems.
Division of Dallas-Based Telecommunications Manufacturer	118	16	4	75%	Possible.
Dallas-Based Telecommunications Manufacturer	137	38	16	57%	Possible.
American Management Systems	113	11	6	45%	Possible.
CIGNA	112	64	40	37%	Inconclusive.
Alcoa (Aluminum Company of America)	148	60	40	33%	Unlikely.
Diamond Shamrock, Inc.	111	30	24	20%	Unlikely.
Duke Power	153	52	34	34%	Unlikely.

(**Note**: Remember that the expectations of a large new project might initially inflate stock price, and bad news made public will tend to deflate stock prices. We did not have the information necessary to determine if stock prices remained depressed after the project.)

4.2.2 Analyzing Earnings Forecasts for Client/Server Threats

Figure 10 is a sample earnings forecast analysis for client/server exposure from one of my clients. Below are the general steps needed to conduct that analysis.

1. Obtain or create a three-year earnings forecast showing the earnings *pie* by product line. I would allocate all overhead to the specific product lines by whatever method is most convenient. This is significant because many projects will promise to decrease expenses, and it is important to be able to judge the impact if these promised expense reductions don't materialize.

2. Obtain a list of key client/server projects under way. This needs to include the project's objectives, budget, and deadline.

3. Lay out the timeline. The primary focus is to identify when the client/server projects must deliver their promised benefits in order to achieve the earnings forecast.

4. Get some objective, outside help to confirm your analysis. You need someone who can tell the difference between a small risk and a threat that requires action. If possible, a certified project management professional would be ideal. At the very least you need a senior consultant with broad information systems experience and lots of *scar tissue*.

We must give the executives in your firm credit for anticipating some degree of problems. You need the outside help to cut through the *foo-foo dust* and objectively determine if any significant risks truly exist.

As you look at the example in Figure 10, you might be tempted to conclude that things will be fine if the client/server computer system is delivered on time, as promised. Note, however, that Product Line A calls for a 70 percent increase in sales volume in three years and no headcount increase in order to meet the forecast. Upon further investigation, I discovered that this goal was unattainable. *Meeting this plan will require the firm to perform at double the productivity level of the industry leader* (measured in sales per employee per day). In and of itself, a doubled productivity level might be possible. Upon further investigation, however, we found that the plan *called for my client to make only one-fifth of the investment in information systems (per employee) made by the industry leader! This project is fundamentally undoable. It never had a chance.*

Do the Right Thing and Lose Your Job. As a final note and commentary on the consulting industry, I will tell you the rest of the story. I was working for one of the top consulting firms in the world. When I discovered these problems I wrote two detailed memoranda insisting that we disclose this risk to the client, even though that disclosure might cost us a $4 million sale. I was immediately dismissed from the project and blacklisted within the firm. I counted fourteen separate incidents when taking this stand resulted in unfounded accusations and rumors against me. I was never assigned another project management role and left the firm some nine months later.

I did not have an avenue to escalate this problem formally. My informal attempts to escalate were only met with more rumors and blacklisting. We were in the middle of a merger, and I was having some health problems so could not really afford to risk my job by telling the client myself. *This is a perfect example of why independent, objective review is needed.* These shareholders will suffer millions of dollars of preventable loss.

4.2.3 Conducting Your Own Cost of Quality Review

Here are steps for proceeding with your own review (an example is provided in Table 10, Section 5, Principle 2):

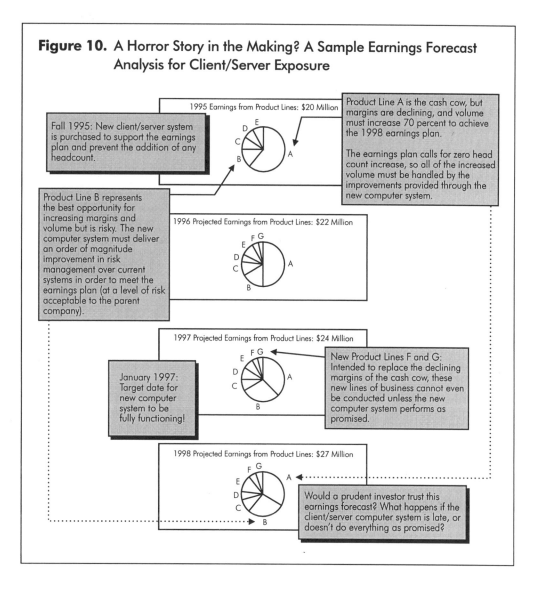

Figure 10. A Horror Story in the Making? A Sample Earnings Forecast Analysis for Client/Server Exposure

1. Review Table 3 entitled The Correlation between Cost of Quality and Root Issues in Section 2 under the Cost of Quality findings. This is your objective. You want to identify all of the major client/server projects within your organization and estimate the total cost of not doing things right the first time. You are also looking to see if the root issues are sound or if any pattern of weakness emerges.

2. Develop a list of key client/server projects. I would recommend investigating anything with a total budget over $100,000. This will probably take some effort and digging. No one is going to be excited about giving out this type of information.

3. Using the Cost of Quality Questionnaire in Appendix E, investigate each project. Again, this will take some digging and effort. I would highly recommend the use of an objective third party at this point. That person will know what to look for in the shortest amount of time. He will also be able to push through the *foo-foo dust* and insist on solid answers.

4. When investigating the total cost of quality, remember that the direct hardware, software, and external labor costs are only the tip of the iceberg. Remember that these projects get funded to reduce expenses and increase revenues. You are looking for the promises made along these lines to get the project funded.

5. Be prepared for multiple iteration. In the book *Quality Is Free*, Philip Crosby advances the cost of quality review concept. He notes that you will generally not get the full picture on the first pass. He expressed the cost of quality as a fraction of total sales and noted that the first review typically came back showing that about 5 percent of total sales were wasted because things were not done right the first time. The second review would be about 12 percent, and ultimately *he found that every cost of quality review showed a total cost to the organization of over 20 percent of sales!*

Keep going until you uncover pain and cost. Some people are very good at hiding such things, but every organization I have dealt with has at least one Horror Story in process. (**Note**: Crosby expresses cost of quality as a percent of total sales. I prefer to express it as a percent of the original project budget. If you prefer to express things as a percent of sales, simply compare the total project budgets and total cost of quality for your firm to your total sales.)

After totaling your present and predicted client/server cost of quality, you should have an idea whether action is justified. The next section looks at the cost/benefit of taking action.

4.3 Understanding What to Do: A High-Level Flow Chart

The details behind the steps depicted in Figure 11 are described in Section 5.

4.4 Weighing the Cost and Benefit of Action

Following is a summary of the key benefits to the organization of pursuing these recommendations:

- Risk: The organization's risk profile is substantially reduced.
- Ability to execute: The ability to execute client/server projects as promised is greatly increased. This means a much higher probability of capturing the revenue increases and cost reductions that justify computer systems in the first place.
- Adapting to change: The organization will become substantially more adept at reacting to change.
- Improvements in other types of projects: The disciplines and standards developed for client/server projects can also be applied to reengineering and product development efforts.
- Improved returns: In Section 2.3, Why Project Management Needs to Become a Core Competency ... we cited a survey conducted by the *Journal of Product Innovation Management* and published in *The Wall Street Journal*. This research shows a clear link between excellence in product development projects and superior financial performance. While we do not yet have similar definitive evidence showing that improved client/server project execution will improve financial returns, this conclusion seems reasonable and justified in light of the evidence presented in this body of research.

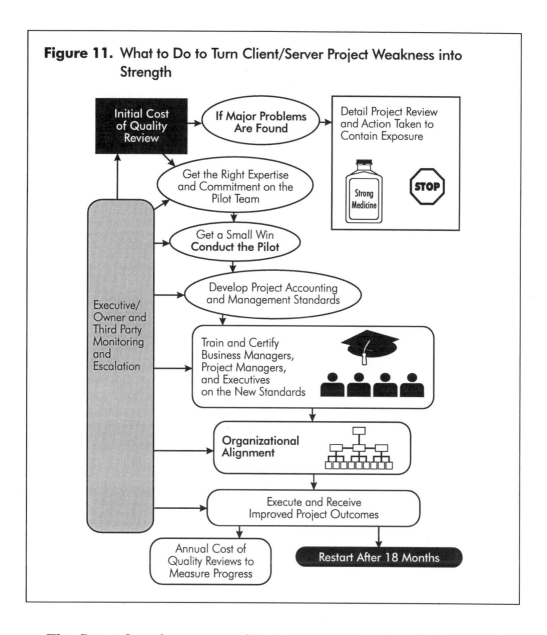

Figure 11. What to Do to Turn Client/Server Project Weakness into Strength

The Costs. One of my current clients is a very typical $500 million manufacturer. I worked with this client to survey existing projects and develop a process for improved computer system project outcomes. Table 9 presents a budget for implementing these recommendations from this case example. (**Note**: The numbers have been altered to prevent any disclosure of confidential information.)

Payback. If we prevent one average Horror Story over the three-year period, the organization will save over $20 million. Investing $735,000 to save $20 million is approximately a twenty-seven-fold payback.

Some good news concerning this initiative:

- This offers a very high potential payback without capital expenditures.
- The pilot approach will allow a rapid verification of results prior to further investment.

- Strong precedents for success exist among the project-driven industries cited above.
- Benefits are long term and can be sustained as a competitive advantage and barrier to competition.

Some bad news:

- While individual projects might be helped in the short term, organizationwide improvements will take multiple years.
- The recommendations are counter to many of the behaviors that got executives where they are. They also call for giving up power and increased accountability. It is unlikely that most will accept these changes willingly.
- Owner/investor/board of directors-level involvement and third party monitoring are probably mandatory, although very hard to come by in larger organizations. While private and smaller firms seem to be more open to participation by the ownership, it is all but impossible in a large public corporation where stock is held by a widely dispersed group of owners who want nothing to do with day-to-day operations. There is some evidence to indicate that this problem is insoluble in most large public corporations.[1]

4.5 Consider Getting Personally Involved

We recognize that shareholders have limited time and prefer not to interfere in day-to-day management matters. Following are the key reasons that shareholders may wish to become more active in this area and ways that this might be accomplished with a minimum of time and difficulty. Reasons for getting personally involved include:

- Little help from the inside: As discussed above, no one internally has a strong motive to take this type of action. Additionally, present auditing and accounting rules don't catch the problems. The leadership integrity issue boils down to leaders advancing their own interests at the expense of the good of the projects and the good of the shareholders. To ask those people to take an active role in regulating themselves would simply not work.
- Major consulting firms are not interested in this type of work: Many people will recognize Dr. Ken Cooper as the father of the wellness and aerobic movements. In the fifties Cooper was trying to decide between a traditional medical career and the radical ideas he held about fitness, wellness, and prevention. His colleagues told him that "there is no profit in health. Only in disease." Cooper went on to father a health and fitness movement, and I think that there are parallels to the situation currently faced by shareholders.

No major consulting firm wants to see a client firm dramatically improve its project management capabilities. I have attempted to get multiple major consulting firms interested in this type of practice but to no avail. One of the reasons that I was not able to interest the large consulting firms is called *leverage*. Consulting firms use their best and brightest people to *close the deal* and sell the customer on using forty-two young, inexpensive consultants as programmers. This is called *leveraging good people*. The consulting services needed for the recommendations we've described are fundamentally *unleveraged*. Junior people are of no value in this situation; this type of work will require only senior people. Anytime you receive a proposal for one senior person and a team of junior people, caution is warranted.

Table 9. A Sample Budget for Implementing These Recommendations for a $500 Million Manufacturer over a Three-Year Period

Area	External Expense (Primarily Consultant Labor)	Internal Expense (Primarily Management and Staff Labor)
Initial Cost of Quality Review	$25,000	$10,000
Building Pilot Team and Conducting Pilot (depends on size of pilot)	$100,000	$50,000
Develop Project Accounting and Management Standards	$50,000	$50,000
Train and Certify Business Managers, Project Managers, and Executives (probably will require additional project managers at higher pay rates)	$25,000	$200,000
Organizational Alignment	$25,000	$50,000
Execution	$25,000	$100,000
Third Party Monitoring and Escalation	$25,000	
Totals	$275,000	$460,000
Total of Both Internal and External	**$735,000**	

(Note: Internal costs are incremental costs over maintaining status quo.)

- Actually counter to consulting firm's interest: As we've seen, project-driven industries have learned to spend more time defining their projects up-front. This is directly counter to the consulting firm's overwhelming desire to get consultants billable as soon as possible.
- Some ways to get involved without an extensive time commitment:
  — Find a way to fund the initial cost of quality review (approximately $25,000) so a solid business case can be made for pursuing further steps.
  — Have a major investor *strongly encourage* the adoption of these steps (being sure to include the provisions for owner reporting and owner escalation safety valve discussed in Section 5, Principle 1, Ownership Involvement and Third Party Monitoring).
  — Present a motion to the board. Remember that some board members are not significant shareholders and so may resist this effort.
  — Present a motion at the stockholders' meeting. (**Note**: It is likely that any significant shareholder involvement will only be required for six months to one year. As the safeguards and standards take effect, the need for a shareholder

presence will drop considerably. See Section 5, Principle 1, Sun Tzu's Rise to Power, for further information.)

If we have learned anything from human history, it is that the owner is ultimately the only one who will consistently look out for her property. Allow me to restate that this is not about technology, it is about the behavior of people. We are currently experiencing a set of changes in the business environment that allows the behavior of some people to jeopardize owner investments. It is up to the owner to take the lead in fixing this problem.

Eight Principles for Turning Weaknesses into Competitive Advantage

See Figure 11 to review the *overall flow* and steps that are needed to implement recommendations made. This section is devoted to eight principles for turning weak client/server project outcomes into a competitive strength.

Principle 1: Ownership Involvement and Third Party Monitoring

This entire book describes the need for greater ownership involvement. Admittedly, few shareholders will want to get involved, but that does not change the facts. To put it bluntly, there is no evidence to indicate that these underlying root problems will go away by themselves. Worse yet would be to delegate the responsibility of improving project outcomes to someone whose agenda may not be that of putting the shareholder first. Following are some additional commentaries from history that further show the need for the authority of the shareholders to be behind any effort to significantly improve project outcomes.

Sun Tzu's Rise to Power. Most business people have heard of this Chinese philosopher and his famous book *The Art of War,* written about 400 B.C. What is not generally known is how Sun Tzu came to be the commanding general of the Kingdom of Wu.[1]

The King of Wu read *The Art of War* and asked Sun Tzu to come to the castle to give a demonstration. The King wanted Sun Tzu to stage a battle using the royal concubines as soldiers and wanted his two favorite concubines to be commanders of the opposing forces. When Sun Tzu explained his orders to the concubines, they dissolved into gales of laughter.

Sun Tzu patiently explained the orders again, and the women again laughed and giggled. Sun Tzu turned to the King and demanded that the commanders of each force, his favorite concubines, be executed for disobeying orders. The King insisted that Sun Tzu had proven his point and that the two women did not really need to be executed. Sun Tzu would not relent. He told the King that, as the appointed leader of troops, there would be occasions where he had to carry out orders that the King might not agree were necessary. Sun Tzu insisted, and the beheadings were carried out.

As you might imagine, the next orders issued by Sun Tzu were carried out very diligently by the remaining concubines. The King named Sun Tzu as his commanding general. The kingdom of Wu absolutely dominated its geographic region for the rest of Sun Tzu's life.

This ancient commentary on human behavior shows why ownership involvement is necessary. Shareholders will have access to some *Sun Tzus*. Somewhere in the organization there will be people who know what needs to be done and want to create value for the shareholder as their first responsibility. Just like the King of Wu, the shareholder will need to back them with authority, even when it may not seem clear why they insist on certain things. Shareholders and executives will also need to protect them from those whose first agenda is not the good of the shareholder.

History, Herbert Simon, and Human Thought Processes. How many historical examples can you cite when those in power gave up power willingly for the good of the organization? How many examples are there of the reverse? Herbert Simon won the Nobel Prize for his work in defining the natural flaws in human thinking.[2] He determined that *human beings need the following conditions for effective decision-making*.

- Generate and evaluate an exhaustive set of alternatives completely and objectively.
- Make selection based on maximized utility or economic outcomes.
- Make decision free from political influence.

In studying human decision-making, Simon also identified how far we typically are from those requirements. The *typical decision process will*:

- generate a small number of alternatives
- partially evaluate some of these alternatives
- use flawed information
- allow subjective biases and political expediency to influence the process
- frequently accept the first acceptable alternate identified.

My research suggests that Simon is not only correct but that he was, in fact, being kind. To my knowledge his work does not openly suggest that leadership integrity is a factor.

I would remind the reader that this sample set of data is far from exhaustive (see Section 6.3 for other cautions), but it might suggest a small addition to Simon's list of how typical decisions are made. The research shows in Section 2.2.7 *that decision-makers in at least half of the Horror Stories were observed behaving in ways that put their personal interests ahead of the good of the shareholder.*

The evidence, the lessons of history, and Noble-Prize winning research all show us that we need to change from the current flawed decision processes to more effective decision processes. *Can you imagine this move happening* without *owner involvement and independent monitoring?*

The Situation Calls for True, *Paycheck* Power. Helen Cooke, a member of the board of directors of the Project Management Institute and a ten-year-plus veteran of information systems project management, describes her experience:

There are several words used in the management literature to describe power. They speak of Personal Power, Expert Power, Associative Power and Endowed (or True) Power. I have been told in many project management situations that I should be able to get people to do the right things through my expertise, personality, the right style or "packaging." These efforts have nearly all ended poorly. By and large, in the case of information systems project management, nothing gets the job done except True, Endowed, Paycheck Power.

I find her perspective identical to mine. If you've had a chance to check my credentials in Appendix I, you probably agree that I've got the expert power in the field of client/server project management. Being male, six-feet, one-inch tall, weighing 295 pounds, and possessing a black belt in karate, I probably qualify as having a degree of personal power as well. Yet my experience is the same as hers: nothing gets the job done in client/server project management except *true power*. We need the visible backing of those with this power in order to get the job done.

The Role and Duties of the Independent Third Party. The United States Department of Defense (DOD) has established that independent third party verification can be added to a project for only 10 percent of the total project cost. The DOD considers this cost well worthwhile for riskier projects.[3]

A similar recommendation was made by a study of 121 military acquisition projects for the Canadian Department of National Defense (DND).[4] This study developed a set of recommendations for dealing with risky projects (whether the risk was technical or cost or deadline oriented). The study concluded that high-risk projects need:
- effective authority for the project manager
- effective issue resolution processes
- tighter technical risk controls through work breakdown structure (WBS) and other advanced control techniques
- increased frequency of monitoring.

Interestingly, the study also noted that the choice of project management tool had no noticeable impact on project outcome. The role of the independent third party that we are recommending is, in large measure, to see that the recommendations of the Canadian DND study are actually implemented (rather than one more *program of the month*).

The Role and Responsibilities of the Third Party. Following are some of the roles and duties that it makes sense for an independent third party to fulfill:
- A safety valve for project problems: As Fran Webster, former editor-in-chief of publications for the Project Management Institute observes: "People who have a mortgage to pay learn to say 'yes sir!' real quick." The evidence cited in Section 2.2.7, on the leadership integrity issue, provides a clear indication that lower-level people who want to do the right things are often suppressed by the questionable behavior of their superiors. The third party judges the issues of a situation based on the project accounting and standards established for the organization (rather than worrying about losing her job). The third party escalates to the shareholders *only if certain critical hurdles are crossed.*
- Provide shareholders with unfiltered information: One of the third party's chief duties is to get information from those doing the work. You will then have the opportunity to hear both the *filtered* and *unfiltered* versions.
- Remain independent and objective: The third party must remain independent of other agendas. If his first priority is to keep dollars coming in to his consulting firm, it is possible to encounter the same pressures that prevented auditors from

escalating project problems during the Horror Stories. You might also find your third party constrained by pressure to keep other consultants billable.

- Minimize shareholder time required and promote the most effective use of that time: The third party can help sort through the technical smokescreens, variety of excuses, obfuscations, and so on.
- Maintain a management performance baseline: The third party can provide shareholders with a reasonable baseline against which to measure management's effectiveness in the area of projects. At a minimum, management needs to be rated against both the state-of-the-art management practices and the organization's performance on projects over the long term. Management also needs to be held accountable for the promises made to secure funding for projects.

The Third Party's Profit Motive. In all likelihood, you have heard or thought of these ideas before, but they have fallen through the cracks. The third party has a profit motive to perform in these areas over the long term.

Summary of What to Do for Principle 1. If possible, get agreement for personal involvement from major shareholders or establish a project committee among the shareholders. (Be very careful about where each committee member's first priority is!) Retain an independent third party to advise, monitor, and keep the shareholders from being buried in the details.

Principle 2: Initial and Ongoing Cost of Quality Reviews

In Section 4.2.3, Conducting Your Own Cost of Quality Review, most of this principle is covered. A sample questionnaire is in Appendix E. Keep in mind that an initial cost of quality review is only a starting point. To be sustained, improvement must be measured on a continuing basis. I believe annual cost of quality reviews are the minimum. This is an ideal task for the independent third party because the profit motive will cause her to help prevent this key task from being forgotten.

Who Do You Interview? The cost of quality review will only be effective if the information comes from those who are doing the work. As we've discussed, they must have a measure of anonymity and immunity from reprisal so they can, at least, feel free to tell the truth. I am in favor of asking for the middle manager's opinion first, then going to the people on the team for the real story. The contrasts between the two versions regarding the health of a particular project should prove enlightening. Table 10 presents a sample summary report for this process.

The summary presented in Table 10 has been prepared from actual Horror Stories and Success Stories (although not all from the same company). It is quite typical of large organizations. One project shows a zero cost of quality, three projects have significant (but probably tolerable) costs of quality, and one project, (D), has the capacity to materially damage the organization. It is in such bad shape that the project team doesn't even know how much has been spent!

The Bottom Line. The exact specifics of this example are unimportant. The real questions are the following. What is the cost of quality in your organization? Do you have any time bombs ticking?

Ongoing Reviews. The research recommends (at a minimum) annual cost of quality reviews to measure progress toward reducing the firm's overall cost of quality and to provide a focal point for continuous improvement.

Table 10. A Sample Cost of Quality Review

Project	Original Project Objectives	Original Direct Project Budget	Total Project Direct Costs Spent to Date	Total Estimated Cost of Quality	Root Issue Score Card
A (See Case 157)	Order Processing System (Increase revenues through improved customer service; reduce operating expenses.)	$700,000	$1,500,000	$1,800,000	凧
B (See Case 134)	Loan Processing System (Increase revenues through improved customer service; reduce operating expenses.)	$1,000,000	$2,000,000	$1,500,000	凧
C (See Case 118)	Convert Financial Systems from Mainframe to Client/Server (Increase revenues through improved information throughout entire corporation; reduce operating expenses.)	$250,000	$400,000	$1,150,000	凧
D (See Case 144)	Product Design and Cost Estimating System (Increase revenues by bringing products to market quicker; reduce operating expenses.)	$8,000,000	n/a	$100,000,000	凧
E (See Texas Instruments Success Story, Section 6.2)	Accounts Receivable Imaging System (Increase revenues through improved collections; reduce operating expenses.)	$500,000	$500,000	None—project is proceeding as expected.	凧
Total Projected Cost of Quality: $104,450,000!					

Principle 3: Getting the Right Expertise on Your Team

Assuming you have conducted a cost of quality review and decided to move forward with building a foundation for improving client/server project outcomes, you need a team. Following are some key people and key areas of expertise that need to be a part of your team.

• Pilot project business unit sponsor and participants: You need a business unit manager who believes that there is a problem and wants to fix it. You will also need support from her people. Look for someone whose business depends on some increased revenues or decreased expenses that will depend on the effective delivery of a client/server project. Also look for those who have been burned in the past; they seem to be more motivated and less susceptible to ridiculous expectations.

• A staff manager that has been trying to implement these types of improvements (a Sun Tzu) but has (probably) not had a lot of measurable success: This person will know the problems, people, and issues. Places to look for this person include reengineering departments, quality departments, and some information systems departments.

- The pilot project manager: You will need someone who is capable and believes that improvement in the status quo is possible. You probably don't want to conduct this pilot without the help of your information systems department, so this is the logical choice. Choose this person carefully! A list of the skills needed by today's project manager appears in Principle 6.
- The need for project-driven industry expertise: As already discussed, you need the outside perspective of someone trained in cross-industry project management. That person needs to understand how project-driven industries are able to consistently manage projects to successful conclusions. A good test of their credentials would be to show them the list of recommended project accounting and management standards shown in Principle 5. Ask them why each recommended standard should or should not be a part of your firm's standards. ("I don't know, but I know how to find out" is an acceptable answer.) I would recommend a certified project management professional, if possible.
- The need for business process design/reengineering expertise: Very few client/server projects simply automate existing business processes. In fact, such a project should be strongly questioned because it will probably not produce many significant benefits. I want to quote Lois Zells, former co-chair of Project Management Institute's Information Systems Specific Interest Group: "The essence of Reengineering boils down to this: You must investigate the existing business processes to the point where you understand what steps must be kept and what steps can be discarded." *I cannot urge this strongly enough; failure to properly cope with the needed business process changes is probably one of the single biggest mistakes made by all of the Horror Stories.*

    I have intentionally omitted a discussion of reengineering in this book because that expertise is available elsewhere. Reengineering is an emerging discipline that suffers from nearly all of the same root project problems that plague client/server. One of the main purposes of the pilot project is to demonstrate that state-of-the-art project management practices can dramatically improve both the client/server and reengineering aspects of these projects. *I would strongly recommend an acid test for your reengineering expert. Can she show you a client/server project that she was involved with that had measurable before and after improvements to the business process?*
- The independent third party: The third party serves as the owner's representative, safety valve, and objective reviewer. It would make sense for this person to also fill the *project-driven industry expertise* role described above.
- (And, ultimately) the technical team members: If we take care of the above priorities first, it has been my experience that the technical team is relatively easy to put together.

I realize that this is a heavy-duty team to put together, but this pilot is no place for half-way measures. The budget that is outlined in Section 4.4, Weighing the Cost and Benefit of Action, provides for this type of expertise. If you can find various people who can fill multiple roles, so much the better.

Principle 4: The Pilot: A Crucial Small Win

Some of the key things to accomplish through the pilot include:
- Develop momentum and credibility for the idea that client/server project outcomes can be substantially improved.

- Sort through the standards shown in Principle 5 to identify the *essential minimum* controls that need to be in place for your particular organization.
- Sort through culture issues of your organization. Determine if they might help or hurt this overall effort and what needs to be done to handle them. For example, some of the Horror Story organizations are extremely political. Since there is a higher tendency in these organizations for promotion of self over the company, more attention and focus will be needed from the independent third party and the shareholder(s).
- Test organization models to find one that works for your unique organization.
- Determine who needs training and the best methods for accomplishing that training.
- Find the warts and flaws in a controlled setting.
- Determine how much *raw power* is needed from executives and shareholders to keep the project focused on the good of the company and undiluted by personal agendas. Note that it is quite likely that shareholder action will be needed only once or twice. Just like Sun Tzu's concubines, the message will get across that you are serious.

Following are some criteria for choosing good pilot projects. Projects that improve revenues and/or reduce expenses in a measurable fashion are far more likely to be recognized as significant. Projects should be small enough to provide measurable results in three to six months and large and complex enough to be credible as a sample win. A good pilot project would be a project that is likely to be skewed by personal agendas in order to test the standards and measures for prevention. There should be a significant reengineering component so that the project management standards can be verified as applicable to situations when significant change is part of the project.

The Responsibilities of the Executive Sponsor. At the risk of restating something you've already heard, Figure 12 represents the foundation that needs to exist for the pilot team to deliver an effective project. The executive sponsor's primary job is to see that this foundation remains solid. The standards shown in Principle 5 are the essence of this foundation.

Principle 5: Developing Project Accounting and Management Standards

We are interested in developing the *essential minimum project accounting and management standards* that will work for your organization. No one is advocating mindless paperwork and bureaucracy. Following are the key areas where your team needs to research and identify the right standards.

Measurable Project Success Definition. As discussed in Section 3.1, on successful project definition, I advocate *performing as promised* or *conformance to specifications*. Whatever standard you adopt, it must be defined and measurable. This implies that the specifications are sufficiently accurate to measure success, which has been a traditional failing of computer projects. One of the reasons the earned value standard needs to be adopted is that it provides workable measures for whether specifications were adequately defined up front.

Basic Project Phase Definition—Concept, Development, Execution, Finish (C/D/E/F). As discussed in Section 3.1, under PMI Key Lessons, this structure is necessary to prevent the *root-of-all-evil* (see Principle 8) trap. Part of this basic phase structure is establishing how much definition is required at each stage before approval is given to move to the next stage. Most of the Horror Stories charged ahead

---

Figure 12. The Project Foundation

ACCOUNTABILITY

Objectivity	Right People	Authority/
	Right Motives	Responsibility
	Right Actions	Match

---

spending money and looking busy without sufficiently defining the project. Following are some key things that need to happen in each phase. (**Note to executives**: These standards are important, but largely tactical. Executives should concentrate their efforts on the next section, Project Foundation Standards.)

- Concept phase (should account for approximately 5 percent of total project budget)
  — order of magnitude cost estimate
  — high-level project plan
  — business case development
  — buy-in and sign-off to proceed.
- Development phase (should account for approximately 20 percent of total project budget) (**Note**: This standard phase refers to development of project specifications—not development of software.)
  — management team in place (project manager, executive sponsor(s), user management, IS management, and so on)
  — definition of work breakdown structure (see Appendix B) and work packages (see Appendix B) defined and broken down to work packets no larger than forty hours of work
  — business unit participation standard
  — resources available as promised standard
  — standards for delivering results in ninety to 180 days
  — estimate refinement and budget development from work breakdown structure (WBS)
  — business requirements analysis and business process design (**Note** that the WBS and work package definition standards require that these business processes be understood to the point when estimates for programming and implementation can be defined in forty-hour chunks. This is a significantly greater degree of definition than has been practiced in the past. It is the principle reason that 20 percent or more of the project budget should be spent in this phase.) Note that this will often require a business process *lab* setting as advocated by Dr. Michael Hammer.[5] This is where new processes are piloted with the users by using paper mock-ups or *quick and dirty* prototypes. *A Guide to the Project Management Body of Knowledge (PMBOK Guide)* suggests that at least 20 percent of the project budget be spent in this area. I differ slightly,

based on my experience with so many projects failing in this area. I would recommend as much as 30 to 40 percent of the project be spent in this phase. The key is to have a defined set of objectives *before we hire the army of programmers in the execution phase*.
— technical solution design begins
— technology and vendor evaluations
— prototype developed and pilot executed
— buy-in and sign-off to proceed. (Again, sign-off for full execution should not take place until the project's objectives and *to-be* business processes are defined.)
• Execution phase (should account for approximately 70 percent of total project budget)
— full project staffing
— technical team training
— full-scale development system(s) purchased and installed
— functional specifications developed from *to-be* business process requirements
— technical solution detailed design
— technical solution development
— test planning and execution
— business process, user procedures, and training documented
— solution implementation
— user training
— production system deployment
— production cutover.
• Finish phase (should account for approximately 5 percent of total project budget)
— clear definition of when project is finished and how maintenance will be transitioned (and to who)
— vendor/supplier contract close out
— evaluation of project overall (estimate to actual, quality, timeliness, and so on)
— individual evaluations
— overall performance evaluation for project (archived to aid future projects).

Project Foundation Standards. These are the standards that executives need to pay particular attention to (although you may need to refer to the above standards for clarification). You've seen these issues in several places. The challenge now is to turn them into effective standards for your organization.

Objectivity Standards. These standards need to ensure that:
• The business case for doing the project will stand objective cost/benefit scrutiny. (Earned value is part of the answer because it improves estimate accuracy.)
• Scope, deliverables and objective definition: Scope and deliverables need to be broken into controllable, defined work packages (less than forty hours each) so that the total effort can be accurately estimated prior to project approval for the execution phase. This usually is a major task of the development phase.
• Budgets, schedules, and deadlines are objectively set based on scope, objectives, and available resources.
• Solution design that is based on objective, solid thinking and able to withstand third party review.
• Resource requirements, availability, and assignment are developed objectively.

Right People, Right Motives, Right Actions Standards. Many of the recommendations throughout this book are designed to help in this area. These include training and certification to ensure competence and third party review to ensure leadership integrity. Your standards and procedures need to ensure that the following

roles are staffed with the right people demonstrating the right motives and taking the right actions:
- involved top executive
- initial and subsequent sponsor(s)
- involved peer-level executives
- project manager
- involved business unit managers
- involved information systems managers
- other involved front line people (business process and requirements people, estimators/designers, users, technical people, and so on)
- externals (consultants, contractors, hardware/software suppliers).

Authority/Responsibility Match Standards. This is where the project manager needs help the most. She needs to have the authority to get the project done right. These types of standards need to ensure that:
- Project manager's sign-off is required for:
  — initial scope/deliverables
  — deadlines
  — budget
  — scope changes (even those pushed by powerful people!)
  — stopping the project.
- Project manager has the following direct project team authorities:
  — hire/fire
  — assignments
  — incentive compensation control
  — capacity to deal with resisters or detractors
  — ability to hold employees/contractors/outsiders or other functional areas accountable for the commitments given by their respective executives.
- Project manager has some degree of discretionary signature authority for the good of the project (e.g., $500).
- Project manager's authority and support from upper management is visible (e.g., reporting level, face-to-face time with executives, the ability to correct erroneous expectations, and so on).
- Project manager's chain of command helps (rather than hurts) his ability to conduct the project in the best interests of the shareholders.
- Project manager cannot be arbitrarily removed from the project if she stands up for the good of the project although a powerful person wants something different.
- Project manager's responsibilities outside the project do not compromise his effectiveness (probably should be at least 70 percent dedicated to the project).
- The organization will reward or penalize the project manager fairly for doing the right things (and the project manager believes it)!

As a final thought in this area, here is a test: Is there anyone the project manager can blame if the project does not perform as promised? There shouldn't be!

Accountability Standards. Overall, accountability consists of the general safeguards to ensure that objectivity, right people, right motives, right actions, and authority/responsibility match standards are adhered to. A few additional accountability standards are necessary to ensure that:

- A *safety valve* exists to escalate significant project problems high enough to ensure that no agenda other than the good of the shareholder prevails. (The independent third party can judge the problem against this set of standards and objectively choose to escalate accordingly.) If they have a solid business reason, project managers and team members need to be able to initiate this safety valve without fear of short- or long-term reprisals.

- Executive sponsor(s) accountability: Executive sponsors often change during the life of the project, and true accountability is often difficult under current methods. The earned value accounting method can specifically measure executives for progress during their periods of ownership. As a final test of executive accountability standards, we need to ask questions such as: "Could they avoid responsibility if things went wrong? Would the organization truly reward them for doing the right things and penalize them for the wrong things?"

Additional Items That Should Be Considered. The following items do not necessarily fall into predefined categories but merit special attention when developing standards for client/server project management.

The Earned Value Method of Accounting and Project Management. I want to again direct you to Section 6.2, the Texas Instruments success stories, for a working example of earned value in a client/server project. As an overview, let me give you my definition: *Earned value project accounting and management is a method of converting work planned and work actually done into dollars so that measurement and control can reliably take place.* This addresses the primary problem of project accounting, which is to accurately *know* how much of the planned work is actually done. Some additional benefits of earned value include:

- Vendors and consultants get paid only what they budgeted for a deliverable—not what they spent. This protects the customer from overruns.

- A clear measurement of the week-to-week progress on actual work done and completed to specifications is available. When progress is not forthcoming it is immediately visible and known by all.

- Project definition diligence prior to approving funds for further work is forced.

- A definition of internal resources is required, and a vehicle for holding people accountable for commitments is also forced.

- A reliable way to predict unacceptable overruns before the project is 20 percent complete is available.[6]

- A proven method for managing complex technology projects is provided.

If only one recommendation from this book is adopted, this should be it. The only downside is that it would be very difficult to do from a book; one needs to be trained and have had experience in actually applying the concepts.

Technical Risk Management Standards—Three Key Questions. Blame-the-technology excuses: I flatly reject as self-serving and lazy the contention that these projects are technically unpredictable. I find no evidence in the management literature or among my experienced peers to indicate that executives and stockholders must tolerate this risk.

If the technology is unpredictable, the first project is to break it down to predictable components! If a technical or project manager cannot recognize when technology is exposing the shareholders to risk, he has no business having managerial authority. *Part of this entire process of implementing project management standards is to create a clear understanding with those proposing projects that predictable outcomes are part of their jobs!*

At this point, Captain Kirk of *Star Trek* fame would say: "Don't mince words with me, Bones. Tell me how you really feel." Having told you how I feel about blame-the-technology excuses, following are three questions that executives and shareholders can ask to determine if technical people have done their due diligence:

- What is the closest possible successful precedent you have been able to find, and what did you learn from studying it? (And what risks are we taking beyond that precedent?)
- How have we confirmed that our planned system will perform under the load of full-scale use?
- Where are our compatibility risks between system components, and how are we managing those risks?

Some Tough Questions for Projects with Large Reengineering Components. The first question to ask is: "How many people will have to materially change the way they do business to use this proposed system?" I've had answers ranging from two to 5,000. As we've discussed earlier, the Horror Stories consistently failed to estimate the magnitude of work involved in large-scale business-process change. Here are some tough requests that can prove whether your reengineering specialists have done their due diligence:

- Show me the process maps for each major business process affected.
- Show me the difference between before and after.
- Show me the specific process steps you have identified as waste.
- Show me how the new process will be done significantly better.

Compensation. One of the greatest travesties of the Horror Stories is that nearly everybody got paid, even though the projects didn't deliver. Whether immediately or over the long term, we need to change to more of a *pay-for-performance, pay-for-value* approach. Fortunately, earned value provides a clear track record of who contributed what value to the project.

I would suggest that we move toward a 70/30 or 60/40 split of salary to incentive. Studies are beginning to show clear improvements in productivity and value creation based on closer links between pay and performance.[7] Note that the individual needs to perceive some upside associated with this loss of security rather than think of it as an arbitrary reduction in salary.

The Continuing Fundamental Problem of Wanting to Do Too Many Projects with a Fixed Pool of Resources. This problem plagues nearly every type of project from client/server to reengineering to product development. Earned value helps a great deal because it forces a definition of internal resources expected. It is only part of the solution, however. If a project requires three critical people from another department three months from now, it is very difficult to guarantee that they will be available.

One possible solution is that when an executive promises that people will be available but doesn't follow through on that promise, *the executive is held responsible for paying for contractors or temporary help* needed to get through the shortage period. Obviously, the executive would have to be well motivated to sign up for this level of accountability.

Another approach being taken by one of my clients is the *portfolio approach*. The basic idea is to maintain a running summary of every computer system, every project, and all of the labor required to complete the existing commitments. Having this portfolio has allowed them to lobby for adequate resources and reprioritize several projects. An important control in this process is a clear definition of when a *new project is approved and added to the portfolio*. This requires an evaluation of the portfolio's ability to absorb the additional resource demands. I should add that this client was a $500 million manufacturer. We got the initial portfolio defined and the data entered in less than two months. The consulting fees were less than $20,000 for the initial work.

Although this portfolio approach has much merit, it has the inherent risks of losing priority and of the information becoming outdated. Maintaining this data is a task that *is probably better suited for a project office* (or some other staff support function) than for people who are daily on the *project firing line*.

Work Authorization Process. As described in the immediately preceding topic, a clear process needs to exist for work authorization. In the real world of an information systems department, project proposals, scope changes, and demands to *fix it now* are flying daily. In this state, it is very easy for a user to want an important new feature but not ever get a definitive answer. The result is (usually) that the user assumes her request is approved simply because she made it.

Once again, earned value has help in this area. A fundamental component is the *scope baseline*, which converts all approved work to dollars. The only way that work can be added is by adding it to the scope baseline, which increases the total cost of the project and is readily visible to all.

Long-Term Benefit Tracking (Earned Value/Earned Benefits). One of the recurring problems of client/server and other information systems projects is that the projects are long over before the benefits are realized. Memories and documentation are fuzzy as to whether the benefits promised were the benefits realized. This fact reduces accountability and contributes to projects being skewed by personal agendas.

I would like to suggest a small extension to the earned value concepts. Earned value tracking stops when the project is over. If we extend the concept to include an evaluation of the actual benefit received against the rigor and baselines of earned value, I believe we have a tool to help encourage long-term accountability and improve performance.

Bill Redmond, a PMI member and long-time certified project management professional, described some of these efforts when he was with Arco Oil & Gas: "We had people assigned to track the specific benefits of each project. This feedback was invaluable, but those people tracking benefits became needed elsewhere and this measurement process fell through the cracks."

This is another role that the independent third party can play over the long term. Imagine the value to a corporation of a five-to-ten year profile on each executive's ability to deliver project benefits as promised!

Buy-in and Participation of Other Departments. The projects that produce the most benefit tend to be cross-departmental projects. A problem arises when one department usually champions the project and others play a supporting role. A large recurring difficulty in the Horror Stories was the underestimation and unavailability of needed people from other departments.

Again, earned value provides a clear vehicle for estimating these resources and holding people accountable for commitments.

Creative Ways to Hold Executives Accountable for Their Promises. Even if you are a shareholder or senior executive with all the power you need, it is frequently difficult to discipline executives without destroying their usefulness. One of my clients came up with several *non-lethal* ways of disciplining senior people who don't live up to their promises. The idea revolves around penalties that hurt status and sting egos but don't really harm the organization. Following are some examples:

- temporary loss of signature authority for expenditures (my favorite)
- temporary loss of perks (car, club memberships, personal secretary, big office, first class travel, and so on)
- assign unpleasant duties (union liaison, OSHA liaison, and so on)
- move part of their responsibilities to others
- insert someone over them
- give the next prestigious assignment to a rival.

Quarterly Peer Reviews. A novel idea suggested by Philip Crosby in *Quality Is Free* is that of a quarterly *peer review* among executives. Each executive would brief peers on the state of each major project and have to defend the project against the critique of peers. This could create a collaborative, learning environment where peer pressure actually works toward improving project outcomes.

Note that a peer group of executives is not going to require each other to adhere to a set of standards that each doesn't believe in. Part of this peer process would have to include input into the initial standards and the opportunity to fix standards that don't work.

An additional benefit of internal discipline may also be possible. If one of the number fails to meet his commitments, the group might impose one of the creative penalties described above.

Principle 6: Grow, Train, and Certify Business Managers, Project Managers, and Executives

The trends we've observed and conclusions drawn certainly suggest that project management needs to become a core area of excellence for each rising manager. These managers will face multiple reengineering, product development, and client/server projects during their careers. Eventually, they will probably have to manage programs (groups of projects). Clearly, training is called for. Following are some starting points for how you might proceed. (**Note**: This assumes that Principles 1–5, particularly the pilot, have been pursued. I would caution against trying to develop and execute large-scale training prior to a successful pilot and definition of standards. While the pilot is discussed before the standards, it is important to remember that testing the standards is a critical aspect of the pilot and must be done before large-scale training takes place.)

The Executive Training and Certification—An Overview.

- Objective: Introduce the executives to the new standards and processes. Present the business case for why this needs to be done. Visibly demonstrate shareholder involvement and authority.

- Mechanics: This will have to be required training. I suggest a one-day minimum, supplemented with videotape training.
- Certification: I believe it is reasonable to require an executive to be certified in the new project accounting and control standards before allowing him to be in charge of projects over, for example, $100,000. The executives will certainly resist this, and shareholder authority will be required to ensure compliance. To deal with the *I don't have time* excuse, the certification can be administered via computer-based testing at the executive's convenience.
- Highlights: The training should focus on how these necessary disciplines will help achieve improved project outcomes and avert disasters in the executive's area.

I also suggest that the cost of quality review already conducted be a major source of focus. To walk the executives through these past internal mistakes and how they will now be prevented should be both interesting and useful.

The Business Unit Manager Training and Certification—An Overview.
- Objective: Introduce the business manager to the new standards and processes. In many cases, business managers ultimately end up managing business-driven projects, so this is an opportunity to build a foundation and help them to at least recognize what they don't know. They will also need to understand the business case for why this needs to be done.
- Mechanics: This will have to be required training. I suggest a one-day minimum, supplemented with videotape training.
- Certification: Certification similar (or identical to) the executive certification can also be administered via computer-based testing at the manager's convenience.
- Highlights: The training should also focus on how these necessary disciplines will help achieve improved project outcomes and avert disasters in the manager's area.

Working from the cost of quality review already conducted should be a major focus, as with the executive training.

The Project Manager Training and Certification—An Overview.
- Objective: Thoroughly train and certify the project manager to implement the new standards.
- Mechanics: This will probably take at least a week but not necessarily all at one time.
- Certification: I do not recommend PMP certification at this point. The project manager needs to be focused on the standards and issues specific to your organization. I believe that this training should be custom developed, and the testing should be rigorous.
- Highlights: If the other recommendations have been adopted, the project manager will now be operating with much greater authority. She will need to learn the benefits and limits of this authority. Rigorous review of the Horror Stories and traps to avoid should be included.

If the shareholder escalation safety valve is going to work, the independent third party and the shareholder have to be present to make it believable.

Skills Needed by Client/Server Project Managers. Following is a listing of the specific skills needed by project managers. I recommend that this serve as a baseline for developing your internal training and growth programs for project managers. The Project Management Institute (see Appendix B, Glossary of Terms and Definitions) has an excellent series of materials that cover most of these disciplines. (**Note 1**: This list also makes a good *tool for interviewing prospective project managers.*) (**Note 2**: I know of no one who is expert in all of these areas. You are looking for generalists with working knowledge of these areas.)

The Hard Skills:
- Earned value method of project accounting and management
- Estimating
- Solution and vendor evaluations
- Scope management and control
  — Work authorization process
  — Scope reporting
- Project planning (work breakdown structure)
- Project scheduling
- Business case, return on investment, feasibility studies
- Project budgets and cost forecasting
- Business process definition, change, and reengineering
- User/business process requirements definition
- System design and development
- Risk quantification and management
- Project management software skills
- Procurement and contracts
- Prototyping (benefits and pitfalls).

The Softer Skills:
- Project team: organizing, motivating, sustaining (internal and external)
- Project team building
- Deliverable planning: the ability to produce user deliverables within ninety days
- Industry/business expertise preferable
- Resource skill and availability assessments
- Coping with the technical personality
- Communication (up, down, sideways, oral, written)
- Facilitated workshops
- Methodologies (good news and bad—don't miss what's important)
- Business unit credibility and rapport
- Survival skills for doing projects with human beings.

Where To Get Help with Training. The PMI magazine (*PM Network*—see Appendix B) advertises many firms that provide PMP and custom training. I have been particularly impressed with the work of Infotech Management of Arlington, Texas, United States. Founder Russ Choyce and principal Ben Settle have both helped me through the massive learning curve for project management.

This is, again, an area where a knowledge of project-driven industry practices is essential. A PMP-certified project manager with experience using earned value is the best source of available expertise.

A Final Thought on Why Project Managers Are Higher up the Management Ladder in Project-Driven Industries. According to an excerpt from a reengineering training session by Dr. Michael Hammer (1994):

> Projects evolve through three main phases requiring differing skills. Initially, it is the "What are we trying to accomplish?" skill set. Secondly, the "How do we solve key problems" skills become prominent. Finally, the "Execution" skills carry through to completion.

If this is the first time you have looked at all of the skills and attributes required by effective project managers, perhaps it is not hard to see why other industries consider the role of project manager such an important one.

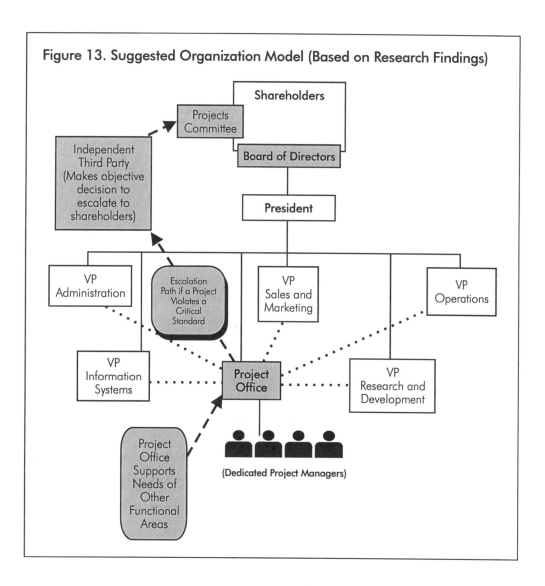

Figure 13. Suggested Organization Model (Based on Research Findings)

Principle 7: Organize for a Solid Project Foundation

Unfortunately, there does not seem to be a definitive organization model for optimizing these types of project outcomes. This will probably need to be an evolving matter and an area calling for more research (see Appendix F).

As a starting point, I'd like to suggest a model based on the earlier-mentioned research, as shown in Figure 13.

Issues to Consider While Organizing. We have discussed a number of special items that need attention in order to turn a weak project management capability into a strong one. When you conduct your first cost of quality review, I suspect the justification for funding this type of support organization and checks and balances will be quite evident. (Remember Philip Crosby's experience in *Quality Is Free*. It is his opinion that a cost of quality review needs to go through three iterations before it has uncovered all of the costs.)

As we've seen throughout the Horror Stories and as documented by the leadership integrity findings, project managers and other mid- to low-level people are often prevented from doing the right things by the agenda of their superiors. This type of reporting structure and *objectivity safety valve* is needed so that:

- Mid-to low-level people have an avenue to see that significant problems are escalated without jeopardizing their jobs or long-term opportunities.
- Personal protection note: These mid- to low-level people do not initiate the escalation. The project management and accounting standards described above call for automatic escalation if critical hurdles are crossed or standards violated. All that the junior people have to do is adhere to the reporting standards, and the rest is automatic. The intent is to largely protect them from the normal repercussions of escalating something above their bosses.
- The independent third party serves as an *objective reality check* on whether the problem has significant enough business consequences to bring to the shareholder project committee.
- The shareholder project committee is necessary because board members are often not significant shareholders. The Horror Story evidence suggests that the board members overseeing these corporations certainly did not exert sufficient diligence and may have acted (or not acted) for personal agendas rather than for the good of shareholders.

Specific Duties of the Project Office

Champion for the Cause of Making Project Management a Core of Excellence.
This excellence should focus on three types of projects: client/server, reengineering, and product development. It should also:

- Create a formal elevation of project management as a business discipline by:
  — separating project management from the technical diciplines of information systems, reengineering, and product development
  — separating project management from the priorities and agendas of other departments such that the good of the shareholders is the only true focus of the project.
- Conduct annual cost of quality reviews to monitor the organization's exposure and to measure progress. This will also serve to provide a clear cost/benefit business case for continued investment in project management excellence.
- Remain part of the escalation process (though escalation is still based on objective hurdles to reduce the potential career downside for individuals).
- Defend the project managers and the project management program from arbitrary budget cuts and layoffs.
- See that project management attracts talented people and ensure that those people are rewarded for doing the right things for shareholders.
  Oversees Standards, Training, Safeguards, and Compliance.
- Develops and monitors project accounting and management standards.
- Develops and administers the required training and certification.
- Tracks project portfolio and resource availability.
- Has the expertise to help business units develop solid contracts with vendors and consultants.

Provides Administrative, Information, and Expertise Support.

- (possibly) Provides administrative support for business unit project managers such as:
  — setting up projects in the standard project management software systems
  — providing data entry services so project manager can direct attention to more important things
  — reporting preparation and interpretation.
- Serves as a central repository for:
  — history of previous projects
  — performance of individuals and executives on those projects
  — state-of-the-art project management techniques and the project management body of knowledge
  — resources for investigating internal and external precedents for particular types of projects.

Provides Dedicated Project Managers and Supports Other Project Managers.

- Develops and grows a core of dedicated project managers.
- Provides experienced, certified, full-time project managers when appropriate (e.g., projects over $100,000 in total cost).
- Provides support for business unit project managers to aid them in doing their own projects.

As you can see, there is much work to be done to move the organization toward effective project outcomes. Some of this work is going on even now in your existing organizations, but it is clearly not operating at critical mass or optimum effectiveness.

Will the Project Office Concept Work? While there are many successful precedents for using project offices in other industries, I have yet to see one surrounding client/server projects in operations-driven companies. This is an area that calls for more research. (See Appendix F for additional items needing more research.)

Two of my clients are attempting project offices for client/server projects at present. While I applaud the attempts, I do not believe they will be successful. In one case, the office appears to be the political creation of someone trying to preserve his job and expand his power base. In the other case, the idea is being initiated internally and is subject to the agenda of the department that is sponsoring it. The research conclusions call for measures to avoid these types of compromises, and neither of these attempts at project offices address that recommendation.

A Final Note on the *Safety Valve* and Shareholder Involvement. It is hoped that the need for these safeguards will diminish over time. The annual cost of quality reviews will be your best measurement as to whether these safeguards remain necessary.

Principle 8: Fads, Traps, and Dirty Tricks to Avoid

As you build your program of improving project effectiveness, there are many traps that lay in wait for the unsuspecting project. Watch for these traps and avoid them if you can. They are mentioned here because they were repeated across multiple Horror Stories.

The Mega-Traps

These four traps are so destructive and so pervasive that they deserve special mention. A common thread of each of these problems is that they precipitate many other traps. If an organization could do nothing more than prevent these four root causes of trouble, project outcomes would be substantially improved.

The *Root-of-All-Evil* (High-Level Project Definition) Trap. The project was not objectively broken down into work packages to the point where scope, resources, budgets, and deadlines could be accurately estimated and changes controlled. Money is approved based on the high-level definition. This situation is very susceptible to being skewed toward personal interests at the expense of the shareholder. This tends to ignite other traps, including the:

- *we think we accomplish too much, too soon, for too little* trap
- *lack of business unit participation* trap
- *the appearance of hard work, progress, and control* trap
- *do whatever it takes to justify previous actions, please those in power, and keep money coming into the project* trap
- *business case is not solid enough to get business unit priority* trap.

Prevention: This mega-trap will be prevented or minimized by the earned value method of project accounting and management, as well as the other standards recommended previously.

"The Project Manager versus *Project Manager*" Trap. This is the trap we have been discussing all along—the difference between the appearance of having a project manager and the reality of having a competent, motivated, empowered *Project Manager* as exists in the project-driven industries. Many of the following traps are precipitated by this mega-trap, including:

- *no empowered, single point of responsibility* trap
- *executive sponsor wants to manage at high level* trap
- all of the traps shown under authority/responsibility match traps.

Prevention: This mega-trap will be prevented by the recommended standards, the project office concept, and the independent third party escalation to shareholders as a safety valve.

The *Putting Self Interest over Shareholder Interest* Trap. As we saw in the discussion on leadership integrity issues (Section 2.2.7), this root problem was directly observed or strongly suspected in at least 50 percent of all Horror Stories. It is at the heart of nearly all that goes wrong with projects.

Prevention: Setting up and adhering to standards, objective third party review, and the escalation safety valve all exist to help prevent this problem.

The *Being Forced to Act* Trap. In Horror Story #109, the French SNCF Railway case, we have an example of the hundreds of millions of dollars of cost that can result from being forced to take action. This quasi-governmental agency allowed itself to get into an exposed, reactive position by procrastinating on replacement of old systems. We can safely conclude that putting off those investments was politically motivated.

Prevention: While nothing can prevent the failures of predecessors, this entire set of recommendations is aimed at safeguards to prevent politically self-serving actions at the expense of the whole. The earned value method of project accounting and management, the independent third party, and the escalation safety valve are all key parts of early warning and prevention.

Some Typical Traps of a Weak Project Foundation

Following are some of the traps repeatedly observed in the Horror Stories. All of the above recommendations are intended to help avoid these traps. If you note projects continuing to fall prey to these traps through your ongoing cost of quality reviews, attention is probably warranted in that particular foundation area.

Objectivity Traps. Following are the types of problems that continually undermine an objective approach to the project:

*   *business case is not solid enough to get business unit priority* trap
*   *everybody else is buying (insert name here)* trap (See Fads. Tends to shortcut diligence.)
*   *pressure to act (or be perceived as acting)* trap
*   *funding of information systems not linked to business unit payback priorities* trap
*   *we think we can accomplish too much, too soon, for too little* trap
*   *lack of business unit participation* trap
*   *immediate hiring and purchase of hardware and software* trap
*   *the appearance of hard work, progress, and control* trap
*   *do whatever it takes to justify previous actions, please those in power, and keep money coming in to the project* trap
*   100 *percent outsourcing of a project that requires a close link to operations* trap
*   *subjective technical solution* trap
*   *executive sponsor wants to manage at high level* trap
*   *technology-driven project* trap (the technical people were incredibly bright and sold management on the idea ...)
*   *information systems-driven project* trap
*   *justify the cost of client/server by unplugging the mainframe* trap
*   *the package software will do everything we need to do* trap
*   *relying on impressions when presented with overly technical and detailed decisions* trap (usually includes time pressure that prevents an appropriate investigation of the details)
*   *political/self-serving budgets and deadlines* trap
*   *just get something in by the end of the quarter* trap.

Accountability Traps.

*   Accountability traps at executive level: See Section 2.2.7 on leadership integrity.
*   Accountability traps below executive level:
    *   — *I'm just smart enough to convince you that I know what I'm doing* trap (vendor sales people, consultants, internal people)
    *   — *OK, I can coast for a while* trap. (Pressure is off, no one knows for sure if the real work is getting done, and all of a sudden you're too far behind to catch up.)

Right People/Right Motives/Right Actions Traps. This root issue is fundamentally about the capability and commitment of the project team (including outsiders). You may also want to refer to the leadership integrity issues discussion in Section 2.2.7 and "The Project Manager versus *Project Manager*" mega-trap at the beginning of this principle. Beyond those items, only one other trap was identified in this area:

*   *promote the up and coming techie to project manager* trap.

Authority/Responsibility Traps.

*   *no single point of responsibility with the capacity to perform* trap
*   *executive sponsor wants to manage at high level* trap
*   *don't bother me, I'm busy running the business* trap
*   *lack of cross-functional executive buy-in* trap

- *delegation in name only* trap—two primary cases:
  — motives pure but interferes with *how-to* details because of general inability to delegate
  — motives not pure; interferes with *how-to* details with the intent to make sure that she always looks good, even at the expense of the project
- *do the right thing and lose your job* trap
- *keep control and make sure you hand off responsibility to a scapegoat* tactic.

The *Prototype/Pilot* Trap. Following is a very skeptical look at the dangers and abuses of prototypes. Under the right controlled conditions, prototypes (or pilots) have enormous value. It would be incorrect to conclude that all canceled prototype/pilot projects are mistakes. Firms of the size studied in this research *should* be investing in technology pilots and taking controlled risks. Prototype/pilot projects that tend to lead to bad outcomes usually exhibit many of the following symptoms:

- The appearance of modest initial costs.
- Approval to proceed without defining work packages to the point that scope, budget, and deadlines can be accurately estimated and controlled.
- Because the initiative is nearly always much larger than it appears at first, the organization as a whole is significantly under-committed to the project.
- The result is often an uncontrolled evolution of project objectives, scope, budgets, and deadlines. It typically includes many unpleasant surprises and often does not settle into the expected consensus and business case.
- Vendor, consultant, and/or insider agendas frequently promote this approach as a means of self-benefit. As the project evolves things will tend to skew further toward the benefit of these personal agendas and away from the good of the shareholder. In the end, when it is clear that the project cannot yield any more personal benefit, those pursuing their own agendas will distance themselves and actively work to avoid blame.
- Even effective prototype efforts contain risks. Business unit managers and executives who are not aware of all of the necessary *behind-the-scenes* work can quickly become frustrated. They know the prototype was developed quickly but become upset at the full time required to deliver a working system. Often these senior people will exert considerable pressure to shorten timetables. If these pressures are combined with the self-serving actions described above, a Horror Story will almost certainly occur. Promises will be made that represent no basis in objective reality. The senior people will think things are under control because they saw them with their own eyes. Enormous resources will be thrown at the project to attempt the impossible and, in the end, more resources will be wasted by those trying to escape accountability.

Fads

Many of the Horror Stories had a noticeable connection to the *fad of the moment* with disastrous results. In fairness, however, we must point out that much overall good has come from things described as fads by some. Most students of management would agree that the quality movement and reengineering have produced significant benefits.

The challenge, then, is to distinguish useful fads from dangerous ones. Following are some of the fad/traps observed among the Horror Stories that seemed to be at the heart of negative consequences:

- *downsizing* fad/trap
- *outsourcing* fad/trap
- *customer information/service system* fad/trap (Consolidated customer information system projects have been the subject of several Horror Stories. It seems that a common component is one department using this project as a vehicle to grab power from other departments.)
- *middleware* fad/trap (Middleware provides ways to improve personal computer access to mainframe data by moving copies of the data to *the middle* on a high-powered server. The concept seemed promising but has yet to consistently pay off.
- *Oracle*: (see Horror Stories #s 102, 108, 119, 128, 137, 148, 153, and 160).

Common Factors of Negative Fads. In examining the above fads that seemed to be linked to negative outcomes among the Horror Stories, the following common elements appeared:

- new technology or consulting technique; flashy, lots of hype
- some high visibility; anecdotal success stories
- opportunity for personal gain (Everyone promoting project stands to win if it goes ahead, regardless of outcome.)
- momentum to move ahead out of balance with an objective business case (Book, article, conference, buddies, or vendors all combine to push idea forward.)
- general absence of ability to objectively investigate details (Just like that great deal on a used car that you better snap up before that other guy does!)
- newness of idea, organizational flux, many parties involved, abundant scapegoats (technical and otherwise).

Common Factors of the Positive Fads. These attributes seem to accompany the fads that prove out over the long term:

- They are dependent on expertise and persistence, not on a product.
- There is some way to objectively validate the outcomes.
- It will not seem too good to be true. People will be forthcoming about the challenges and barriers.

Dirty Tricks

Here are some dirty tricks that emerged from the Horror Stories.

Software Vendor Promises. In the spring of 1995 I was working for one of the leading suppliers of client/server software. The firm decided to change direction and dismissed me and several other project managers. The explanation we were given was: "The firm can't make a profit if we have to assume project management responsibility. We just want to sell software."

This left several customer contracts in the lurch, and I had a sense that we weren't alone in this problem. I wondered if this might be an industry trend. Later that year I surveyed thirteen leading suppliers of client/server software via letter and telephone follow-up. I interviewed senior financial managers to reduce the chances of getting biased information from a sales or marketing person. I ultimately talked with people from nine firms. Under conditions of anonymity, I learned that:

- Three software firms had tried managing projects for their customers and exited that business.
- Three software firms intentionally designed their strategies to avoid assuming project management responsibilities for their customers.
- Three software firms are still attempting to manage projects for customers and having great difficulty.

First conclusion: No software firm contacted claimed to be profitably and effectively managing client/server projects for their customers. (I interviewed financial people in all but one case.)

The ratio analysis: Now let's add one more piece of information to understand a root cause. I consulted the Robert Morris Associates' 1994 *Annual Statement Studies* to determine if relative profit margins could be a root issue, and I found that:

- Consulting services firms average about 20 percent return on investment (before taxes).
- Pre-packaged software firms average over 50 percent return on investment (before taxes).

We need to remember that some package software firms are hideously profitable and many fail, which distorts these ratios somewhat.

Second conclusion: Selling the software is several times more profitable than providing the services to manage projects effectively.

Overall Conclusions for Dealing with Software Vendors. There is no compelling evidence that software vendors can manage client/server projects effectively for customers on a consistent basis (based on the standards identified in this book.) There is ample evidence that they cannot (as measured against the standards of project effectiveness contained in this book).

Software vendors have significant financial incentives to do or say *whatever it takes* to sell the software. Good intentions aside, it is simply several times more profitable to sell software than deliver the services required to make that software effective. I suspect that you will conclude, as I have, that contracts with software vendors are an important area where the organization must understand and adhere to standards.

Consulting Firms Tend to Exhibit a *Revenues First, Customer Second* Set of Behaviors. Despite the public pronouncements of most consulting firms and the heroic efforts of some individuals, the *revenues first* mentality usually prevails (at the customer's expense). I have personally been required to withhold critical information from customers three times because it might jeopardize revenues. (See Horror Stories 117, 159, and the case described in section 4.2.2, Analyzing Earnings Forecasts for Client/Server Threats). Those three instances ultimately cost shareholders somewhere between $10 million and $100 million.

Certainly, the free enterprise system exists because of the profit motive. The key is discovering when the consultant's profit motive conflicts with your best interests.

Here is an example: Recall that the project-driven industries tend to spend 30 percent or more of a project's budget before they hire the army of people and kick into high gear. Horror Stories 136, 137, 144, 145, 153, and 159 involved major consulting firms that appear to have assigned an army of bodies to the project right away, directly violating the proven practices of the project-driven industries. Could that behavior have anything to do with getting those people billable quickly? Look at the price paid by shareholders!

The Warm-Fuzzy Doesn't Show up in the Contract. Consultants and software vendors know that you have severe time pressure, and they use that against you. Any normal human being is going to be overwhelmed by the mass of complexity in one of these projects. The most natural thing to do in this situation is to look at the high level, take a read on the people, and see if it feels right. You will notice an abundance of very impressive people when you are making your decision, but you often won't see those people around when it is time for the vendor or consultant to perform as promised.

I have personally witnessed situations when the expectations formed by these high-level executive overviews are blatantly wrong. Worse yet, I—and others like me—am constrained from telling customers the truth and correcting those errors. What happens in the end is that the high-level, warm-fuzzy does not end up in the contract. What ends up in the contract is hard, cold language that has proven over time to protect the vendor or consultant's interests.

Recommendation: As the Department of Defense (see under Principal 1, The Role and Duties of the Independent Third Party) found out, getting an objective third party validation adds less than 10 percent to a project's total cost. I suspect that every one of the executives in the Horror Stories would gladly pay ten times that amount to have prevented their personal nightmares.

If the Project Is Going Bad, Bring in Heavy Hitters, Smoke, And Mirrors; Blame Previous Project Manager. Most people can sense when this is happening but don't have a way to confirm it. My suggestion is to take the above research and, in particular, the proven techniques from the project-driven industries, and test the actions of those who are claiming they will save the day.

Bank on Customers Believing That Litigation Is Not Worth the Hassle. You will note that relatively few of the Horror Stories resulted in litigation. I have personally been in a situation when my job was to prevent my firm (the software and consulting services vendor) from being sued. The reality is that we should have been sued, but I had an enormous body of evidence showing our good faith attempts to resolve the problem and the customer's lack of legitimate action. In the end, we were not sued largely because it would have exposed the executive sponsor's incompetence.

On May 8, 1995, *Computerworld* ran an article by Brian McWilliams titled Defying the Giant. It revisits the first case when IBM was held accountable for damages to one of its customers. The article describes a six-year legal battle between a small jewelry firm, Catamore Enterprises, with $7 million in annual sales, and IBM. In 1976 a jury awarded Catamore approximately $11 million. The fight was long and costly, but Catamore persevered. Although Catamore prospered and was ultimately sold in 1981 with annual sales of about $130 million, most firms would have *cut their losses* much earlier. This was a landmark case in bringing accountability to computer system promises.

Overall, the evidence is compelling that we need standards for vendor and consultant contracts. Through a combination of standards, arbitration, and litigation, we need to hold vendors and consultants firmly responsible for performing as promised.

Computer Project Sales 101: Find Political Pressure to Do Something Quickly. Some years ago when I was with Sperry Univac and just out of college, I was taught this founding principle for all capital project sales. Every pressure that sales people have is to produce *quickly*. I believe this leads them to hunt for situations that already are fundamentally unsound. By my definition, a computer project that is initiated for any reason other than the good of the shareholder is a bad computer project.

Something else to remember is that vendors cultivate internal champions for their products. This again tends to lead to projects being done and products being purchased for the wrong reasons. One more time, we see why these recommendations need serious consideration.

A Summary: Turning Weakness to Competitive Advantage

The Perseverance of Sun Tzu

As you move forward in your efforts to improve project outcomes, be patient. All of the evidence indicates that it will take time and significant shareholder and executive support to make these changes, but it can be done. I would like to ask you to remember how Sun Tzu came to be the commanding general of the kingdom of Wu (see Principle 1). He first had to do some unpleasant things. Thereafter, however, he and the King of Wu dominated the landscape for decades.

I can promise a little initial unpleasantness as you implement this program. Many executives will take offense at both the loss of authority and the safety-valve check on their integrity. These standards will cause up-front, objective scrutiny of what people want to do, how they will do it, and why. It is human nature to resent these things. This is one reason you must have a significant *small win* in the pilot to prove that all of this pain does pay off.

A key reason for using earned value is the ability to accurately forecast unacceptable overruns before the project is 20 percent complete. In all likelihood, some of the first few projects will have to be canceled. People will tend to test the limits and (at best) only pay lip service to the standards. They will probably ridicule the *new program of the month*. That will change when the first project is canceled. When the first project is canceled so early in its life, you will have the attention of the organization, just as Sun Tzu got the attention of the concubines by beheading their leaders.

Restart after Eighteen Months. Why does Philip Crosby (*Quality Is Free*) advocate restarting in eighteen months? Assuming the initiative is successful, the project managers will be given greater and greater responsibility and will lose their most essential personal resource—time to do the job right.

Without an ongoing stream of project managers and the continuous improvement of project standards, the organization will fall back into its previous ways. This is another role that the third party can fill because his profit motive will serve as a reminder to restart after eighteen months.

Effectiveness While Competitors Flounder. Please refer again to Horror Story #101, American Airlines (The Confirm Project), a $160 million disaster. Note that this project involved a partnership between American, Budget, Hilton Hotels, and Marriott on a joint reservations system.

Now look at the Hyatt Hotels Success Story #525 in Section 6.2. During the same time frame, Hyatt executed a reservations system project that was completed on time, under budget, and resulted in substantial improvements to customer service. It appears that Hyatt Hotels generally prospered while its competitors suffered. (However, Hyatt is a private firm, and we have not been able to verify this independently.)

During the period when the disastrous consequences of this project became public (1993/94) American Airlines' stock experienced a drop from $72 to $48; Hilton

Hotels' stock experienced a drop from $75 to $48; and Marriott experienced a drop from $32 to $24. *All three of these public firms lost at least 25 percent of their stock value in a matter of months while at least one competitor prospered.*

As mentioned earlier, many factors affect stock price, and we cannot conclude from this evidence alone that the Horror Story directly caused this loss of shareholder value. Taken in context with the rest of the research, however, this link seems likely. This book is by no means the end of the matter. Appendix F shows the areas where we need further research. My hope is that you will agree that this material is a start in the right direction. *You have the opportunity to choose to be a Hyatt.*

The Cases—Horror Stories, Success Stories, and Study Methods

6.1 Horror Stories

This section provides a summary sheet for the key issues of each Horror Story. If you have questions about how the information was developed or defined, refer to Section 6.3 for a discussion of the study methods. As you review these Horror Stories, here are some things to keep in mind; these items tend to be the most revealing:
- project outcome
- original budget
- total cost of quality
- the root issue scorecard.

(**Caution**: Don't get too hung up on specific dollar figures. What really counts is whether there might be a Horror Story brewing in your organization!)

Look for root issue patterns:
- Do you agree that these root issue problems form a pattern?
- Do you believe, as I do, that failure in these root issues leads directly to higher costs of quality?
- Are you willing to take some action to deal with them (even if it is unpopular action)?

CASE PROFILE: AMERICAN AIRLINES (THE CONFIRM PROJECT)		
Case ID: 101	Industry: Transportation	Data Source: Interview with a team member in *The Dallas Morning News,* 1994.
Type of Project: Joint venture on airline reservations system. Significant client/server component. Partners included Budget, Hilton, and Marriott.		**Project Outcome:** Joint venture dissolved, litigation, some ongoing attempt to use system. $160,000,000 (or more) in wasted project costs and litigation settlement.

COST OF QUALITY

Direct Project Costs:	*Costs of Unrealized Objectives:*
Original Budget: n/a Total Spent to Date: n/a Estimate of Wasted Direct Project Costs: $160,000,000	Organization did not receive benefits as promised or encountered extra expense in the following areas: - divestiture costs - cost reductions not captured - lost revenues - extreme turmoil - time lost to lawsuit, scapegoating. Estimated Costs of Unrealized Objectives: $300,000,000
	TOTAL COST OF QUALITY: $460,000,000 (estimated by adding wasted project costs to costs of unrealized objectives)

ROOT ISSUE SCORECARD

Objectivity Right People   Authority/
             Right Motives Responsibility
             Right Actions Match

Root Issue Scoring: The study team deemed that the root, foundational issues of this project were sufficiently well addressed to darken the "legs" of the Root Issue Scorecard in the following areas:

- None

ROOT ISSUES

Objectivity Problems:	**Right People/Right Motives/Right Actions Problems:**
- Project proceeded without scope and deliverable definition - Indescrimate scope creep and changes - Technical design not objective.	- Arrogance - Enamored with technology - Management roles granted on a political basis.
Authority/Responsibility Problems:	**Accountability Problems:**
- Technical manager(s) fired for pointing out problems.	- Extreme scope expansion - When things went wrong, undue management attention went to protecting personal interests.

CASE PROFILE: EAST COAST-BASED TELECOMMUNICATIONS FIRM

Case ID: 102	Industry: Manufacturing	Data Source: Multiple interviews with executives supplying people to project between 1993 and 1995.

Type of Project:	Project Outcome:
Client/Server customer service/information system, worldwide, using Oracle.	Project originally was driven from Dallas-based division. Extreme delay, confusion, and loss of customer good will were encountered. Customer service department fell back to old systems; project was stopped and control transferred to East Coast. At last report, no useable deliverables had been produced, and future of project is uncertain.

COST OF QUALITY

Direct Project Costs:	Costs of Unrealized Objectives:
Original Budget: n/a Total Spent to Date: $65,000,000 Estimate of Wasted Direct Project Costs: $65,000,000	Organization did not receive benefits as promised or encountered extra expense in the following areas: - lost incremental revenues from improved marketing and customer service - lost customers - unrealized cost savings in customer service area. Estimated Costs of Unrealized Objectives: $65,000,000
	TOTAL COST OF QUALITY: $130,000,000 (estimated by adding wasted project costs to costs of unrealized objectives)

ROOT ISSUE SCORECARD   ROOT ISSUES

Objectivity   Right People   Authority/
           Right Motives   Responsibility
           Right Actions   Match

Root Issue Scoring: The study team deemed that the root, foundational issues of this project were sufficiently well addressed to darken the "legs" of the Root Issue Scorecard in the following areas:

- None

Objectivity Problems:	Right People/Right Motives/Right Actions Problems:
- Technical design was not objectively defined to the point of addressing global business processes and centralized data requirements. - Scope was not objectively broken down into work packages to the point where scope and resources could be accurately estimated and changes controlled.	- Technically driven without considering customer interaction - Personal agendas to "have client/server on resume" may have adversely affected project.

Authority/Responsibility Problems:	Accountability Problems:
	- Putting project "on hold" and transferring control to East Coast may have been a maneuver to protect those responsible.

CASE PROFILE: FEDERAL RESERVE BANK OF DALLAS		
Case ID: 103	**Industry: Government**	**Data Source:** Personal interview with project participant in 1993.
Type of Project: Multiple client/server applications were abandoned as unstable and consolidated back onto centralized mainframe.		**Project Outcome:** n/a

COST OF QUALITY

Direct Project Costs: Original Budget: n/a Total Spent to Date: n/a Estimate of Wasted Direct Project Costs: $50,000,000	***Costs of Unrealized Objectives:*** Organization did not receive benefits as promised or encountered extra expense in the following areas: Estimated Costs of Unrealized Objectives: n/a
	TOTAL COST OF QUALITY: $50,000,000 (estimated by adding wasted project costs to costs of unrealized objectives)

ROOT ISSUE SCORECARD   ROOT ISSUES

n/a

Root Issue Scoring: The study team deemed that the root, foundational issues of this project were sufficiently well addressed to darken the "legs" of the Root Issue Scorecard in the following areas:

- Insufficient data to score project

Objectivity Problems: - Decision to abandon client/server probably indicates a host of underlying root problems. - Decision to abandon client/server in favor of mainframe goes strongly against industry trends (though possibly a good idea). However, IBM has dominated the mainframes of the Fed for so long that its influence may have affected the objectivity of this unusual decision.	**Right People/Right Motives/Right Actions Problems:** - Could not sufficiently control and support disparate client/server platforms and applications in distributed environment.
Authority/Responsibility Problems:	**Accountability Problems:**

CASE PROFILE: MIDWESTERN INSURANCE CARRIER		
Case ID: 104	**Industry:** Insurance	**Data Source:** *InfoWorld* (June 28, 1993).
Type of Project: Client/server insurance processing systems.		**Project Outcome:** n/a

COST OF QUALITY

Direct Project Costs:	*Costs of Unrealized Objectives:*
Original Budget: $5,000,000 Total Spent to Date: $15,000,000 Estimate of Wasted Direct Project Costs: $10,000,000	Organization did not receive benefits as promised or encountered extra expense in the following areas: - unrealized cost reductions in processing areas - lost incremental revenues from improved customer service. Estimated Costs of Unrealized Objectives: $30,000,000
	TOTAL COST OF QUALITY: $40,000,000 (estimated by adding wasted project costs to costs of unrealized objectives)

ROOT ISSUE SCORECARD   ROOT ISSUES

n/a

Objectivity Problems: - Scope was not broken down into work packages to the point of being able to objectively estimate scope, resources, budgets, and deadlines or control changes.	Right People/Right Motives/Right Actions Problems: - Significant lack of experience.
Authority/Responsibility Problems:	Accountability Problems:

Root Issue Scoring: The study team deemed that the root, foundational issues of this project were sufficiently well addressed to darken the "legs" of the Root Issue Scorecard in the following areas:

- Insufficient data to score project

CASE PROFILE: EAST COAST HEALTH CARE FIRM		
Case ID: 105	**Industry: Health Care**	**Data Source:** *InfoWorld* (June 28, 1993).
Type of Project: Client/server strategic network development.		**Project Outcome:** Project canceled.

COST OF QUALITY

Direct Project Costs:	*Costs of Unrealized Objectives:*
Original Budget: n/a Total Spent to Date: $10,000,000 Estimate of Wasted Direct Project Costs: $10,000,000	Organization did not receive benefits as promised or encountered extra expense in the following areas: Estimated Costs of Unrealized Objectives: n/a
	TOTAL COST OF QUALITY: $10,000,000 (estimated by adding wasted project costs to costs of unrealized objectives)

ROOT ISSUE SCORECARD   ROOT ISSUES

n/a

Root Issue Scoring: The study team deemed that the root, foundational issues of this project were sufficiently well addressed to darken the "legs" of the Root Issue Scorecard in the following areas:

- Insufficient data to score project

Objectivity Problems:	Right People/Right Motives/Right Actions Problems:
Authority/Responsibility Problems:	**Accountability Problems:** - After eighteen months, outsourcer was found to have no design methodology in place and no records for the work done to date. Vendor assured client that completion was just around the corner. Client disagreed and scrapped the project.

CASE PROFILE: McGaw, Inc.

Case ID: 106	Industry: Medical Supplies	Data Source: Alice LaPlante, The Big Deal About Thinking Small, *Forbes, ASAP* (approx. 1993), page 22.

Type of Project: Downsizing from mainframe.	Project Outcome: "Brought the company to its knees."

COST OF QUALITY

Direct Project Costs:	*Costs of Unrealized Objectives:*
Original Budget: n/a Total Spent to Date: $5,000,000 Estimate of Wasted Direct Project Costs: $2,500,000	Organization did not receive benefits as promised or encountered extra expense in the following areas: - unrealized cost savings - lost customers - lost revenues from diversion of management attention. Estimated Costs of Unrealized Objectives: $5,000,000
	TOTAL COST OF QUALITY: $7,500,000 (estimated by adding wasted project costs to costs of unrealized objectives)

ROOT ISSUE SCORECARD

Root Issue Scoring: The study team deemed that the root, foundational issues of this project were sufficiently well addressed to darken the "legs" of the Root Issue Scorecard in the following areas:

- **None**

ROOT ISSUES

Objectivity Problems:
- Ninety-day estimate by original consultant was wholly subjective.
- Technical design relied on vendor promises and trusted unproven systems with vital data—Chief Executive Officer pushed project due in some measure of the "fad factor" rather than an objective balance between business case, scope, budget, and deadlines.

Right People/Right Motives/Right Actions Problems:
- Clear evidence of competence problems.

Authority/Responsibility Problems:

Accountability Problems:

CASE PROFILE: VERY LARGE CENTRAL UNITED STATES BANK

Case ID: 107	Industry: Financial Services	Data Source: Author was assigned to turn project around in 1994.

Type of Project:
Combination of client/server, imaging, and mainframe systems to support a reengineering project.

Project Outcome: When author took over the project it was about $1,000,000 over original budget, a year late, and suffering extreme morale problems. An audit projected an additional $1,800,000 in costs, bringing the total projected price to $4,000,000. Project was shelved and ultimately canceled. The customer-vendor dispute was ultimately settled without litigation.

COST OF QUALITY

Direct Project Costs:	Costs of Unrealized Objectives:
Original Budget: $1,200,000 Total Spent to Date: $2,200,000 Estimate of Wasted Direct Project Costs: $2,200,000	Organization did not receive benefits as promised or encountered extra expense in the following areas: - unrealized cost savings through headcount reduction and reduced turnover. Estimated Costs of Unrealized Objectives: $4,000,000
	TOTAL COST OF QUALITY: $6,200,000 (estimated by adding wasted project costs to costs of unrealized objectives)

ROOT ISSUE SCORECARD

Objectivity   Right People   Authority/
         Right Motives   Responsibility
         Right Actions   Match

Root Issue Scoring: The study team deemed that the root, foundational issues of this project were sufficiently well addressed to darken the "legs" of the Root Issue Scorecard in the following areas:

- **Accountability**

- **Right People/Right Motives/ Right Actions**

ROOT ISSUES

Objectivity Problems:
- Business case was based on invalid technical assumptions and pushed through primarily for the personal agenda of executive sponsor.
- See *prototype/pilot* trap in Section 5, Principle 8: "Fads, Traps, and Dirty Tricks..."
- Scope was not sufficiently broken down to work packages such that scope, budget, and deadlines could be reliably estimated and controlled (until the author took over the project).
- Business unit rejected information system's initial estimate of $5,000,000 for project and chose to attempt to do it on its own for $1,200,000. This decision severely compromised the technical design.
- Many other problems.

Right People/Right Motives/Right Actions Problems:
- Prevailing culture was extreme arrogance and adversarial relationships with vendors.
- Project manager did not have experience for the job.
- Project manager was tall, good looking, hardworking, and loyal. He kept very busy and produced a lot of detail. This produced the appearance that the project was under control when it was not.
- Executive sponsor was clearly dominated by personal agenda and self interest.

continued on next page

ROOT ISSUES *(continued)*

Authority/Responsibility Problems:	Accountability Problems:
- To save money, responsibilities were split between business unit, the information systems department, the reengineering consultant, and the software vendor. The executive sponsor believed that she could control the project with very limited personal involvement. The result was that no one really took ownership of the entire project, and everyone had three other organizations to blame.	- The customer accepted an initial time and materials contract from the software vendor for $800,000 in services. Since the project ultimately proved to require $4,000,000 in services, both the vendor and customer deserved to be held accountable for severe lapses in judgment. A portion of that accountability did hit home.

Additional items of note:

- This project suffered from the *prototype/pilot* trap. See Section 5, Principle 8: "Fads, Traps, and Dirty Tricks..." for more details.

- The situation of valiant but futile efforts to save a doomed project is a recurring example. The author made a number of contributions to this project but also made the ultimate mistake of accepting an un-doable assignment. See Horror Story #162, $500 Million Mega Project in Trouble, for more details.

CASE PROFILE: DFW AIRPORT BOARD

Case ID: 108	Industry: Government	Data Source: Personal interviews with new executive sponsor and ex-employee during 1994.

Type of Project:	Project Outcome:
Conversion from mainframe/mini-computer client/server using Oracle financial software.	During 1994, project experienced turbulence, high turnover, and executive sponsor turnover and was over one year behind. Current status is not known.

COST OF QUALITY

Direct Project Costs:	Costs of Unrealized Objectives:
Original Budget: n/a Total Spent to Date: $2,000,000 (estimate) Estimate of Wasted Direct Project Costs: $1,000,000	Organization did not receive benefits as promised or encountered extra expense in the following areas: - unrealized cost savings in operations and administrative areas - lost incremental revenue from parking and airline fees. Estimated Costs of Unrealized Objectives: $2,000,000
	TOTAL COST OF QUALITY: $3,000,000 (estimated by adding wasted project costs to costs of unrealized objectives)

ROOT ISSUE SCORECARD   ROOT ISSUES

Objectivity   Right People   Authority/
              Right Motives Responsibility
              Right Actions Match

Root Issue Scoring: The study team deemed that the root, foundational issues of this project were sufficiently well addressed to darken the "legs" of the Root Issue Scorecard in the following areas:

- **None**

Objectivity Problems:
- Scope, budgets, and deadlines were set for political reasons.

Note: The new executive sponsor had ample opportunity to fire the project manager and blame him for all the project's problems. Instead, the sponsor chose to stick with the project manager and provide him conditions where he could be successful.

Unfortunately, this behavior seems to be the exception rather than the rule.

Right People/Right Motives/Right Actions Problems:
- Project manager was a consultant who was accomplished at "vision," facilitating, and other soft skills but not able to deliver solid progress on objectives.
- Outright resistance was prevalent.
- Pseudo-governmental nature of organization compromised the needed "get it done" attitude at both the front line and the executive sponsor level.

Authority/Responsibility Problems:
- Previous executive sponsors may have sought control of project when it looked good and jettisoned project when it might hurt them politically.

Accountability Problems:
- Previous executive sponsor(s) may have allowed project to languish while he was in transition.

CASE PROFILE: FRENCH SNCF RAILWAY

Case ID: 109	Industry: Transportation	Data Source: Maguy Day, *The Dallas Morning News* article (December 14, 1993).

Type of Project:	Project Outcome:
Reservations and rail traffic management system (partially mainframe and partially client/server.	Extreme customer dissatisfaction and public attack. Public image of railway destroyed. Rush hour waits went from 30 minutes to 2.5 hours. Passengers were routed out of their way *and* paid higher fares. Complete cities were lost.
	The Railway posted a $600,000,000 loss in 1992 and may have posted a loss as high as $1,200,000,000 in 1993.

COST OF QUALITY

Direct Project Costs:	Costs of Unrealized Objectives:
Original Budget: n/a Total Spent to Date: $244,000,000 Estimate of Wasted Direct Project Costs: $100,000,000	Organization did not receive benefits as promised or encountered extra expense in the following areas: - extreme loss of existing customers - loss of incremental revenues - unrealized cost savings. (Note: This is more of a "guesstimated" cost than validated. The study team has no experience with the intricacies of a state-subsidized railway within a troubled national economy. In reality, this figure is probably quite conservative.) Estimated Costs of Unrealized Objectives: $300,000,000
	TOTAL COST OF QUALITY: $400,000,000 (estimated by adding wasted project costs to costs of unrealized objectives)

ROOT ISSUE SCORECARD   ROOT ISSUES

ACCOUNTABILITY

Objectivity Right People Authority/
          Right Motives Responsibility
          Right Actions   Match

Root Issue Scoring: The study team deemed that the root, foundational issues of this project were sufficiently well addressed to darken the "legs" of the Root Issue Scorecard in the following areas:

- **None**

Objectivity Problems:	Right People/Right Motives/Right Actions Problems:
- Firm forced itself into an exposed, reactive position by procrastinating on replacement of the old system. - The assumption was made that American Airlines' reservations system would work for the French rail system, but it could not handle the complexity and volumes necessary.	- Disastrous decision to provide only six days training to ticket agents leads to questions of project team competence *or* short sighted cost containment by executives.
Authority/Responsibility Problems:	**Accountability Problems:**

continued on next page

ROOT ISSUES *(continued)*

Other Items of Note:

- American Airlines VP dismissed these problems as "Mere growing pains."
- The French public was presented with a radical culture change by this system. The French were used to cheap, predictable state-subsidized mass transit. This new system was used as a platform to force the transition to a "for profit" railway.

Ignoring substantial cultural differences is a common mistake in international projects. Whether this culture clash was by accident or design, the results were certainly painful for France.

- For more information on projects done by American Airlines and its subsidiaries, see Horror Story #101, American Airlines (The Confirm Project).

CASE PROFILE: GREYHOUND

Case ID: 110	Industry: Transportation	Data Source: Multiple interviews with project participants between 1991 and 1994.

Type of Project:	Project Outcome:
Bus scheduling and operations management on a client/server system.	Users were not sufficiently involved in the system's design. System had to be redeveloped because it did not meet the user's needs.

COST OF QUALITY

Direct Project Costs:	Costs of Unrealized Objectives:
Original Budget: n/a Total Spent to Date: $2,000,000 Estimate of Wasted Direct Project Costs: $2,000,000	Organization did not receive benefits as promised or encountered extra expense in the following areas: - unrealized cost savings in scheduling and operations labor, fuel, and maintenance - lost incremental revenues due to improved customer service and better marketing. Estimated Costs of Unrealized Objectives: $1,500,000
	TOTAL COST OF QUALITY: $3,500,000 (estimated by adding wasted project costs to costs of unrealized objectives)

ROOT ISSUE SCORECARD

Objectivity   Right People   Authority/
         Right Motives   Responsibility
         Right Actions   Match

Root Issue Scoring: The study team deemed that the root, foundational issues of this project were sufficiently well addressed to darken the "legs" of the Root Issue Scorecard in the following areas:

- **Accountability**

ROOT ISSUES

Objectivity Problems:	Right People/Right Motives/Right Actions Problems:
- Arrogance, presumption, and technology focus may have led to the belief that the users weren't needed. - User participation may have been sought but not given due to business unit not prioritizing the project's business case.	- Lack of user involvement may indicate that the project team was not competent.
Authority/Responsibility Problems:	**Accountability Problems:**

Other Items of Note:

- The original project manager was in charge of the rewrite; some degree of accountability was present.

CASE PROFILE: DIAMOND SHAMROCK		
Case ID: 111	**Industry: Energy**	**Data Source:** 1995 interview with supervisor of existing project manager.
Type of Project: Client/server imaging system to support contracts.		**Project Outcome:** As of 1995, at least one year late.

COST OF QUALITY

Direct Project Costs:	**Costs of Unrealized Objectives:**
Original Budget: $1,000,000 Total Spent to Date: $3,000,000 Estimate of Wasted Direct Project Costs: $2,000,000	Organization did not receive benefits as promised or encountered extra expense in the following areas: - unrealized cost savings from reduced administrative labor - reduced risk profile due to easier access to contractual documents. Estimated Costs of Unrealized Objectives: $1,000,000
	TOTAL COST OF QUALITY: $3,000,000 (estimated by adding wasted project costs to costs of unrealized objectives)

ROOT ISSUE SCORECARD   ROOT ISSUES

n/a

Root Issue Scoring: The study team deemed that the root, foundational issues of this project were sufficiently well addressed to darken the "legs" of the Root Issue Scorecard in the following areas:

- Insufficient data to score project

Objectivity Problems: - Probably suffered from the *prototype/pilot* trap (see Section 5, Principle 8: Fads, Traps, and Dirty Tricks. ...). - Scope was not objectively broken down into work packages such that deliverables, budgets, and deadlines could be estimated and changes controlled.	**Right People/Right Motives/Right Actions Problems:**
Authority/Responsibility Problems:	**Accountability Problems:**

CASE PROFILE: CIGNA

Case ID: 112	Industry: Insurance	Data Source: Alice LaPlante, The Big Deal About Thinking Small, *Forbes, ASAP* (Approx. 1993), page 22.

Type of Project:	Project Outcome:
Downsizing from mainframe to client/server system.	Project is late and 30 percent over budget.

COST OF QUALITY

Direct Project Costs:	Costs of Unrealized Objectives:
Original Budget: $3,000,000 Total Spent to Date: $4,000,000 Estimate of Wasted Direct Project Costs: $1,000,000	Organization did not receive benefits as promised or encountered extra expense in the following areas: - unrealized cost savings from reduced mainframe costs. Estimated Costs of Unrealized Objectives: $3,000,000
	TOTAL COST OF QUALITY: $4,000,000 (estimated by adding wasted project costs to costs of unrealized objectives)

ROOT ISSUE SCORECARD   ROOT ISSUES

n/a

Root Issue Scoring: The study team deemed that the root, foundational issues of this project were sufficiently well addressed to darken the "legs" of the Root Issue Scorecard in the following areas:

- **Insufficient data to score project**

Objectivity Problems:	Right People/Right Motives/Right Actions Problems:
- Numerous false starts indicate that scope was not objectively broken down into work packages sufficient to define deliverables, deadlines, and budgets. - Choosing immature technology indicates that the technical design was not objectively defined. - Project probably suffered from the *justify the cost of client/server by unplugging the mainframe* trap. See Section 5, Principle 8: Fads, Traps, and Dirty Tricks. ...	- Friction between information systems and business unit employees.
Authority/Responsibility Problems:	**Accountability Problems:**

CASE PROFILE: AMERICAN MANAGEMENT SYSTEMS

Case ID: 113	Industry: Computer Software and Services	Data Source: Alice LaPlante, The Big Deal About Thinking Small, *Forbes, ASAP* (Approx. 1993), page 22.

Type of Project:	Project Outcome:
Downsizing of mainframe financial systems to client/server.	Original budget has been doubled; project not finished yet.

COST OF QUALITY

Direct Project Costs:	*Costs of Unrealized Objectives:*
Original Budget: $1,000,000 Total Spent to Date: $2,000,000 Estimate of Wasted Direct Project Costs: $1,000,000	Organization did not receive benefits as promised or encountered extra expense in the following areas: - unrealized cost savings from removing mainframe. Estimated Costs of Unrealized Objectives: $1,000,000
	TOTAL COST OF QUALITY: $2,000,000 (estimated by adding wasted project costs to costs of unrealized objectives)

ROOT ISSUE SCORECARD   ROOT ISSUES

n/a

Root Issue Scoring: The study team deemed that the root, foundational issues of this project were sufficiently well addressed to darken the "legs" of the Root Issue Scorecard in the following areas:

- Insufficient data to score project

Objectivity Problems:	Right People/Right Motives/Right Actions Problems:
- Significant unanticipated support costs indicate that the technical design was not objectively defined. - Project probably suffered from the *justify the cost of client/server by unplugging the mainframe* trap. See Section 5, Principle 8: Fads, Traps, and Dirty Tricks. ...	
Authority/Responsibility Problems:	**Accountability Problems:**

CASE PROFILE: EAST COAST HEALTHCARE PRODUCTS PROVIDER		
Case ID: 114	**Industry: Medical Supplies**	**Data Source:** 1993 personal audit of project by author.
Type of Project: Client/server beta project to give users better access to mainframe financial data.		**Project Outcome:** Loss of credibility for project champion and vendor. Very little usable result.

COST OF QUALITY

Direct Project Costs: Original Budget: $100,000 Total Spent to Date: $500,000 Estimate of Wasted Direct Project Costs: $400,000	**Costs of Unrealized Objectives:** Organization did not receive benefits as promised or encountered extra expense in the following areas: - lost incremental revenues from better marketing - unrealized cost reductions in accounting processes. Estimated Costs of Unrealized Objectives: $200,000
	TOTAL COST OF QUALITY: $600,000 (estimated by adding wasted project costs to costs of unrealized objectives)

ROOT ISSUE SCORECARD   ROOT ISSUES

ACCOUNTABILITY

Objectivity | Right People Right Motives Right Actions | Authority/ Responsibility Match

Root Issue Scoring: The study team deemed that the root, foundational issues of this project were sufficiently well addressed to darken the "legs" of the Root Issue Scorecard in the following areas:

- **Accountability**

Objectivity Problems:
- Project was technology driven rather than business driven. It was purchased without an objective understanding of the capabilities and how they would benefit the project.
- Scope was never objectively broken down into work packages sufficient to define deliverables, deadlines, budgets, and control changes.
- Business case was not objectively balanced with scope and budget.
- Software vendor had significant power and pushed hard for this beta project.
- Project suffered from the *prototype/pilot* trap. See Section 5, Principle 8: Fads, Traps, and Dirty Tricks. ...
- Customer's intent to use a beta system for real business unit benefits was risky, at best.

Right People/Right Motives/Right Actions Problems:

Authority/Responsibility Problems: | **Accountability Problems:**

Other Items of Note:
- Project champion suffered internal credibility loss and was held accountable at least in some degree.

CASE PROFILE: NATIONS BANK

Case ID: 115	Industry: Financial	Data Source: 1993 interview with manager of project team members.

Type of Project:	Project Outcome:
Development of consolidated customer information system on client/server platform project done by Perot Systems outsourcing firm.	Multi-year delay in implementation. Perot Systems dismissed from project. Project restarted internally.

COST OF QUALITY

Direct Project Costs:	*Costs of Unrealized Objectives:*
Original Budget: n/a Total Spent to Date: $500,000 Estimate of Wasted Direct Project Costs: $250,000	Organization did not receive benefits as promised or encountered extra expense in the following areas: - lost incremental revenues from improved customer service and better marketing - unrealized cost reductions in customer service areas. Estimated Costs of Unrealized Objectives: $500,000
	TOTAL COST OF QUALITY: $750,000 (estimated by adding wasted project costs to costs of unrealized objectives)

ROOT ISSUE SCORECARD

Objectivity   Right People   Authority/
           Right Motives   Responsibility
           Right Actions   Match

Root Issue Scoring: The study team deemed that the root, foundational issues of this project were sufficiently well addressed to darken the "legs" of the Root Issue Scorecard in the following areas:

- **Accountability**

ROOT ISSUES

Objectivity Problems:	Right People/Right Motives/Right Actions Problems:
- Because delivered system could not handle necessary data volumes, it is clear that the technical design was not objective.	
Authority/Responsibility Problems:	**Accountability Problems:**

Other Items of Note:

- Consolidated customer information system projects have been the subject of several disaster stories. See *customer information/service systems* fad/trap, Section 5, Principle 8: Fads, Traps, and Dirty Tricks. ... for more details.

CASE PROFILE: SOUTH-CENTRAL UNITED STATES RETAIL ENERGY PRODUCTS FIRM

Case ID: 116	Industry: Energy	Data Source: 1995 interview with project team member.

Type of Project:	Project Outcome:
Client/server imaging system for land records; project partially outsourced.	One-year delay of payback, lost time discovering rework; vendor had to absorb $500,000 of rework.

COST OF QUALITY

Direct Project Costs:	Costs of Unrealized Objectives:
Original Budget: n/a Total Spent to Date: n/a Estimate of Wasted Direct Project Costs: n/a	Organization did not receive benefits as promised or encountered extra expense in the following areas: - unrealized cost savings from reduced administrative labor - reduced legal risk due to better control of contracts. Estimated Costs of Unrealized Objectives: $250,000
	TOTAL COST OF QUALITY: $250,000 (estimated by adding wasted project costs to costs of unrealized objectives)

ROOT ISSUE SCORECARD   ROOT ISSUES

Objectivity   Right People   Authority/
      Right Motives   Responsibility
      Right Actions   Match

Root Issue Scoring: The study team deemed that the root, foundational issues of this project were sufficiently well addressed to darken the "legs" of the Root Issue Scorecard in the following areas:

- **Accountability:** Strong contract with vendor resulted in vendor absorbing $500,000 overrun.

- **Right People/Right Motives/ Right Actions:** As a part of the project team, the vendor should be credited for fulfilling its obligations.

Objectivity Problems:	Right People/Right Motives/Right Actions Problems:
- Since 50 percent of the outsourcer's work had to be redone, it is likely that the technical design was not objective. - Since poor user involvement was cited, either the business case or resource estimates must have been faulty.	- Inadequate testing questions project team competence.
Authority/Responsibility Problems: - Project suffered a dilution of authority by attempting to split responsibilities. See the *outsourcing* trap, Section 5, Principle 8, Fads, Traps, and Dirty Tricks. ... for more details.	**Accountability Problems:**

CASE PROFILE: SOUTH-CENTRAL UNITED STATES OIL AND GAS FIRM #2		
Case ID: 117	**Industry:** Energy	**Data Source:** Author served as project manager in 1993.
Type of Project: Client/server beta project to give accounting users better access to mainframe financial data.		**Project Outcome:** Project exceeded budget by tenfold. Extreme delay in receiving benefits. Multiple managers and executives left firm abruptly.

COST OF QUALITY

Direct Project Costs: Original Budget: $25,000 Total Spent to Date: $250,000 Estimate of Wasted Direct Project Costs: $225,000	**Costs of Unrealized Objectives:** Organization did not receive benefits as promised or encountered extra expense in the following areas: - reduced costs of accounting labor - reduced overall organization costs due to better information. Estimated Costs of Unrealized Objectives: $250,000
	TOTAL COST OF QUALITY: $475,000 (estimated by adding wasted project costs to costs of unrealized objectives)

ROOT ISSUE SCORECARD

Objectivity   Right People   Authority/
           Right Motives   Responsibility
           Right Actions   Match

Root Issue Scoring: The study team deemed that the root, foundational issues of this project were sufficiently well addressed to darken the "legs" of the Root Issue Scorecard in the following areas:

- **Accountability:** Project sponsor was significantly embarrassed and left firm.

- **Right People/Right Motives/ Right Actions:** Project team was very capable.

ROOT ISSUES

Objectivity Problems:

- Project was technology driven rather than business driven. It was purchased without an objective understanding of the capabilities and how they would benefit the project.
- Scope was never objectively broken down into work packages sufficient to define deliverables, deadlines, budgets, and control changes.
- Business case was not objectively balanced with scope and budget.
- Software vendor had significant power and pushed hard for this beta project.
- Project suffered from the *prototype/ pilot* trap. See Section 5, Principle 8: Fads, Traps, and Dirty Tricks. ...
- Customer's intent to use a beta system for real business unit benefits was risky, at best.

Right People/Right Motives/Right Actions Problems:

Authority/Responsibility Problems:

- Repeated recommendations from project team were ignored by sponsor.

Accountability Problems:

- Vendor's project team discovered a work-around that would greatly assist the customer but was not allowed to disclose it. The work-around was a better solution than the vendor's product and would jeopardize future sales!

CASE PROFILE: Division of Dallas-Based Telecommunications Manufacturer

Case ID: 118	Industry: Manufacturing	Data Source: 1994 personal interview with fired MIS manager.

Type of Project:	Project Outcome:
Conversion of financial and customer service applications from mainframe to client/server.	Project was ultimately completed. Business unit was forced to use it with disastrous consequences. MIS manager was fired as scapegoat; division was ultimately broken up and absorbed into other operating units.

COST OF QUALITY

Direct Project Costs:	Costs of Unrealized Objectives:
Original Budget: $250,000 Total Spent to Date: $400,000 Estimate of Wasted Direct Project Costs: $150,000	Organization did not receive benefits as promised or encountered extra expense in the following areas: - unrealized customer service cost savings - lost incremental revenues from improved customer service - organizational breakup. Estimated Costs of Unrealized Objectives: $1,000,000
	TOTAL COST OF QUALITY: $1,150,000 (estimated by adding wasted project costs to costs of unrealized objectives)

ROOT ISSUE SCORECARD

Objectivity | Right People Right Motives Right Actions | Authority/ Responsibility Match

Root Issue Scoring: The study team deemed that the root, foundational issues of this project were sufficiently well addressed to darken the "legs" of the Root Issue Scorecard in the following areas:

- **Accountability:** Rightly or wrongly, someone (the project manager) was held accountable.

ROOT ISSUES

Objectivity Problems:
- Technology driven, inappropriate standardization, underfunded project management function, many others.
- Project suffered greatly from the *just get something in by the end of the quarter* trap. See Section 5, Principle 8: Fads, Traps, and Dirty Tricks. ...
- This project may have suffered from the *customer information/ service system* fad/trap. See Section 5, Principle 8: Fads, Traps, and Dirty Tricks. ...

Right People/Right Motives/Right Actions Problems:

Authority/Responsibility Problems:
- The project manager was experienced and capable. His recommendations were ignored, and he was forced into the position of going along with a failing project or losing his job if he protested too loudly.

Accountability Problems:
- Executive sponsor inherited project and distanced himself. When things went badly he used the project manager as a scapegoat. See the discussion of the *keep control and make sure you hand off responsibility to a scapegoat* tactic in Section 5, Principle 8: Fads, Traps, and Dirty Tricks. ...

CASE PROFILE: DALLAS-BASED INSURANCE AGENCY

Case ID: 119	Industry: Insurance	Data Source: 1994 personal interview with executive sponsor.

Type of Project:	Project Outcome:
Conversion from mini-computer to Oracle financials on client/server.	Multi-year delay in implementation. Project manager and entire team were replaced.

COST OF QUALITY

Direct Project Costs:	Costs of Unrealized Objectives:
Original Budget: estimated $100,000 Total Spent to Date: $200,000 Estimate of Wasted Direct Project Costs: $100,000	Organization did not receive benefits as promised or encountered extra expense in the following areas: - unrealized cost savings in administration and operations - lost incremental revenues from improved customer service and marketing. Estimated Costs of Unrealized Objectives: $200,000
	TOTAL COST OF QUALITY: $300,000 (estimated by adding wasted project costs to costs of unrealized objectives)

ROOT ISSUE SCORECARD   ROOT ISSUES

Objectivity   Right People   Authority/
          Right Motives   Responsibility
          Right Actions   Match

Root Issue Scoring: The study team deemed that the root, foundational issues of this project were sufficiently well addressed to darken the "legs" of the Root Issue Scorecard in the following areas:

- **Accountability**

Objectivity Problems:	Right People/Right Motives/Right Actions Problems:
- Poor project management was given as primary reason for project problems. Although true reasons are unknown, it is likely that this project suffered from "The Project Manager versus *Project Manager*" trap. See Section 5, Principle 8: Fads, Traps, and Dirty Tricks. ...	
Authority/Responsibility Problems:	**Accountability Problems:**

CASE PROFILE: LOCKHEED

Case ID: 120	Industry: Defense Contractor	Data Source: Alice LaPlante, The Big Deal About Thinking Small, *Forbes, ASAP* (Approx. 1993), page 22.

Type of Project:	Project Outcome:
Downsizing materials procurement application from mainframe to client/server.	Original estimate was fifteen months and $175,000. Currently at twenty-four months and $350,000.

COST OF QUALITY

Direct Project Costs:	*Costs of Unrealized Objectives:*
Original Budget: $175,000 Total Spent to Date: $350,000 Estimate of Wasted Direct Project Costs: $175,000	Organization did not receive benefits as promised or encountered extra expense in the following areas: - unrealized cost savings in materials purchases and reduced administrative costs - lost incremental revenues from improved customer service. Estimated Costs of Unrealized Objectives: $350,000
	TOTAL COST OF QUALITY: $525,000 (estimated by adding wasted project costs to costs of unrealized objectives)

ROOT ISSUE SCORECARD   ROOT ISSUES

n/a

Root Issue Scoring: The study team deemed that the root, foundational issues of this project were sufficiently well addressed to darken the "legs" of the Root Issue Scorecard in the following areas:

- Insufficient data to score project

Objectivity Problems:	Right People/Right Motives/Right Actions Problems:
- This project suffered from the *root-of-all-evil* (high-level project definition) trap: Project was not objectively broken down into work packages to the point where scope, resources, budgets, and deadlines could be accurately estimated and changes controlled. See Section 5, Principle 8: Fads, Traps, and Dirty Tricks. ...	
Authority/Responsibility Problems:	**Accountability Problems:**

CASE PROFILE: DATA GENERAL

Case ID: 121	Industry: Manufacturing	Data Source: 1993 personal audit of project.

Type of Project:	Project Outcome:
Client/server beta project to give users better access to mainframe financial data and to further the marketing partnership with the software vendor.	Software vendor gave product to Data General to promote a partnership. Because it was free, project was given very little attention and resources. It ultimately yielded little benefit.

COST OF QUALITY

Direct Project Costs:	*Costs of Unrealized Objectives:*
Original Budget: $25,000 (internal labor costs only; Data General was given software by vendor and provided its own hardware) Total Spent to Date: $100,000 Estimate of Wasted Direct Project Costs: $75,000	Organization did not receive benefits as promised or encountered extra expense in the following areas: - internal labor costs to do project were significantly higher than planned - unrealized cost savings in accounting area. Estimated Costs of Unrealized Objectives: $50,000
	TOTAL COST OF QUALITY: $125,000 (estimated by adding wasted project costs to costs of unrealized objectives)

ROOT ISSUE SCORECARD

ACCOUNTABILITY

Objectivity · Right People Right Motives Right Actions · Authority/ Responsibility Match

Root Issue Scoring: The study team deemed that the root, foundational issues of this project were sufficiently well addressed to darken the "legs" of the Root Issue Scorecard in the following areas:

- **Right People/Right Motives/ Right Actions**

ROOT ISSUES

Objectivity Problems:	Right People/Right Motives/Right Actions Problems:
- Project was technology driven rather than business driven. It was purchased without an objective understanding of the capabilities and how they would benefit from the project. - Scope was never objectively broken down into work packages sufficient to define deliverables, deadlines, budgets, and control changes. - Business case was not objectively balanced with scope and budget. - Software vendor had significant power and pushed hard for this beta project. - Project suffered from the *prototype/ pilot* trap. See Section 5, Principle 8: Fads, Traps, and Dirty Tricks. ... - Customer's intent to use a beta system for real business unit benefits was risky, at best.	

Authority/Responsibility Problems:	Accountability Problems:
	- Because it was free, the project was given very little attention and resources. No one was held particularly responsible.

Other Items of Note: If viewed as an internal project only, this was a clear failure. If viewed as an investment in a marketing partnership it might be viewed as a successful failure. Data General learned that the software vendor's product looked very good up-front but didn't really deliver much of value.

CASE PROFILE: INFORMATION INDUSTRIES, INC.

Case ID: 122	Industry: Personnel Services	Data Source: Personal management of project during 1987 and 1988.

Type of Project:	Project Outcome:
Converting mainframe human resources applications to client/server. Substantial incremental features crept into the project due to poor scope control.	Project was badly mismanaged by all parties, including the author. After multi-year delays and uncontrolled changes the author's firm went out of business and could not complete the project. The author's personal failure on this project ten years ago provided substantial motivation to learn how to produce consistently positive client/server project outcomes.

COST OF QUALITY

Direct Project Costs:	Costs of Unrealized Objectives:
Original Budget: $25,000 Total Spent to Date: $100,000 Estimate of Wasted Direct Project Costs: $75,000	Organization did not receive benefits as promised or encountered extra expense in the following areas: - lost incremental revenues due to better marketing - unrealized cost savings from reduced administrative labor. Estimated Costs of Unrealized Objectives: $100,000
	TOTAL COST OF QUALITY: $175,000 (estimated by adding wasted project costs to costs of unrealized objectives)

ROOT ISSUE SCORECARD   ROOT ISSUES

Objectivity Right People / Right Motives / Right Actions Authority/ Responsibility Match

Root Issue Scoring: The study team deemed that the root, foundational issues of this project were sufficiently well addressed to darken the "legs" of the Root Issue Scorecard in the following areas:

- Accountability: The author's firm remained financially liable for not delivering on promised applications.

- Authority/Responsibility Match: The author and the customer's project manager had the authority needed. They just didn't have the expertise to complete the project effectively.

Objectivity Problems:
- Trying to do too much on too limited of a budget, extreme volatility of user requirements, third party default on programming contract.
- Project suffered from the *prototype/pilot* trap. See Section 5, Principle 8: Fads, Traps, and Dirty Tricks. ...

Right People/Right Motives/Right Actions Problems:
- This project suffered from the *promote the up and coming techie to project manager* trap. See Section 5, Principle 8: Fads, Traps, and Dirty Tricks. ...

Authority/Responsibility Problems:

Accountability Problems:

CASE PROFILE: THE ENVELOPE MAN

Case ID: 123	Industry: Manufacturing	Data Source: Personal management of project during 1987 and 1988.

Type of Project:	Project Outcome:
Manufacturing order processing on client/server platform. Substantial incremental features crept into the project due to poor scope control.	Project was badly mismanaged by all parties, including the author. After multi-year delays and uncontrolled changes the author's firm went out of business and could not complete the project.
	The author's personal failure on this project ten years ago provided substantial motivation to learn how to produce consistently positive client/server project outcomes.

COST OF QUALITY

Direct Project Costs:	Costs of Unrealized Objectives:
Original Budget: $25,000	Organization did not receive benefits as promised or encountered extra expense in the following areas:
Total Spent to Date: $75,000	- lost incremental revenues due to better marketing
Estimate of Wasted Direct Project Costs: $50,000	- unrealized cost savings from reduced order processing and fulfillment labor.
	Estimated Costs of Unrealized Objectives: $100,000
	TOTAL COST OF QUALITY: $150,000 (estimated by adding wasted project costs to costs of unrealized objectives)

ROOT ISSUE SCORECARD   ROOT ISSUES

Objectivity   Right People   Authority/
              Right Motives Responsibility
              Right Actions Match

Root Issue Scoring: The study team deemed that the root, foundational issues of this project were sufficiently well addressed to darken the "legs" of the Root Issue Scorecard in the following areas:

- **Accountability**

- **Authority/Responsibility Match**

Objectivity Problems:	Right People/Right Motives/Right Actions Problems:
Client would not allocate sufficient professional resources, presumption factor, technology driven; vendor defaulted on third party software contract.	
Authority/Responsibility Problems:	**Accountability Problems:**

CASE PROFILE: SOUTH-CENTRAL UNITED STATES OIL AND GAS FIRM #3

Case ID: 124	Industry: Energy	Data Source: 1995 personal interview with project participant.

Type of Project:	Project Outcome:
Client/server imaging system for the management of gas contracts including significant conversion of history to new system.	Ninety-day delay in implementation; system integrator went out of business.

COST OF QUALITY

Direct Project Costs:	**Costs of Unrealized Objectives:**
Original Budget: $400,000 estimate Total Spent to Date: $400,000 estimate Estimate of Wasted Direct Project Costs: $0 (approx. $100,000 overage absorbed by system integrator)	Organization did not receive benefits as promised or encountered extra expense in the following areas: - unrealized cost savings from reduced administrative labor - reduced legal risk due to better control of contracts. Estimated Costs of Unrealized Objectives: $50,000
	TOTAL COST OF QUALITY: $50,000 (estimated by adding wasted project costs to costs of unrealized objectives)

ROOT ISSUE SCORECARD

Objectivity   Right People   Authority/
        Right Motives   Responsibility
        Right Actions   Match

Root Issue Scoring: The study team deemed that the root, foundational issues of this project were sufficiently well addressed to darken the "legs" of the Root Issue Scorecard in the following areas:

- **Accountability:** Strong contracts required the system integrator to absorb rework.

- **Authority/Responsibility Match:** A ninety-day delay on this type of project is a relative success in many ways. It is likely that authority and responsibility were matched.

ROOT ISSUES

Objectivity Problems:	**Right People/Right Motives/Right Actions Problems:**
- Project probably suffered from the *prototype/pilot* trap. See Section 5, Principle 8: Fads, Traps, and Dirty Tricks. ... - Inadequate systems design by system integrator indicates that this project probably suffered from the *100 percent outsourcing...* trap. See Section 5, Principle 8: Fads, Traps, and Dirty Tricks. ...	- Rework absorbed by system integrator indicates poor quality of initial work.
Authority/Responsibility Problems:	**Accountability Problems:**

CASE PROFILE: A SUBSIDIARY OF SOUTHLAND CORP. (MERRIT FOODS)		
Case ID: 125	**Industry: Public Warehouse**	**Data Source:** Personal management of project during 1987 and 1988.
Type of Project: Inventory control for public warehouse on client/server platform.		**Project Outcome:** Project was suffering from the default of the programming firm when the author's firm took over the project. Project was badly mismanaged by all parties, including the author. The customer was not willing to pay for what it wanted, and the author was not experienced enough to walk away from the project. After multi-year delays and uncontrolled changes the author's firm went out of business and could not complete the project. The author's personal failure on this project ten years ago provided substantial motivation to learn how to produce consistently positive client/server project outcomes.

COST OF QUALITY

Direct Project Costs:	*Costs of Unrealized Objectives:*
Original Budget: $25,000 Total Spent to Date: $50,000 Estimate of Wasted Direct Project Costs: $25,000	Organization did not receive benefits as promised or encountered extra expense in the following areas: - lost incremental revenues due to improved customer service - unrealized cost savings in warehouse and administrative labor. Estimated Costs of Unrealized Objectives: $50,000
	TOTAL COST OF QUALITY: $75,000 (estimated by adding wasted project costs to costs of unrealized objectives)

ROOT ISSUE SCORECARD   ROOT ISSUES

ACCOUNTABILITY

Objectivity Right People Authority/
             Right Motives Responsibility
             Right Actions Match

continued on next page

Root Issue Scoring: The study team deemed that the root, foundational issues of this project were sufficiently well addressed to darken the "legs" of the Root Issue Scorecard in the following areas:

- **Accountability:** Customer contracts provided that the customer actually lost relatively little due to programming firm defaults.

- **Authority/Responsibility Match:** Customer's project manager and executive sponsor had the needed authority.

ROOT ISSUES *(continued)*

Objectivity Problems:	**Right People/Right Motives/Right Actions Problems:**
- Project suffered from *root-of-all-evil* trap. See Section 5, Principle 8: Fads, Traps, and Dirty Tricks. ... - Failure to objectively balance scope, budget, and deadlines up-front allowed customer and author to believe that the high level objectives could be accomplished for a limited budget. This created a declining spiral of scope increases, delays, cost overruns, hostility, and ultimately the default of multiple third parties. - Project also suffered from the *technology-driven project* trap. See Section 5, Principle 8: Fads, Traps, and Dirty Tricks. ...	- Customer's project manager was excessively cost focused and combative. - Two different programming firms (including author's) defaulted on project.
Authority/Responsibility Problems:	**Accountability Problems:**

CASE PROFILE: ***DELETED FROM STUDY—NOT RELEVANT***		
Case ID: 126	Industry:	Data Source:
Type of Project:		Project Outcome:

COST OF QUALITY

Direct Project Costs:	Costs of Unrealized Objectives:
	TOTAL COST OF QUALITY:

ROOT ISSUE SCORECARD   ROOT ISSUES

Objectivity Problems:	Right People/Right Motives/Right Actions Problems:
Authority/Responsibility Problems:	Accountability Problems:

CASE PROFILE: SOUTH-CENTRAL UNITED STATES PHARMACEUTICAL LABORATORY		
Case ID: 127	**Industry: Health Care**	**Data Source:** 1994 interview with project manager.
Type of Project: Client/server-based executive information system.		**Project Outcome:** Extreme delay and confusion, users would not use system, ultimately no useful benefits.

COST OF QUALITY

Direct Project Costs:	**Costs of Unrealized Objectives:**
Original Budget: n/a Total Spent to Date: n/a Estimate of Wasted Direct Project Costs: n/a	Organization did not receive benefits as promised or encountered extra expense in the following areas: Estimated Costs of Unrealized Objectives: n/a
	TOTAL COST OF QUALITY: N/A (estimated by adding wasted project costs to costs of unrealized objectives)

ROOT ISSUE SCORECARD   ROOT ISSUES

n/a

Root Issue Scoring: The study team deemed that the root, foundational issues of this project were sufficiently well addressed to darken the "legs" of the Root Issue Scorecard in the following areas:

- Insufficient data to score project

Objectivity Problems:	**Right People/Right Motives/Right Actions Problems:**
- Project suffered from no separate budget and no clear objectives, indicating the *root-of-all-evil* trap, Section 5, Principle 8: Fads, Traps, and Dirty Tricks. ... - Project also suffered from an ineffective information system sponsor and did not have a business unit sponsor, possibly indicating the *information systems-driven* project trap. See Section 5, Principle 8: Fads, Traps, and Dirty Tricks. ... for more details. - The developers were not allowed to investigate user needs beyond cursory level, indicating both the *business case is not solid enough to get business unit priority* trap and the *root-of-all-evil* trap because the business unit never agreed to the objectively defined amount of resources it would need to provide to accomplish the project. See Section 5, Principle 8: Fads, Traps, and Dirty Tricks. ... for more details.	
Authority/Responsibility Problems:	**Accountability Problems:**

CASE PROFILE: BURLINGTON COAT FACTORY

Case ID: 128	Industry: Retail	Data Source: Alice LaPlante, The Big Deal About Thinking Small, *Forbes, ASAP* (Approx. 1993), page 22.

Type of Project:	Project Outcome:
Downsizing from mainframe to client/server using Oracle.	Lost significant business and credibility with internal Burlington merchandising managers.

COST OF QUALITY

Direct Project Costs:	*Costs of Unrealized Objectives:*
Original Budget: n/a Total Spent to Date: n/a Estimate of Wasted Direct Project Costs: n/a	Organization did not receive benefits as promised or encountered extra expense in the following areas: Estimated Costs of Unrealized Objectives: n/a
	TOTAL COST OF QUALITY: N/A (estimated by adding wasted project costs to costs of unrealized objectives)

ROOT ISSUE SCORECARD   ROOT ISSUES

n/a

Root Issue Scoring: The study team deemed that the root, foundational issues of this project were sufficiently well addressed to darken the "legs" of the Root Issue Scorecard in the following areas:

- **Insufficient data to score project**

Objectivity Problems:	Right People/Right Motives/Right Actions Problems:
- Due to understaffing, the project team had to freeze the mainframe merchandising database while developing the Oracle database. This indicates the *root-of-all-evil* trap, Section 5, Principle 8: Fads, Traps, and Dirty Tricks. ...	
Authority/Responsibility Problems:	**Accountability Problems:**

CASE PROFILE: ROGERS GROUP

Case ID: 129	Industry: Construction	Data Source: Thomas Hoffman, Users Share Stories of Downsizing Pros, Cons, *Computerworld* (Approx. 1994).
Type of Project: Move from IBM mainframe to client/server.		**Project Outcome:**

COST OF QUALITY

Direct Project Costs:	*Costs of Unrealized Objectives:*
Original Budget: n/a Total Spent to Date: n/a Estimate of Wasted Direct Project Costs: n/a	Organization did not receive benefits as promised or encountered extra expense in the following areas: Estimated Costs of Unrealized Objectives: n/a
	TOTAL COST OF QUALITY: N/A (estimated by adding wasted project costs to costs of unrealized objectives)

ROOT ISSUE SCORECARD ROOT ISSUES

n/a

Root Issue Scoring: The study team deemed that the root, foundational issues of this project were sufficiently well addressed to darken the "legs" of the Root Issue Scorecard in the following areas:

- Insufficient data to score project

Objectivity Problems:	Right People/Right Motives/Right Actions Problems:
- Extreme cost overruns in telecommunications area. Merger of server supplier set entire project back materially. This precipitated a transition over an eighteen-month period to a wholly new server technology. See the *subjective technical solution* trap and *downsizing* fad/trap in Section 5, Principle 8: Fads, Traps, and Dirty Tricks. ... - Multi-year delays nearly always indicate the *root-of-all-evil* trap. See Section 5, Principle 8: Fads, Traps, and Dirty Tricks. ... for more details.	
Authority/Responsibility Problems:	**Accountability Problems:**

CASE PROFILE: National Trucking Services

Case ID: 130	Industry: Trucking	Data Source: 1994 personal interview with project team member.

Type of Project: Migration of mainframe applications to client/server.	Project Outcome: At last report, decision was reversed and company is moving applications back to mainframe.

COST OF QUALITY

Direct Project Costs:	*Costs of Unrealized Objectives:*
Original Budget: $200,000 (very rough estimate) Total Spent to Date: $500,000 (very rough estimate) Estimate of Wasted Direct Project Costs: $300,000 (very rough estimate)	Organization did not receive benefits as promised or encountered extra expense in the following areas: - lost incremental revenues from improved customer service - unrealized cost savings from reduced administrative labor - possible reduction in bad debt losses. Estimated Costs of Unrealized Objectives: $200,000 (very rough estimate)
	TOTAL COST OF QUALITY: $500,000 (very rough estimate) (estimated by adding wasted project costs to costs of unrealized objectives)

ROOT ISSUE SCORECARD

n/a

Root Issue Scoring: The study team deemed that the root, foundational issues of this project were sufficiently well addressed to darken the "legs" of the Root Issue Scorecard in the following areas:

- Insufficient data to score project

ROOT ISSUES

Objectivity Problems:	Right People/Right Motives/Right Actions Problems:
- Project suffered from the *root-of-all-evil* trap, charging ahead based on high-level project definition, cost estimates, schedules, technical designs, and so on. See Section 5, Principle 8: Fads, Traps, and Dirty Tricks. ... for more details. - Project probably suffered from the *technology-driven project* trap. See Section 5, Principle 8: Fads, Traps, and Dirty Tricks. ...	
Authority/Responsibility Problems:	**Accountability Problems:**

CASE PROFILE: Midwestern Real Estate Services Firm

Case ID: 131	Industry: Real Estate Services	Data Source: 1995 interview with a project team member.

Type of Project:	Project Outcome:
Client/server imaging, accounts payable workflow application.	Confusion, delay, ill will. Ultimate outcome not known.

COST OF QUALITY

Direct Project Costs:	Costs of Unrealized Objectives:
Original Budget: Estimated at $400,000	Organization did not receive benefits as promised or encountered extra expense in the following areas:
Total Spent to Date: n/a	
Estimate of Wasted Direct Project Costs: n/a	Estimated Costs of Unrealized Objectives: n/a
	TOTAL COST OF QUALITY: N/A (estimated by adding wasted project costs to costs of unrealized objectives)

ROOT ISSUE SCORECARD

ROOT ISSUES

n/a

Root Issue Scoring: The study team deemed that the root, foundational issues of this project were sufficiently well addressed to darken the "legs" of the Root Issue Scorecard in the following areas:

- Insufficient data to score project

Objectivity Problems:	Right People/Right Motives/Right Actions Problems:
	- Multiple competing agendas by client, consultant, vendor, and subcontractor damaged the project.

Authority/Responsibility Problems:	Accountability Problems:
- Absence of experienced, single point-of-responsibility project manager with adequate authority indicates the *no single point of responsibility* trap. See Section 5, Principle 8: Fads, Traps, and Dirty Tricks. ... for more details. - Probably also suffered from the *executive sponsor wants to manage at high level* trap. See Section 5, Principle 8: Fads, Traps, and Dirty Tricks. ...	

CASE PROFILE: EAST COAST PHARMACEUTICAL FIRM

Case ID: 132	Industry: Medical Supplies	Data Source: 1995 interview with project team member.

Type of Project:
Client/server imaging system for credit/invoice processing. Complex routing and matching.

Project Outcome:
Vendor absorbed substantial overage, significant delay.

COST OF QUALITY

Direct Project Costs:	Costs of Unrealized Objectives:
Original Budget: Estimated at $400,000 Total Spent to Date: n/a Estimate of Wasted Direct Project Costs: n/a	Organization did not receive benefits as promised or encountered extra expense in the following areas: - lost incremental revenues due to improved customer service - unrealized cost savings in accounting areas. Estimated Costs of Unrealized Objectives: $200,000
	TOTAL COST OF QUALITY: $200,000 (estimated by adding wasted project costs to costs of unrealized objectives)

ROOT ISSUE SCORECARD

Objectivity Right People   Authority/
             Right Motives Responsibility
             Right Actions Match

Root Issue Scoring: The study team deemed that the root, foundational issues of this project were sufficiently well addressed to darken the "legs" of the Root Issue Scorecard in the following areas:

- **Accountability:** Contract with vendor was strong enough that vendor absorbed overage.

ROOT ISSUES

Objectivity Problems:	Right People/Right Motives/Right Actions Problems:
- Project suffered from nebulous direction, unclear objectives, and lack of scope containment. These symptoms all point to the *root-of-all-evil* problem. See Section 5, Principle 8: Fads, Traps, and Dirty Tricks. ...	- Project manager used methodology and lists by rote. - Absence of experienced project manager indicates "The Project Manager versus *Project Manager*" trap. See Section 5, Principle 8: Fads, Traps, and Dirty Tricks. ... for more details.
Authority/Responsibility Problems:	Accountability Problems:

CASE PROFILE: SOUTHEASTERN UNITED STATES ELECTRIC UTILITY

Case ID: 133	Industry: Energy	Data Source: 1995 interview with member of project team.

Type of Project:
Client/server imaging system, multiple applications.

Project Outcome:
Some delay, confusion, ill will.

COST OF QUALITY

Direct Project Costs:
Original Budget: Estimated at $400,000
Total Spent to Date: n/a
Estimate of Wasted Direct Project Costs: n/a
($35,000 overage absorbed by vendor)

Costs of Unrealized Objectives:
Organization did not receive benefits as promised or encountered extra expense in the following areas:
- unrealized cost savings in accounting areas.

Estimated Costs of Unrealized Objectives: $100,000

TOTAL COST OF QUALITY: $100,000
(estimated by adding wasted project costs to costs of unrealized objectives)

ROOT ISSUE SCORECARD

Objectivity   Right People   Authority/
              Right Motives Responsibility
              Right Actions Match

Root Issue Scoring: The study team deemed that the root, foundational issues of this project were sufficiently well addressed to darken the "legs" of the Root Issue Scorecard in the following areas:

- **Accountability:** Contract with vendor was strong enough that vendor absorbed overage.

- **Objectivity:** Although some problems did exist, the relatively low overage indicates some level of objectivity.

ROOT ISSUES

Objectivity Problems:
- Problems associated with changing technology indicate the *subjective technical solution* trap. See Section 5, Principle 8: Fads, Traps, and Dirty Tricks. ... for more details.

Right People/Right Motives/Right Actions Problems:

Authority/Responsibility Problems:
- Absence of empowered, experienced project management indicates "The Project Manager versus *Project Manager*" trap. See Section 5, Principle 8: Fads, Traps, and Dirty Tricks. ...

Accountability Problems:

CASE PROFILE: WEST COAST SAVINGS AND LOAN

Case ID: 134	Industry: Financial	Data Source: 1995 interview with project team member.

Type of Project:
Client/server imaging systems for loan processing and other financial services applications.

Project Outcome:
Customer has gone through at least two and possibly three imaging systems vendors. At last report, customer was threatening litigation, though it is clear that the customer's mistakes are significant as well.

COST OF QUALITY

Direct Project Costs:
Original Budget: Estimated at $1,000,000
Total Spent to Date: $2,000,000
Estimate of Wasted Direct Project Costs: $1,000,000
(significant overage absorbed by vendor)

Costs of Unrealized Objectives:
Organization did not receive benefits as promised or encountered extra expense in the following areas:
- unrealized cost savings in loan processing and other administrative areas
- lost incremental revenues from improved customer service
- extra costs from changing vendors and contentious nature of project.

Estimated Costs of Unrealized Objectives: $500,000

TOTAL COST OF QUALITY: $1,500,000
(estimated by adding wasted project costs to costs of unrealized objectives)

ROOT ISSUE SCORECARD

Objectivity | Right People Right Motives Right Actions | Authority/ Responsibility Match

Root Issue Scoring: The study team deemed that the root, foundational issues of this project were sufficiently well addressed to darken the "legs" of the Root Issue Scorecard in the following areas:

- **Accountability:** Contract with vendor was strong enough that vendor absorbed overage.

ROOT ISSUES

Objectivity Problems:
- Project suffered from the *prototype/pilot* trap. See Section 5, Principle 8: Fads, Traps, and Dirty Tricks. ... for more details.
- Project suffered from the *root-of-all-evil* trap. See Section 5, Principle 8: Fads, Traps, and Dirty Tricks. ... for more details.

Right People/Right Motives/Right Actions Problems:
- Internal personnel clearly were bent on blaming vendors for all problems and contributing to a combative environment.

Authority/Responsibility Problems:
- Project probably suffered from the *100 percent outsourcing...* trap. See Section 5, Principle 8: Fads, Traps, and Dirty Tricks. ...

Accountability Problems:

CASE PROFILE: REINSURANCE FIRM

Case ID: 135	Industry: Insurance	Data Source: 1995 personal interview with project team member.

Type of Project: Imaging, underwriting workflow, multi-city.	Project Outcome: Client sponsor lost credibility; three-month delay, ill will, consternation, rework.

COST OF QUALITY

Direct Project Costs:	Costs of Unrealized Objectives:
Original Budget: Estimated at $600,000 Total Spent to Date: n/a Estimate of Wasted Direct Project Costs: n/a ($200,000 overage absorbed by vendor)	Organization did not receive benefits as promised or encountered extra expense in the following areas: - unrealized cost savings in underwriting process and other administrative areas - lost incremental revenues from improved customer service. Estimated Costs of Unrealized Objectives: $200,000
	TOTAL COST OF QUALITY: $200,000 (estimated by adding wasted project costs to costs of unrealized objectives)

ROOT ISSUE SCORECARD

Root Issue Scoring: The study team deemed that the root, foundational issues of this project were sufficiently well addressed to darken the "legs" of the Root Issue Scorecard in the following areas:

- **Accountability:** Even though the vendor changed strategy away from fixed price mid-project and vendor's resources were constrained, the contract with vendor was strong enough that vendor absorbed overage.

- **Objectivity:** Because the customer was not severely damaged by the project, a degree of objectivity must have been present.

ROOT ISSUES

Objectivity Problems: - Vendor was blinded by large project and sold project fixed price, fixed schedule. - Project also suffered from the *information systems-driven* project trap. See Section 5, Principle 8: Fads, Traps, and Dirty Tricks. ... for more details.	Right People/Right Motives/Right Actions Problems:
Authority/Responsibility Problems:	**Accountability Problems:**

CASE PROFILE: QUASI-GOVERNMENTAL AGENCY

Case ID: 136	Industry: Government	Data Source: 1993 personal interview with manager of project team members.

Type of Project:
Client/server point-of-sale system with back office systems for 400 retail locations.

Project Outcome:
Original three-year $7,000,000 estimate given in late eighties. After $11,000,000 spent, customer fired consulting firm. As of 1993, total spent at $15,000,000 with first sites to be implemented in summer 1995.

Big Six Consulting firm fired the partner and staff, and the office was shut down.

COST OF QUALITY

Direct Project Costs:	Costs of Unrealized Objectives:
Original Budget: $7,000,000 Total Spent to Date: $15,000,000 Estimate of Wasted Direct Project Costs: $8,000,000	Organization did not receive benefits as promised or encountered extra expense in the following areas: - lost incremental sales from improved customer service - unrealized cost savings from reduced administrative labor and reduced inventory losses - extra costs from disastrous nature of project. Estimated Costs of Unrealized Objectives: $20,000,000
	TOTAL COST OF QUALITY: $28,000,000 (estimated by adding wasted project costs to costs of unrealized objectives)

ROOT ISSUE SCORECARD

Objectivity   Right People   Authority/
Right Motives   Responsibility
Right Actions   Match

Root Issue Scoring: The study team deemed that the root, foundational issues of this project were sufficiently well addressed to darken the "legs" of the Root Issue Scorecard in the following areas:

- Authority/Responsibility Match: Apparently the project manager(s) had the authority needed, but it wasn't used correctly.

ROOT ISSUES

Objectivity Problems:
- Consultant and customer decided to build their own programming *tools* but did not really have the experience to do so. However, the technical people were incredibly bright and sold management on the idea. Project clearly suffered from the *root-of-all-evil* trap, the *technology-driven project* trap, and the *subjective technical solution* trap. See Section 5, Principle 8: Fads, Traps, and Dirty Tricks. ...
- It is very possible that some deadlines and budgets were mandated for political/self serving reasons. See the *political/self serving budgets and deadlines* trap in Section 5, Principle 8: Fads, Traps, and Dirty Tricks. ...

Authority/Responsibility Problems:

Right People/Right Motives/Right Actions Problems:
- Having many of the resources needed yet failing so badly may either question the competence of the project manager or may indicate that the project manager existed in name only. See "The Project Manager versus *Project Manager*" trap, Section 5, Principle 8: Fads, Traps, and Dirty Tricks. ... for more details.

Accountability Problems:
- Accountability was defused through continual shuffling of executive in charge (may have been intentional).
- The project clearly suffered from inattention during the middle phases. See the *OK, I can coast for a while* trap, Section 5, Principle 8: Fads, Traps, and Dirty Tricks. ... for more details.

CASE PROFILE: DALLAS-BASED TELECOMMUNICATIONS MANUFACTURER

Case ID: 137	Industry: Manufacturing	Data Source: 1993 and 1994 interviews with a project team member and the executive sponsor.

Type of Project:	Project Outcome:
Conversion of all financial and manufacturing applications from mainframe to client/server using Oracle.	Executive sponsor had to go before board twice to explain delays and scope changes. Multi-year delay in receiving benefits.

COST OF QUALITY

Direct Project Costs:	Costs of Unrealized Objectives:
Original Budget: Estimated at $2,000,000 Total Spent to Date: Estimated at $3,500,000 Estimate of Wasted Direct Project Costs: Estimated at $1,500,000	Organization did not receive benefits as promised or encountered extra expense in the following areas: - unrealized cost savings in all areas of administrative tasks - unrealized cost savings in improved inventory utilization and improved control of product costs - lost incremental revenues due to improved customer service - extra costs due to extended nature of project and conflicts. Estimated Costs of Unrealized Objectives: $10,000,000
	TOTAL COST OF QUALITY: $11,500,000 (estimated by adding wasted project costs to costs of unrealized objectives)

ROOT ISSUE SCORECARD

Objectivity   Right People   Authority/
              Right Motives Responsibility
              Right Actions Match

Root Issue Scoring: The study team deemed that the root, foundational issues of this project were sufficiently well addressed to darken the "legs" of the Root Issue Scorecard in the following areas:

- **Accountability:** The executive sponsor at least had to go in front of the board to account for the delays and problems.

ROOT ISSUES

Objectivity Problems:

- Sales people sold aggressive schedule based on Oracle meeting dates and stability of Alpha code. See the *Oracle* fad, Section 5, Principle 8: Fads, Traps, and Dirty Tricks. ... for more details.
- Scope was too large, deadlines too quick, and project dependent on risky technology. See the *root-of-all-evil* trap. See also the *subjective technical solution* trap in Section 5, Principle 8: Fads, Traps, and Dirty Tricks. ...

Right People/Right Motives/Right Actions Problems:

- Indications were that internal project management was weak at mid to low levels. See "The Project Manager versus *Project Manager*" trap, Section 5, Principle 8: Fads, Traps, and Dirty Tricks. ... for more details.

continued on next page

ROOT ISSUES *(continued)*

Authority/Responsibility Problems:	Accountability Problems:
- Executive sponsor was presented with a summary of the major risks the project was running during the project's mid-point. These recommendations were ignored.	

Other Items of Note:

The author has on file a similar mainframe horror story for this firm. In that case, under-attention to information systems issues caused an $11,000,000 inventory write-off. Speculation exists that, because the major shareholder (and CEO) of the firm comes from an engineering and operations background, insufficient attention is given to information systems and other necessary functions. See the *don't bother me, I'm busy running the business* trap, Section 5, Principle 8: Fads, Traps, and Dirty Tricks. ... for more details.

CASE PROFILE: ACCOR SA (FRANCE)

Case ID: 138	Industry: Travel Agency	Data Source: *Open Computing* (January 1995).

Type of Project:	Project Outcome:
Joint venture reservations system between Accor SA and Volkswagen (multi-country).	Initially implemented system could only handle 50 percent of the annual four million reservations. Two million customers had to be diverted to manual or other systems. Extreme opportunity costs and partnership turmoil. Six to eight months delay to rectify problem.

COST OF QUALITY

Direct Project Costs:	*Costs of Unrealized Objectives:*
Original Budget: n/a Total Spent to Date: n/a Estimate of Wasted Direct Project Costs: n/a	Organization did not receive benefits as promised or encountered extra expense in the following areas: - lost incremental revenues - extra costs from coping with project volatility. Estimated Costs of Unrealized Objectives: $10,000,000
	TOTAL COST OF QUALITY: $10,000,000 (This cost of unrealized objectives was estimated by assuming an average commission of $50 per reservation. Since two million reservations were diverted to manual or other systems during the initial implementation, it was assumed that 10 percent of those two million reservations were lost to competitors. Therefore, 200,000 lost reservations times $50 equals $10,000,000 in lost revenues.)

ROOT ISSUE SCORECARD

Root Issue Scoring: The study team deemed that the root, foundational issues of this project were sufficiently well addressed to darken the "legs" of the Root Issue Scorecard in the following areas:

- **Accountability:** The evidence of an internal effort to kill the project indicates that at least some level of accountability existed.

ROOT ISSUES

Objectivity Problems:	Right People/Right Motives/Right Actions Problems:
- Although the article referencing this case speaks largely of the cultural lesson and mistakes, it is important to note that in Horror Case #115, Perot systems was a part of a similar situation where the initially delivered system could not handle the performance load. See the *root-of-all-evil* trap in Section 5, Principle 8: Fads, Traps, and Dirty Tricks. ...	
Authority/Responsibility Problems:	Accountability Problems:

Other Items of Note:

Cultural Lessons: Entrepreneurial culture at Accor SA conflicted with old line, autocratic culture at Volkswagen. Volkswagen's management and unions had not bought in. When technical throughput problems were encountered, Volkswagen (unions and management) tried to kill the project. Consulting firm (Perot) did not realize that unions in semi-socialist countries are substantially more powerful than in the United States.

CASE PROFILE: MIDWESTERN REINSURANCE FIRM

Case ID: 139	Industry: Insurance	Data Source: 1995 interview with project team member.

Type of Project:	Project Outcome:
Client/server imaging system with front and back office processing for reinsurance. Very aggressive real-time access to information with fourteen remote sites.	Extreme vendor/consultant/client friction. Ernst & Young dismissed from project. Original project was so overly ambitious that it could never really be done. Current state of the project is unknown.

COST OF QUALITY

Direct Project Costs:	Costs of Unrealized Objectives:
Original Budget: estimated at $2,000,000 Total Spent to Date: estimated at $4,000,000 Estimate of Wasted Direct Project Costs: $2,000,000	Organization did not receive benefits as promised or encountered extra expense in the following areas: - lost incremental sales due to improved customer service and improved marketing - unrecognized cost savings in insurance application processing and other administrative areas - extra costs due to volatility of project. Estimated Costs of Unrealized Objectives: $10,000,000
	TOTAL COST OF QUALITY: $12,000,000 (estimated by adding wasted project costs to costs of unrealized objectives)

ROOT ISSUE SCORECARD

Objectivity Right People Authority/
Right Motives Responsibility
Right Actions Match

Root Issue Scoring: The study team deemed that the root, foundational issues of this project were sufficiently well addressed to darken the "legs" of the Root Issue Scorecard in the following areas:

- **Accountability:** Since the consulting firm was dismissed, at least some level of accountability existed.

ROOT ISSUES

Objectivity Problems:
- Technology fixation and absence of detailed application specifications indicate the *technology-driven project* and *root-of-all-evil* traps. See Section 5, Principle 8: Fads, Traps, and Dirty Tricks. ... for more details.
- Project also probably suffered from the *subjective technical solution* trap. See Section 5, Principle 8: Fads, Traps, and Dirty Tricks. ... See also the *prototype/pilot* trap.

Right People/Right Motives/Right Actions Problems:
- Consultant ignored vendor's technical cautions and proceeded to build a system based on the arrogant presumption that the consultant knew better. See the *I'm just smart enough to convince you that I know what I'm doing* trap, Section 5, Principle 8: Fads, Traps, and Dirty Tricks. ... for more details.

Authority/Responsibility Problems:
- See the *no single point of responsibility* trap, Section 5, Principle 8: Fads, Traps, and Dirty Tricks. ... for more details.
- Severe responsibility and expectation miscommunication.

Accountability Problems:

CASE PROFILE: FEDERAL AGENCY, AUSTIN, TEXAS

Case ID: 140	Industry: Government	Data Source: 1995 personal interview with project team member.

Type of Project:	Project Outcome:
Client/server imaging system, central repository for accounts payable vouchers, nationwide.	Integrator nearly lost certification for providing federal government systems. Substantial confusion and delay. Project was ultimately completed.

COST OF QUALITY

Direct Project Costs:	Costs of Unrealized Objectives:
Original Budget: estimated at $200,000 Total Spent to Date: estimated at $300,000 Estimate of Wasted Direct Project Costs: $100,000	Organization did not receive benefits as promised or encountered extra expense in the following areas: - unrealized cost savings in administrative labor for processing accounts payable. Estimated Costs of Unrealized Objectives: $200,000
	TOTAL COST OF QUALITY: $300,000 (estimated by adding wasted project costs to costs of unrealized objectives)

ROOT ISSUE SCORECARD   ROOT ISSUES

Objectivity Right People   Authority/
            Right Motives Responsibility
            Right Actions Match

Root Issue Scoring: The study team deemed that the root, foundational issues of this project were sufficiently well addressed to darken the "legs" of the Root Issue Scorecard in the following areas:

- **Accountability:** Strong contracts with the integrator prevented significant loss to the agency.

Objectivity Problems:
- Project probably suffered from the *100 percent outsourcing* trap and the *root-of-all-evil* traps. See Section 5, Principle 8: Fads, Traps, and Dirty Tricks. ... for more details.
- The system integrator apparently fell into the *subjective technical solution* trap, Section 5, Principle 8: Fads, Traps, and Dirty Tricks. ... for more details.

Right People/Right Motives/Right Actions Problems:
- Integrator was undertrained and undersupported by software vendor. Application was designed in a vacuum without review by experienced technicians. See the *I'm just smart enough to convince you that I know what I'm doing* trap, Section 5, Principle 8: Fads, Traps, and Dirty Tricks. ... for more details.

Authority/Responsibility Problems:

Accountability Problems:

CASE PROFILE: INDEPENDENT TELEPHONE COMPANY

Case ID: 141	Industry: Telecommunications	Data Source: 1995 and 1996 personal interviews with project manager and multiple others familiar with the situation.

Type of Project:	Project Outcome:
Large-scale conversion of mainframe systems to client/server. Over seventy individual projects.	A cost of quality review is pending. Projects total value exceeds $250,000,000 and is widely held to be in serious trouble.

COST OF QUALITY

Direct Project Costs:	*Costs of Unrealized Objectives:*
Original Budget: $250,000,000 Total Spent to Date: n/a Estimate of Wasted Direct Project Costs: n/a	Organization did not receive benefits as promised or encountered extra expense in the following areas: Estimated Costs of Unrealized Objectives: $875,000,000 (estimate very rough due to magnitude)
	TOTAL COST OF QUALITY: $875,000,000 (estimated by adding wasted project costs to costs of unrealized objectives)

ROOT ISSUE SCORECARD   ROOT ISSUES

n/a

Objectivity Problems:	Right People/Right Motives/Right Actions Problems:

Root Issue Scoring: The study team deemed that the root, foundational issues of this project were sufficiently well addressed to darken the "legs" of the Root Issue Scorecard in the following areas:

- **Insufficient data to score project**

Authority/Responsibility Problems:	Accountability Problems:

CASE PROFILE: EAST COAST-BASED LONG DISTANCE CARRIER

Case ID: 142	Industry: Telecommunications	Data Source: 1994 personal management of project.

Type of Project:	Project Outcome:
Client/server imaging system for accounts payable, two sites.	Author was dismissed from project in first week for insisting on scope and risk management controls. At last report, the original timetable is at least doubled, and client is attempting to blame vendor and force refund (with no contractual basis for claim).

COST OF QUALITY

Direct Project Costs:	Costs of Unrealized Objectives:
Original Budget: $400,000 Total Spent to Date: n/a Estimate of Wasted Direct Project Costs: n/a	Organization did not receive benefits as promised or encountered extra expense in the following areas: - unrecognized cost savings in accounts payable labor - unrecognized cost savings through better control of accounts payable. Estimated Costs of Unrealized Objectives: $400,000
	TOTAL COST OF QUALITY: $400,000 (estimated by adding wasted project costs to costs of unrealized objectives)

ROOT ISSUE SCORECARD

Objectivity | Right People Right Motives Right Actions | Authority/ Responsibility Match

Root Issue Scoring: The study team deemed that the root, foundational issues of this project were sufficiently well addressed to darken the "legs" of the Root Issue Scorecard in the following areas:

- None

ROOT ISSUES

Objectivity Problems:
- Vendor and client rushed through pre-sales effort without due diligence. Client paid for software up-front. See the *root-of-all-evil* trap and the *I'm just smart enough to convince you that I know what I'm doing* trap, Section 5, Principle 8: Fads, Traps, and Dirty Tricks. ... for more details.
- This project also suffered from the *prototype/pilot* trap. See Section 5, Principle 8: Fads, Traps, and Dirty Tricks. ... for more details.

Right People/Right Motives/Right Actions Problems:
- Extreme arrogance, rudeness, and political maneuvering dominated customer's behavior. Client made ridiculous assumptions about timetables and levels of effort, ignoring vendor's attempts to correct expectations.

Authority/Responsibility Problems:
- Author insisted on scope and risk controls and was dismissed from project in the first week. See the *do the right thing and lose your job* trap in Section 5, Principle 8: Fads, Traps, and Dirty Tricks. ...

Accountability Problems:
- As far as was observable, no accountability arose for the internal project manager and others who were maneuvering for personal gain.
- The customer paid the software vendor for the system up-front (to get a great deal) and lost any real accountability short of litigation.

CASE PROFILE: DALLAS/FORT WORTH AREA CITY GOVERNMENT

Case ID: 143	Industry: Government	Data Source: 1995 personal management of project.

Type of Project:
Client/server imaging system for work order tracking. Ultimately, workflow management and mainframe communications were added. Customer insisted on using homemade, non-supported equipment to save a few dollars.

Project Outcome:
Project was underfunded and included extreme technical risks. Author insisted on the resolution of these issues before proceeding. Customer had to go back for more money and release vendor from technical liability. Customer dismissed author as project manager. At last report, project has proceeded with great difficulty.

COST OF QUALITY

Direct Project Costs:
Original Budget: $40,000
Total Spent to Date: n/a
Estimate of wasted Direct Project Costs: n/a

Costs of Unrealized Objectives:
Organization did not receive benefits as promised or encountered extra expense in the following areas:
- unrealized cost reductions in work order labor.

Estimated Costs of Unrealized Objectives: $50,000

TOTAL COST OF QUALITY: $50,000
(estimated by adding wasted project costs to costs of unrealized objectives)

ROOT ISSUE SCORECARD

Objectivity   Right People   Authority/
      Right Motives   Responsibility
      Right Actions   Match

Root Issue Scoring: The study team deemed that the root, foundational issues of this project were sufficiently well addressed to darken the "legs" of the Root Issue Scorecard in the following areas:

- **None**

ROOT ISSUES

Objectivity Problems:
- Sales process allowed customer to believe that vendor would make system work on non-supported hardware at no extra charge. Sales person also removed the workflow and communications options to reduce the cost but didn't tell everyone.

Right People/Right Motives/Right Actions Problems:
- The customer project manager appeared to have a clear belief that he could push the vendor into absorbing unreasonable costs and risks.

Authority/Responsibility Problems:
- Author insisted on scope and risk controls and was dismissed from project. See the *do the right thing and lose your job* trap in Section 5, Principle 8: Fads, Traps, and Dirty Tricks. ...

Accountability Problems:
- The vendor and the customer were both saved thousands of dollars in project trouble through the author's actions. However, the salesman and the customer's project manager both greatly resented the author's actions.

CASE PROFILE: ULP, Des Plaines, IL

Case ID: 144	Industry: Manufacturing	Data Source: *Computerworld* (May 8, 1995).

Type of Project:	Project Outcome:
Client/server system for engineering design and cost estimating applications.	$8,000,000 spent; no production system produced. $100,000,000 lawsuit pending against Andersen Consulting. Project moved to two smaller integrators.

COST OF QUALITY

Direct Project Costs:	Costs of Unrealized Objectives:
Original Budget: $8,000,000 Total Spent to Date: n/a Estimate of Wasted Direct Project Costs: (included in lawsuit damages)	Organization did not receive benefits as promised or encountered extra expense in the following areas: (damages claimed by lawsuit) Estimated Costs of Unrealized Objectives: $100,000,000
	TOTAL COST OF QUALITY: $100,000,000 (estimated as the damages claimed in the lawsuit)

ROOT ISSUE SCORECARD

ACCOUNTABILITY

Objectivity | Right People | Authority/
| Right Motives | Responsibility
| Right Actions | Match

Root Issue Scoring: The study team deemed that the root, foundational issues of this project were sufficiently well addressed to darken the "legs" of the Root Issue Scorecard in the following areas:

- **None:** Although there is no evidence to indicate that any of the root issues were done right, a certain amount of perspective is called for. In many situations, Andersen Consulting has performed as promised. Judgment needs to be withheld until the litigation is settled.

ROOT ISSUES

Objectivity Problems:	Right People/Right Motives/Right Actions Problems:
- Andersen contract called for delivering prototypes. ULP expected much more, alleging defective deliverables, misrepresentation, extensive budget overruns, and extensive delays. Project almost certainly suffered from the *root-of-all-evil* trap, the *prototype/pilot* trap, and most of the other traps. See Section 5, Principle 8: Fads, Traps, and Dirty Tricks. ... for more details.	
Authority/Responsibility Problems:	**Accountability Problems:**

CASE PROFILE: BOSTON MARKET (BOSTON CHICKEN)

Case ID: 145	Industry: Restaurant	Data Source: *Computerworld* (May 8, 1995).

Type of Project:	Project Outcome:
Client/server system; application not disclosed.	$5,000,000 spent, project scrapped. Ernst & Young has pared back its presence at Boston Market.

COST OF QUALITY

Direct Project Costs:	*Costs of Unrealized Objectives:*
Original Budget: n/a Total Spent to Date: $5,000,000 Estimate of Wasted Direct Project Costs: $5,000,000	Organization did not receive benefits as promised or encountered extra expense in the following areas: - unrealized cost savings - lost incremental revenues due to better marketing. Estimated Costs of Unrealized Objectives: $10,000,000
	TOTAL COST OF QUALITY: $15,000,000 (estimated by adding wasted project costs to costs of unrealized objectives)

ROOT ISSUE SCORECARD

Objectivity   Right People   Authority/
          Right Motives   Responsibility
          Right Actions   Match

Root Issue Scoring: The study team deemed that the root, foundational issues of this project were sufficiently well addressed to darken the "legs" of the Root Issue Scorecard in the following areas:

- **None:** Although there is no evidence to indicate that any of the root issues were done right, a certain amount of perspective is called for. Ernst and Young has performed creditably in many other assignments.

ROOT ISSUES

Objectivity Problems:	Right People/Right Motives/Right Actions Problems:

Authority/Responsibility Problems:	Accountability Problems:

Other items of note:

Mismatch of size: Integrator's large-scale, structured approach did not fit smaller company and project. Big six, big integrator downsides include:
- Client usually has to accept a large percentage of inexperienced people as part of project team.
- Big integrators are solidly entrenched in their methods and structures. They are uncomfortable with a flexible, pick, choose, and customize approach.

CASE PROFILE: ***DELETED FROM STUDY - NOT RELEVANT***		
Case ID: 146	Industry:	Data Source:
Type of Project:		Project Outcome:

COST OF QUALITY

Direct Project Costs:	Costs of Unrealized Objectives:
	TOTAL COST OF QUALITY:

ROOT ISSUE SCORECARD   ROOT ISSUES

n/a

Objectivity Problems:	Right People/Right Motives/Right Actions Problems:
Authority/Responsibility Problems:	Accountability Problems:

CASE PROFILE: CELLULAR SERVICE SUBSIDIARY OF FORMER BELL OPERATING COMPANY

Case ID: 147	Industry: Telecommunications	Data Source: Project team interviews from 1994 through 1996.

Type of Project:	Project Outcome:
Consolidation of multiple billing systems.	Deliverables drastically scaled back to attempt to meet deadline; initial pilots proceeding with some difficulty and some success.

COST OF QUALITY

Direct Project Costs:	Costs of Unrealized Objectives:
Original Budget: $12,000,000 Total Spent to Date: $120,000,000 plus Estimate of Wasted Direct Project Costs: $108,000,000	Organization did not receive benefits as promised or encountered extra expense in the following areas: - unrealized cost savings of consolidations and client/server over mainframe - lost customers - lost incremental revenues - annual report notes strong increase in revenues but omits discussion of costs or profits. Estimated Costs of Unrealized Objectives: $100,000,000
	TOTAL COST OF QUALITY: $208,000,000 (estimated by adding wasted project costs to costs of unrealized objectives)

ROOT ISSUE SCORECARD   ROOT ISSUES

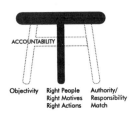

ACCOUNTABILITY

Objectivity   Right People   Authority/
Right Motives   Responsibility
Right Actions   Match

Root Issue Scoring: The study team deemed that the root, foundational issues of this project were sufficiently well addressed to darken the "legs" of the Root Issue Scorecard in the following areas:

- **Right People/Right Motives/ Right Actions**

Objectivity Problems:	Right People/Right Motives/Right Actions Problems:
- Technical design not objective. - Business case not objective. - Scope/deliverables not objectively defined up front. - Budget, deadlines, and scope not objectively balanced.	- Executives appear to have been promoting project for their own benefits.
Authority/Responsibility Problems:	**Accountability Problems:**
- Executives mandated contractor, system supplier, deadlines, and scope without full buy-in from those responsible for the work.	- Executives have avoided accountability to date. - High personnel turnover may indicate scapegoating.

CASE PROFILE: ALCOA

Case ID: 148	Industry: Manufacturing	Data Source: *Computerworld* (April 29, 1996).

Type of Project:	Project Outcome:
Replace SAP R/3 client/server systems with Oracle worldwide across twenty-two business units.	In process.

COST OF QUALITY

Direct Project Costs:	**Costs of Unrealized Objectives:**
Original Budget: $100,000,000 Total Spent to Date: n/a Estimate of Wasted Direct Project Costs: n/a	Organization did not receive benefits as promised or encountered extra expense in the following areas: Estimated Costs of Unrealized Objectives: n/a
	TOTAL COST OF QUALITY: N/A (estimated by adding wasted project costs to costs of unrealized objectives)

ROOT ISSUE SCORECARD   ROOT ISSUES

n/a

Root Issue Scoring: The study team deemed that the root, foundational issues of this project were sufficiently well addressed to darken the "legs" of the Root Issue Scorecard in the following areas:

- **Insufficient data to score project**

Objectivity Problems:	Right People/Right Motives/Right Actions Problems:
- Decision to use SAP R/3 may have been less than objective. - Decision to use Oracle worldwide may be path of convenience or politically driven rather than the objective thing to do.	
Authority/Responsibility Problems:	Accountability Problems:

CASE PROFILE: ANDERSEN CONSULTING INTERNAL PROJECT		
Case ID: 149	**Industry: Consulting Services**	**Data Source:** Project participant interview, 1995.
Type of Project: Convert a software development tool from OS/2 to Windows.		**Project Outcome:** Severely underestimated and one year late. Did not really work when delivered. Outcome caused Andersen to beef up project management in affected areas.

COST OF QUALITY

Direct Project Costs:	**Costs of Unrealized Objectives:**
Original Budget: n/a Total Spent to Date: n/a Estimate of Wasted Direct Project Costs: n/a	Organization did not receive benefits as promised or encountered extra expense in the following areas: Estimated Costs of Unrealized Objectives: n/a
	TOTAL COST OF QUALITY: N/A (estimated by adding wasted project costs to costs of unrealized objectives)

ROOT ISSUE SCORECARD   ROOT ISSUES

n/a

Objectivity Problems: - Scope was not objectively defined or contained.	**Right People/Right Motives/Right Actions Problems:**
Authority/Responsibility Problems:	**Accountability Problems:**

Root Issue Scoring: The study team deemed that the root, foundational issues of this project were sufficiently well addressed to darken the "legs" of the Root Issue Scorecard in the following areas:

- Insufficient data to score project

CASE PROFILE: ASSOCIATES FINANCIAL		
Case ID: 150	**Industry: Financial**	**Data Source:** 1995 interview with project team member.
Type of Project: Client/server components of loan administration systems.		**Project Outcome:** Attempted rapid application development (RAD), but deliverables were late and system required substantial rework.

COST OF QUALITY

Direct Project Costs:	*Costs of Unrealized Objectives:*
Original Budget: n/a Total Spent to Date: n/a Estimate of Wasted Direct Project Costs: n/a	Organization did not receive benefits as promised or encountered extra expense in the following areas: Estimated Costs of Unrealized Objectives: n/a
	TOTAL COST OF QUALITY: N/A (estimated by adding wasted project costs to costs of unrealized objectives)

ROOT ISSUE SCORECARD   ROOT ISSUES

n/a

Objectivity Problems: - Initial scope and changes not objectively managed. - Initial design not objective, causing rework. - Non-objective budget constraints may have caused the rework.	**Right People/Right Motives/Right Actions Problems:** - Business unit and information systems conflicts contributed to delays.
Authority/Responsibility Problems:	**Accountability Problems:**

Root Issue Scoring: The study team deemed that the root, foundational issues of this project were sufficiently well addressed to darken the "legs" of the Root Issue Scorecard in the following areas:

- Insufficient data to score project

CASE PROFILE: CALIFORNIA DEPARTMENT OF MOTOR VEHICLES

Case ID: 151	Industry: Government	Data Source: *Application Development Trends* (January 1995)

Type of Project:	Project Outcome:
Client/server driver's license and registration system to replace mainframe system.	Started in 1987. Canceled in 1993.

COST OF QUALITY

Direct Project Costs:	Costs of Unrealized Objectives:
Original Budget: n/a Total Spent to Date: $45,000,000 Estimate of Wasted Direct Project Costs: $45,000,000	Organization did not receive benefits as promised or encountered extra expense in the following areas: - unrealized improvements in the cost and rapid response of the data processing department. Estimated Costs of Unrealized Objectives: $50,000,000
	TOTAL COST OF QUALITY: $95,000,000 (estimated by adding wasted project costs to costs of unrealized objectives)

ROOT ISSUE SCORECARD

Objectivity | Right People Right Motives Right Actions | Authority/ Responsibility Match

Root Issue Scoring: The study team deemed that the root, foundational issues of this project were sufficiently well addressed to darken the "legs" of the Root Issue Scorecard in the following areas:

- None

ROOT ISSUES

Objectivity Problems:	Right People/Right Motives/Right Actions Problems:
- Lack of objective balance between scope and schedule. - Lack of objective definition of work packages (needed to define scope, objectives, system design, and change control). - Lack of objective business case. - No user involvement could mean that the resources needed for user input were never provided.	- Project was allowed to proceed without clear accountability and support from executive management. - No user involvement raises serious competence questions.
Authority/Responsibility Problems:	**Accountability Problems:**
- Those responsible were never confident that the technical design would work. - Project proceeded without the support of the data processing management.	- Project phases and deliverables may have been altered to escape accountability. - Some individuals probably attempted to skew the project for personal gain but were not held accountable.

CASE PROFILE: CENTRAL UNITED STATES PHARMACEUTICAL MANUFACTURER

Case ID: 152	Industry: Manufacturing	Data Source: 1995 interview with project team member.

Type of Project:	Project Outcome:
Client/server SAP accounting and manufacturing systems implementation worldwide (approximately five sites).	One site was actually implemented successfully, but other sites were never deployed, including a revolt by the Consumer Products division. Substantial delays. Company was divested before system could be fully deployed. Speculation that system delays contributed to divestiture.

COST OF QUALITY

Direct Project Costs:	**Costs of Unrealized Objectives:**
Original Budget: n/a Total Spent to Date: n/a Estimate of Wasted Direct Project Costs: n/a	Organization did not receive benefits as promised or encountered extra expense in the following areas: Estimated Costs of Unrealized Objectives: n/a
	TOTAL COST OF QUALITY: N/A (estimated by adding wasted project costs to costs of unrealized objectives)

ROOT ISSUE SCORECARD   ROOT ISSUES

Objectivity   Right People   Authority/
               Right Motives   Responsibility
               Right Actions   Match

Root Issue Scoring: The study team deemed that the root, foundational issues of this project were sufficiently well addressed to darken the "legs" of the Root Issue Scorecard in the following areas:

- **None**

Objectivity Problems: - Scope not objectively broken up into near-term deliverables. - Schedule, scope, and resources required from business unit may not have been objectively balanced.	**Right People/Right Motives/Right Actions Problems:** - Business unit people did not buy in to resources/time needed to complete system.
Authority/Responsibility Problems:	**Accountability Problems:**

CASE PROFILE: DUKE POWER

Case ID: 153	Industry: Energy	Data Source: *Computerworld* (February 26, 1996).

Type of Project:	Project Outcome:
Client/server customer service/information system using Oracle.	Canceled after told it would take two years more than original two-year estimate. Charge of $12,000,000 against 1995 revenue. Work redirected to replacement system, which won't be complete until year 2000.

COST OF QUALITY

Direct Project Costs:	*Costs of Unrealized Objectives:*
Original Budget: $13,000,000 (estimate) Total Spent to Date: Estimate at least $25,000,000 Estimate of Wasted Direct Project Costs: $12,000,000 ($12,000,000 in 1995 write-off alone)	Organization did not receive benefits as promised or encountered extra expense in the following areas: - lost future customers (deregulation will allow competition for customers) - lost cost reductions in customer service - lost incremental revenues through better marketing - higher cost and longer timeframe of replacement system. Estimated Costs of Unrealized Objectives: $75,000,000
	TOTAL COST OF QUALITY: $87,000,000 (estimated by adding wasted project costs to costs of unrealized objectives)

ROOT ISSUE SCORECARD

Objectivity | Right People Right Motives Right Actions | Authority/ Responsibility Match

Root Issue Scoring: The study team deemed that the root, foundational issues of this project were sufficiently well addressed to darken the "legs" of the Root Issue Scorecard in the following areas:

- **None**

ROOT ISSUES

Objectivity Problems:	Right People/Right Motives/Right Actions Problems:
- Lack of objective technical design. - Lack of objective balance between scope, budget, and deadlines. - Lack of objective work package definition to define scope and control change.	- Technology prevailed over business priority. - Is a recurring pattern with Oracle noticeable?

Authority/Responsibility Problems:	Accountability Problems:
- Probably experienced standard difficulties of a fully outsourced project that supports an internal process. Those responsible were outside and could not wield the requisite authority.	- Did not discover the degree of project problems until deadline elapsed. - Oracle may have gotten paid even though it did not deliver as promised.

CASE PROFILE: FIDELITY INVESTMENTS

Case ID: 154	Industry: Financial	Data Source: James S. Hirsch, *The Wall Street Journal* (June 11, 1996).

Type of Project:	Project Outcome:
Client/server system for financial trading from home computers.	Normally strong in systems, Fidelity has had extreme delays and (arguably) spent $40,000,000 on the same system that competitors have developed for one-tenth of the cost.

COST OF QUALITY

Direct Project Costs:	Costs of Unrealized Objectives:
Original Budget: n/a Total Spent to Date: $40,000,000 Estimate of Wasted Direct Project Costs: $30,000,000	Organization did not receive benefits as promised or encountered extra expense in the following areas: - lost future customers in an expanding market - lost present customers due to weakness of existing system that must be used until new one is ready. Estimated Costs of Unrealized Objectives: $80,000,000
	TOTAL COST OF QUALITY: $110,000,000 (estimated by adding wasted project costs to costs of unrealized objectives)

ROOT ISSUE SCORECARD

ACCOUNTABILITY

Objectivity | Right People Right Motives Right Actions | Authority/ Responsibility Match

Root Issue Scoring: The study team deemed that the root, foundational issues of this project were sufficiently well addressed to darken the "legs" of the Root Issue Scorecard in the following areas:

- **Accountability**

ROOT ISSUES

Objectivity Problems:	Right People, Right Motives,. Right Actions Problems:
- Deadlines set when prototype presented to chairman were not objective. - Scope, business case, and deadlines not objectively balanced up-front. - Work packages were not objectively defined to the point of an accurate estimate. - Technical design not objectively validated up-front.	- Extreme turnover may indicate scapegoating. - Internal culture clashes and turf wars contributed to delays.
Authority/Responsibility Problems:	**Accountability Problems:**
- Project manager did not have authority to define and contain scope and changes.	- Since competitors were able to develop similar offerings for one tenth the cost, project's problems should have been visible and prevented earlier.

CASE PROFILE: FoxMeyer Corp. (Delta Project)

Case ID: 155	Industry: Medical Supplies	Data Source: Interview with employee, *The Dallas Morning News,* multiple articles in 1995–96.

Type of Project:	Project Outcome:
Client/server computerized information system (probably migration from IBM outsourcing).	As of 2/2/96, company claims that $20,000,000 of planned $40,000,000 savings has been realized but is disappointed with delay.

COST OF QUALITY

Direct Project Costs:	*Costs of Unrealized Objectives:*
Original Budget: $10,000,000 (estimated) Total Spent to Date: $15,000,000 (estimated) Estimate of Wasted Direct Project Costs: $5,000,000	Organization did not receive benefits as promised or encountered extra expense in the following areas: - unrealized cost savings; the delay in cost reduction is probably attributable to annual outsourcing cost savings being realized slower than expected. Estimated Costs of Unrealized Objectives: $20,000,000
	TOTAL COST OF QUALITY: $25,000,000 (estimated by adding wasted project costs to costs of unrealized objectives)

ROOT ISSUE SCORECARD

Objectivity   Right People   Authority/
              Right Motives Responsibility
              Right Actions Match

Root Issue Scoring: The study team deemed that the root, foundational issues of this project were sufficiently well addressed to darken the "legs" of the Root Issue Scorecard in the following areas:

- None

ROOT ISSUES

Objectivity Problems:	Right People/Right Motives/Right Actions Problems:
Authority/Responsibility Problems	Accountability Problems:

Other Events of Note

8/91	IPO at $14.50 a share.
8/92	Fraud by executives at major customer costs firm roughly $40 million.
1993	Reported that mainframe data center outsourced to IBM.
3/93	FY 1992 sales at $3.2 billion.
3/95	FY 1995 sales over $5 billion but no profits.
2/96	Reports $45.7 million loss attributed to a $59.9 million loss from new automated distribution center.
2/96	President resigns.
by 7/96	Public reports that: - Share price has gone from a high near $30 to less than $12. - Automated distribution center has given away $18 million in product. - Firm is seeking turnaround expert, having discussions with potential buyers, considering taking company private, and so on.

CASE PROFILE: DALLAS-BASED INSURANCE FIRM

Case ID: 156	Industry: Insurance	Data Source: 1995 interview with project team member.

Type of Project:	Project Outcome:
Client/server imaging system for processing insurance claims.	After two years, process was returned to manual operation because business discovered it was cheaper to do manually!

COST OF QUALITY

Direct Project Costs:	Costs of Unrealized Objectives:
Original Budget: n/a Total Spent to Date: n/a Estimate of Wasted Direct Project Costs: n/a	Organization did not receive benefits as promised or encountered extra expense in the following areas: Estimated Costs of Unrealized Objectives: n/a
	TOTAL COST OF QUALITY: N/A (estimated by adding wasted project costs to costs of unrealized objectives)

ROOT ISSUE SCORECARD

Objectivity   Right People   Authority/
         Right Motives   Responsibility
         Right Actions   Match

Root Issue Scoring: The study team deemed that the root, foundational issues of this project were sufficiently well addressed to darken the "legs" of the Root Issue Scorecard in the following areas:

- None

ROOT ISSUES

Objectivity Problems:
- Business case was not objective.
- Solution design was not objective.

Right People/Right Motives/Right Actions Problems:
- Automating an existing manual process with no improvements raises competency questions.

Authority/Responsibility Problems:
- If project manager knew the process needed to be improved, he didn't have the authority to see it through.

Accountability Problems:
- If no process benefits were gained and the process cost less to do manually, someone approved this project but never expected to be held accountable for the outcome.

CASE PROFILE: EAST COAST MEDICAL TESTING FIRM		
Case ID: 157	Industry: Medical Services	Data Source: 1995 interview with project team member.
Type of Project: Client/server order entry system for fifty locations.		Project Outcome: Twelve months late. Client had been outsourcing. Decided to bring systems back in-house.

COST OF QUALITY

Direct Project Costs:	Costs of Unrealized Objectives:
Original Budget: $700,000 Total Spent to Date: $1,500,000 Estimate of Wasted Direct Project Costs: $800,000	Organization did not receive benefits as promised or encountered extra expense in the following areas: - lost customers - lost incremental revenues due to improved levels of service and marketing. Estimated Costs of Unrealized Objectives: $1,000,000
	TOTAL COST OF QUALITY: $1,800,000 (estimated by adding wasted project costs to costs of unrealized objectives)

ROOT ISSUE SCORECARD   ROOT ISSUES

Objectivity   Right People   Authority/
               Right Motives   Responsibility
               Right Actions   Match

Root Issue Scoring: The study team deemed that the root, foundational issues of this project were sufficiently well addressed to darken the "legs" of the Root Issue Scorecard in the following areas:

- None

Objectivity Problems: - Deadline and scope not objectively reconciled up-front. - Work packages not sufficiently defined to accurately estimate deadlines and control changes to scope. - Resource estimates were not objectively defined, resulting in understaffing and delays.	Right People/Right Motives/Right Actions Problems: - Estimator was inexperienced.
Authority/Responsibility Problems:	Accountability Problems: - Consultants were paid even though system was late and doubled the budget.

CASE PROFILE: UPPER MIDWEST STEEL MANUFACTURER

Case ID: 158	Industry: Manufacturing	Data Source: Participated in project in 1995.

Type of Project:	Project Outcome:
Client/server maintenance system for three steel mills.	Project was seen as last hope of major cost reduction, or divestiture would result.
	Some good efforts went into project, and one plant may have what it takes to persevere. However, the system was sold (and purchased) more in response to political/survival issues than as a function of an objective assessment of the right things to do.
	At last report in late 1995, it is extremely unlikely that this project will ever produce a return on its promises.

COST OF QUALITY

Direct Project Costs:	Costs of Unrealized Objectives:
Original Budget: $40,000,000	Organization did not receive benefits as promised or encountered extra expense in the following areas:
Total Spent to Date: n/a	- maintenance cost reductions will not be realized as promised
Estimate of Wasted Direct Project Costs: $40,000,000	- incremental revenues from higher production uptime will not be realized
	- reductions in waste and rework costs will not be realized.
	Divestiture is highly probable.
	Estimated Costs of Unrealized Objectives: $120,000,000

	TOTAL COST OF QUALITY: $160,000,000
	(estimated by adding wasted project costs to costs of unrealized objectives)

ROOT ISSUE SCORECARD   ROOT ISSUES

Objectivity   Right People   Authority/
          Right Motives   Responsibility
          Right Actions   Match

Root Issue Scoring: The study team deemed that the root, foundational issues of this project were sufficiently well addressed to darken the "legs" of the Root Issue Scorecard in the following areas:

- None

Objectivity Problems:	Right People/Right Motives/Right Actions Problems:
Authority/Responsibility Problems:	**Accountability Problems:**

CASE PROFILE: LARGE UNITED STATES SERVICE FIRM		
Case ID: 159	**Industry: Services**	**Data Source:** Personal involvement in project in 1995.

Type of Project:	Project Outcome:
Two-part client/server system to support significant new product line and improve existing operations.	Although this firm is widely considered a technology leader, this project never had a chance. At last report, project is running at least eighteen months late and cannot possibly accomplish the high-level promises made to get the project initially approved and keep it alive.

COST OF QUALITY

Direct Project Costs:	Costs of Unrealized Objectives:
Original Budget: Approximately $4,000,000 Total Spent to Date: Estimated at $10,000,000 Estimate of Wasted Direct Project Costs: $6,000,000	Organization did not receive benefits as promised or encountered extra expense in the following areas: - eighteen-month delay in receiving full revenues from new product line - increased costs of accommodating new product ramp up with old systems. Estimated Costs of Unrealized Objectives: $100,000,000
	TOTAL COST OF QUALITY: $106,000,000 (estimated by adding wasted project costs to costs of unrealized objectives)

ROOT ISSUE SCORECARD   ROOT ISSUES

ACCOUNTABILITY

Objectivity Right People   Authority/
         Right Motives Responsibility
         Right Actions Match

Root Issue Scoring: The study team deemed that the root, foundational issues of this project were sufficiently well addressed to darken the "legs" of the Root Issue Scorecard in the following areas:

- **Right People/Right Motives/ Right Actions**

Objectivity Problems:	Right People/Right Motives/Right Actions Problems:
- Scope, budget, and deadlines were not objectively balanced up-front. - The business case was not objective up-front. Substantial effort went to finding justification for the project after it was under way. - Scope and deliverables were broken down to objective work packages sufficient to define scope, control changes, and accurately estimate resources. - Technical design was based on "whatever could be sold internally" rather than objective requirements. - This initiative was sold to management as the creation of an information systems function within a business unit. Creation of this department was justified by pointing to the slow response of the existing information systems department and the outrageous, subjective claims of the executive sponsor (who was formerly with Andersen Consulting).	- Although many excellent people were on the project, the executive sponsor would not accept any recommendations that jeopardized his personal agenda of "look good at all costs and get as much responsibility as possible." - As far as was observable, the executive sponsor never made a single credible decision that promoted the good of the shareholder over his personal agenda.

continued on next page

ROOT ISSUES *(continued)*

Authority/Responsibility Problems:	Accountability Problems:
- Although multiple senior project managers were on the project and knew what needed to be done, they clearly had no authority to do so. - The executive sponsor continually meddled in the project team's area of responsibility. The interference typically surrounded items where the sponsor might look bad. This caused extensive wasted rework on prototypes, documents, presentations, and so on. - At one point the author insisted on scope and deadline sign-off authority. Shortly thereafter he was demoted to a supporting role and another, substantially less vocal project manager was placed over him. This project manager also happened to be a former subordinate of the executive sponsor. - It was clear to all involved that any firm disagreement with the sponsor or escalation of issues beyond him would be met with immediate demotion or dismissal.	- At last report, the executive sponsor has not been held responsible for his actions. - It appears that the boss of the executive sponsor has positioned himself so that the executive sponsor takes the blame if things go wrong. In like manner, the executive sponsor maintained several scapegoats among his project managers and team leaders. - The systems integration firm involved supplied as many as ten people to the project at one time. The possibility of losing these revenues caused the integration firm's management to decline repeated requests to escalate the problems above the executive sponsor. - The fact that such a sequence of events could exist and jeopardize $100 million or more in revenues is outrageous. The author's understanding is that the new product line was touted to investors and the potential for securities law violations exist. If promises were made to prospective shareholders for new revenues by certain dates, and the board of directors was aware of the true state of these two computer projects, it is possible that Federal Director Liability Laws, Title 18, Code 1030, may have been violated.

Other Items of Note:

- The author and two other experienced project managers were nominally responsible for the two projects.
- The executive sponsor focused his primary energies on looking good, building his organization, and self promotion. He would drastically alter or add to the projects on a moment's whim if he perceived some personal gain from doing so.
- All three senior project managers vigorously pursued escalation of issues to no avail. True resolution of these issues was suppressed by both the executive sponsor and the management of the systems integration firm that supplied the three senior project managers.
- All three senior project managers left the project and were replaced by people that were substantially less vocal about the problems of the project.

CASE PROFILE: CENTRAL UNITED STATES BUILDING PRODUCTS MANUFACTURER		
Case ID: 160	Industry: Manufacturing	Data Source: Interviews with CFO and other employees between 1994 and 1996.
Type of Project: Multiple attempts to implement client/server manufacturing systems, including Oracle, Masterpac, and ASI.		Project Outcome:

COST OF QUALITY

Direct Project Costs:	Costs of Unrealized Objectives:
Original Budget: n/a Total Spent to Date: n/a Estimate of Wasted Direct Project Costs: n/a	Organization did not receive benefits as promised or encountered extra expense in the following areas: - unrealized cost reductions - lost incremental revenues due to improved marketing and customer service - wasted hardware, software, and people costs. Estimated Costs of Unrealized Objectives: $100,000,000
	TOTAL COST OF QUALITY: $100,000,000 (estimated by adding wasted project costs to costs of unrealized objectives)

ROOT ISSUE SCORECARD   ROOT ISSUES

n/a

Root Issue Scoring: The study team deemed that the root, foundational issues of this project were sufficiently well addressed to darken the "legs" of the Root Issue Scorecard in the following areas:

- **Insufficient data to score project**

Objectivity Problems: - Organization appears to be highly political. It is likely that the poor system decisions made were the product of self-promotion instead of an objective balance between business case, solution design, scope, budget, and deadlines.	Right People/Right Motives/Right Actions Problems:
Authority/Responsibility Problems:	Accountability Problems:

Other Items of Note:

- The firm went public in 1996. It is possible that some or all of the executives and owners profited substantially even though such glaring mismanagement examples exist.

CASE PROFILE: PPP (Largest Health Insurance Provider in United Kingdom)		
Case ID: 161	**Industry: Insurance**	**Data Source:** *Imaging in Insurance* (June 1994).
Type of Project: Client/server imaging system pilot for insurance back office processing application.		**Project Outcome:** Canceled after two years because pilot did not produce suitable returns.

COST OF QUALITY

Direct Project Costs:	*Costs of Unrealized Objectives:*
Original Budget: n/a Total Spent to Date: $7,500,000 Estimate of Wasted Direct Project Costs: $7,500,000	Organization did not receive benefits as promised or encountered extra expense in the following areas: - unrealized cost savings in administrative labor. Estimated Costs of Unrealized Objectives: $3,250,000
	TOTAL COST OF QUALITY: $10,750,000 (estimated by adding wasted project costs to costs of unrealized objectives)

ROOT ISSUE SCORECARD   ROOT ISSUES

n/a

Root Issue Scoring: The study team deemed that the root, foundational issues of this project were sufficiently well addressed to darken the "legs" of the Root Issue Scorecard in the following areas:

- Insufficient data to score project

Objectivity Problems: This case illustrates the potential traps of *prototype/pilot* projects. See details in Section 5, Principle 8: Fads, Traps, and Dirty Tricks. ...	Right People/Right Motives/Right Actions Problems:
Authority/Responsibility Problems:	Accountability Problems:

| **CASE PROFILE:** $500 MILLION MEGA-PROJECT IN TROUBLE (NAME NOT DISCLOSED) |

| **Case ID:** 162 | **Industry:** n/a | **Data Source:** Jean Stafford (a project participant between 1993 and 1995), *Computerworld* (September 4, 1995). |

Type of Project:	**Project Outcome:**
Very large system with mainframe, minicomputer, and client/server components involving hundreds of programmers and many departments.	Jean Stafford was called in to audit project and determine what was wrong. Her recommendations cited the need for dramatic improvements in technology and change management processes. She warned of potential five-year delays. Stafford's recommendations were largely ignored until a failed customer demonstration. Some of her recommendations were adopted but current state of project is unknown.

COST OF QUALITY

Direct Project Costs:	**Costs of Unrealized Objectives:**
Original Budget: $250,000,000 (estimate) Total Spent to Date: $500,000,000 Estimate of Wasted Direct Project Costs: $250,000,000	Organization did not receive benefits as promised or encountered extra expense in the following areas: Estimated Costs of Unrealized Objectives: n/a
	TOTAL COST OF QUALITY: $250,000,000 (estimated by adding wasted project costs to costs of unrealized objectives)

ROOT ISSUE SCORECARD   ROOT ISSUES

Objectivity   Right People   Authority/
              Right Motives Responsibility
              Right Actions Match

Root Issue Scoring: The study team deemed that the root, foundational issues of this project were sufficiently well addressed to darken the "legs" of the Root Issue Scorecard in the following areas:

- None

Objectivity Problems:	**Right People/Right Motives/Right Actions Problems:**
- Scope was not broken down into work packages sufficient to control change requests. Midway through the project the customer decided to move significant portions of the project from the mainframe to client/server, creating enormous delays and rework.	- People on project were parochial and focused on their own department's measurements rather than the project's good. - Managers objected to the turf invasion by the auditor. - A detrimental preference for technology over business issues hurt the project. People resisted the creation of basic business process maps as "a waste of good programming time."
Authority/Responsibility Problems:	**Accountability Problems:**

continued on next page

ROOT ISSUES *(continued)*

Other Items of Note:

- Stafford broke with tradition and put together a team of frontline people to investigate the problems rather than the standard approach of interviewing the managers of those doing the work.

- The foundational, strategic issues of the project were in such bad shape that the project never had a chance. She should have recognized this up-front.

However, *in fairness to Stafford*, this points out a recurring problem: Those who are close enough to the work to understand the foundational, strategic issues:

a) almost never have the authority to affect those strategic issues

b) generally have basic personalities that avoid confrontation.

To ask these people to stand up to senior executives and insist on the correction of strategic project flaws is impractical.

To further expect that they will risk their jobs by declining assignments to flawed projects borders on ludicrous.

Stafford performed quite predictably. She dug in and identified tactical improvements that she could make in the technology and change management processes.

Unfortunately, the bottom line is that this tactical improvement furthers the illusion that the project can still be saved but does not address the underlying root issues.

Author's Note: I found myself in a nearly identical situation in 1994 (see Horror Story #107), and I made the same mistakes that Stafford did. My impetus to conduct this root cause study came substantially from the personal trauma of that project.

6.2 Success Stories

The following pages contain some examples of things that went well. They are presented here to provide some encouragement, perspective, and lessons.

While we did not study these cases in detail, the reader should find some helpful tips and suggestions. Note that we do not have budget or cost of quality data on these projects, so we cannot assume that they are fully successful based only on the information presented.

These success stories come from some of my personal projects, interviews with project participants, and publicly available information. The two Texas Instruments success stories were written for publication in *PM Network*, published by the Project Management Institute.

6.2.1 An Earned Value Success Story at Texas Instruments

The following article is reproduced with the permission of the Project Management Institute. This article first appeared in the December 1995 issue of *PM Network*.

Client/Server and Imaging:
On Time, On Budget, As Promised!
Part I: The Client's Perspective

Tom Ingram, PMP

Early in 1994, Texas Instruments (TI) was looking for a way to move its accounts receivable function toward a paperless office. Client/server imaging technology was the answer. The resulting project made aggressive use of new technology and is currently in use in the United States and Europe, with worldwide operations soon to follow (see Figure 1). The project benefited from strong cooperation between Texas Instruments and ViewStar, the technology supplier and consultant. Best of all, the project came in on time and on budget.

In an effort to view the project from the client's perspective, I interviewed Texas Instrument's project team after the consultant's portion of the project was completed. What follows are the team's observations and recommendations for future projects.

The accompanying article, written from the consultant's perspective, describes several advanced project management techniques advocated by the Project Management Institute (PMI) in the context of an actual client/server project.

Framework for Analyzing This Case

The June 1994 *Project Management Journal* included my article, Managing Client/Server and Open Systems Projects: A 10-Year Study of 62 Mission-Critical Projects. Since that publication, I have conducted additional research into forty-eight *horror stories*, resulting in a total of 110 client/server cases reviewed.

The difference between the success stories and the horror stories boiled down to four foundational concepts:

1. *objectivity,* with regard to scope, budget, deadlines, and solution design
2. *experienced* people at all levels in the project
3. *authority to match responsibility*—the people who know the right things to do need the clout to get those things done
4. *accountability* sufficient that all parties either perform as promised or are visibly, undeniably held responsible.

Executive responsibility is the fundamental issue. The successful projects had executives that did not allow projects to proceed unless a solid foundation was present. The horror stories consistently charged forward with key omissions and those executives ultimately paid the price.

This research has been augmented by seven other published studies on client/server project studies. This article presents the TI project in the context of the key foundational concepts identified by this body of research.

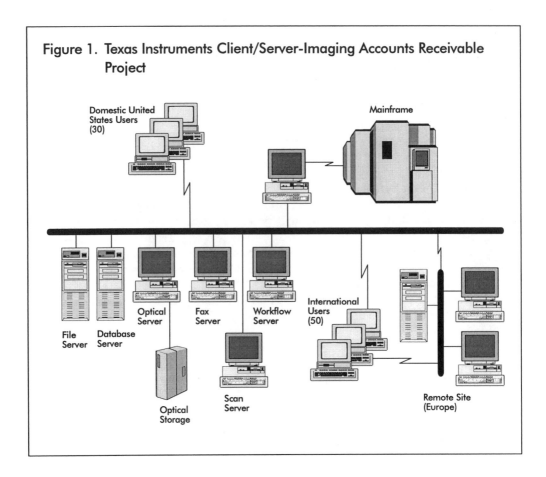

Figure 1. Texas Instruments Client/Server-Imaging Accounts Receivable Project

Texas Instruments' Project Team

The team was composed of Stan Sigle, project manager, Paul Conner, team leader, and Chris Fowler, team member. Sigle has been with TI for eleven years in various information systems roles. Although new to client/server, he has a strong project management background and is a PMI member. He is currently studying for the PMP certification (see sidebar, Texas Instruments, Project Management, and PMI). Sigle's primary contributions to the project were his strong project management experience and in-depth knowledge of TI's internal environment.

Conner, a five-year TI employee, and Fowler, with TI for four years, worked jointly on all aspects of the project. Both contributed the negotiating and people skills needed to work with the users, internal groups, and supplier project team. Their strong technical skills allowed them to perform most of the design as well as to contribute in areas ranging from gathering customer requirements to hardware and software installation to programming in the supplier's development language.

All three members of the team exerted considerable effort on internal technical standards and procurement. They maintained a *whatever-it-takes* attitude throughout the project and demonstrated a strong ability to work cooperatively with the supplier to solve problems.

Texas Instruments, Project Management, and PMI

With roots in the semiconductor industry, Texas Instruments has been pursuing effective project management for its entire existence. During the preparation of the accompanying articles I had the opportunity to meet with several TI employees and discuss their company's approach to project management and its relationship with the Project Management Institute. The TI staff members I interviewed for this article are part of TI's Semiconductor Information Systems & Services (IS&S) organization. Semiconductor IS&S views the operating divisions, called business units, as their customers. We discussed project management in both the business units and the information systems function. The following discussion sheds some light on the direction and practices of what many would consider one of the premier project management firms in Dallas.

PMI's Contribution

According to Mark Bruno, Open Business Systems program office manager and president of the Dallas Chapter of the Project Management Institute, TI has approximately twenty PMI members and participants, two in the process of PMP certification and three fully certified PMPs. He feels that TI has become quite good at the "hard skills" of project management: cost, schedule, and risk management as well as quality programs. "Our participation in PMI has helped increase TI's awareness of the value of project manager professional development," he explains. "It has also helped TI improve in some of the 'softer' areas of project management, such as communication, contracts, human resources, and leadership."

PMI advocates skills development for project managers in all of these categories. Most of these topics are incorporated into the nine knowledge areas collectively known as *A Guide to the Project Management Body of Knowledge* (*PMBOK Guide*).

Regarding scope management, Winston Baker, Open Business Systems program director, comments: "Scope creep is the number one problem that I see continually plaguing projects." Mark Bruno adds: "TI recognizes the importance of scope management through the entire project life cycle. This also includes the corporate culture within which these projects take place."

TI is an excellent example of a corporation pursuing improvement on many fronts, the kind of balanced, ongoing improvement in many areas recommended by PMI for effective project management.

Information Systems and Project Management

Client/Server and Open Systems. Bruno explains that "TI is currently undergoing a significant effort in the client/server area called open business systems (OBS). This includes network infrastructure, applications, outsourcing, and change management. Some of the underlying principles within this initiative include moving toward a buy rather than build mentality and a complete reengineering of how our information technology division fulfills its role of providing information systems to business units.

"Texas Instruments has taken project management very seriously for a long time," Bruno continues. "Our software development methodology is based on the 'best practices' identified over many years, including the Carnegie-Mellon Software Engineering Institute capability maturity model. We have a project management methodology developed over the years as a product of generally accepted project management principles and from our roots in the defense industry."

TI has also recently embraced ISO 9000 certification and the Defense Systems Group has won the Malcolm Baldrige Quality Award. The most telling factor of all is that the software development and project management methodologies are integrated and take place in a corporate culture that seriously pursues quality. The company also has multiple mandatory classes for project managers, covering leadership, financial management, project tools, and methodology.

Gene Nance, senior member of technical staff, Semiconductor Group, IS&S, comments on the increasing importance of project management: "I currently have a project where full funding and support are waiting on the assignment of a certified project manager. We have not yet fully defined what we consider a 'certified' project manager. The PMP certification being offered by PMI is under active consideration."

Studying Areas For Improvement. Nance says that as their customers have studied themselves and worked to articulate what they want, three items rise to the surface concerning project management:

1. Improved project manager skills, which would include methodology, tools, and certification.
2. Standardization of such items as the project process or templates, names of data elements, and common language across the broad spectrum of product groups in the Semiconductor organization. "Metrics are also a target for standardization, but are currently in the process of being defined," Nance says. "Another area of standardization under strong consideration is determining thresholds for organizational commitment before funding projects," he adds.
3. Data management, which includes accumulating the right metric data accurately over time. "We need to be able to roll up the numbers and learn lessons from previous projects," Nance says.

Capability Maturity Model. The Software Engineering Institute (SEI) of Carnegie-Mellon University has developed a method of assessing an organization's capability and maturity in the process of developing software. It includes several measures related specifically to project management. After a survey is conducted, the results are boiled down to a 1 to 5 rating showing the organization's overall maturity, with 5 representing a very mature organization. This is called the capability maturity model (CMM).

Chris Plant, business systems analyst, Semiconductor Group, IS&S, discusses the CMM: "Another indicator of how seriously we take project management is shown by our involvement with the software development capability maturity model. Our IS&S division has attained a Level 2 rating and is targeting accomplishment of Level 3 certification by the end of 1995. Portions of our Defense Systems Group have already attained a Level 3 certification." It should be noted that, as of SEI's last publication, with some 250 organizations surveyed, only sixty-five had attained Level 2 or above.

How Much Control? Winston Baker comments: "One of the large issues that we are continually wrestling with is the degree of management and control we are going to impose on a project. With a $20 million project that is visible and carries a substantial price of failure, it is easy. We apply the 'best of breed' tools, consultants, full-time project managers, and all of the expertise that you would expect from TI. It is much harder in the case of a $1 million project. By the time you put the full 'best practices' in place, the project is over."

A Lesson Learned. Baker continues: "We had a project in the $1 million range that had a 'go live date' of June 1. Everyone was quite optimistic about this new project and its wonderful benefits. The 'bands played daily in the halls' and conversations could be observed in every corner trumpeting the glories of this project. On May 30 the bad news was broken that the project would be delayed thirty days. Under this project's circumstances the delay was unfortunate but acceptable and no one was overly concerned. However, on June 29, another announcement came forth that the project would be delayed another thirty days. At this point 'management' stepped in. The project was ultimately delivered in another three or four months. The project management sin in this case was not the delays. The sin was not knowing about or communicating the delays until the last moment. Texas Instruments may be different, but I have rarely seen people punished for waving a flag early in a project, saying that it's going to take longer and cost more than we anticipated. I have seen careers ruined, however, over not knowing problems until the last minute."

Business Units and Project Management

Mark Bruno explains: "The business units have developed classes and methodologies as they have applied project management concepts to the business of developing technology products. Our Semiconductor Group is the forerunner in this area." The Semiconductor Group accounts for $8 billion worth of Texas Instruments' annual $11 billion revenues. Nance adds: "One of the reasons we are particularly interested in the management of software projects is that semiconductor products, by their nature, tend to include lots of software."

Bull's-Eye Tracking. Nance continues: "One of the symptoms that we have observed and are currently working on is that our organization has several very large, multiyear projects as well as a great number of smaller projects. We observed that, surprisingly enough, the smaller projects were getting done while critical path items for the larger projects would frequently slip. We believe that the larger projects suffer from a loss of visibility and priority over time. In a large, multiproject environment such as ours, it is also very difficult for managers to avoid over-committing their resources. One of the steps that we've taken to address this issue is quarterly 'bull's-eye tracking.' Other people might call them milestones or deliverables, but we use the term 'bull's-eye.' Organizations now are responsible for the percentage of their bull's-eyes that are attained on a quarterly basis."

When asked whether the bull's-eye was based on dates or costs, Nance replied: "We fundamentally focus on meeting our dates to support new product introductions and other critical competitive product advantages. While no one enjoys a cost overrun, we believe that overrunning the cost for an internal project is far preferable to missing a product introduction hurdle. We have seen research that quantifies and supports this belief."

Need for Professional Project Management. "One of the things that our customer is beginning to see is that professional project management skills are needed," Chris Plant explains. "Our current structure revolves around a project leader who is, at heart, a technical product development person. The project plan allocates 10 percent of the leader's time to project management issues, but it ends up being 2 percent or less. The result is project problems that we now believe could have been prevented if a person with certified project management skills was materially involved."

Quality Definition. "The definition of quality at the Semiconductor Group goes somewhat beyond the classic 'conformance to specifications,'" Plant comments. "We consider that quality also involves helping to determine the right specifications in sufficient detail such that the designer and the customer agree. The measurement of that agreement is whether material surprises arise within the project."

While the above comments do not necessarily reflect Texas Instruments as a whole, it is obvious that TI is doing many things right in the project management arena. As an outside project manager chartered with implementing a client/server imaging system for TI (see accompanying article), I can also add that the way TI does business "strongly encourages" its suppliers and contractors to improve their project management and quality practices. Many organizations would be well served to emulate TI's example.

What Went Well

Objectivity. Lack of objectivity in key decisions is one of the most common root problems that plagues client/server projects. Decisions surrounding the business case for doing the project, scope, budgets, deadlines, and solution design need to be ruthlessly examined for bias and lack of due diligence. Fortunately, TI did a number of things right:

Business case: Team leader Conner commented that the team presented the proposal to the vice-president based on decreasing the days outstanding of accounts receivable by one day on a worldwide basis. The members also contended that this technology would help TI increase the volume of accounts receivable work without adding staff. The vice-president bought the idea without going through detailed financial justifications—partly because a one-day reduction in accounts receivable for TI worldwide would justify this system many times over. The business case, though abbreviated, was rooted in sound business judgment and presented potential order-of-magnitude returns.

As the project was being rolled out to production, project manager Sigle, encouraged by good user response, began to feel confident that the system would deliver the benefits promised. TI was pushing the envelope with this technology, and the project team had to work very closely with the standards group. It was necessary to arrive at a tailored approach that met both quality goals and real-world expectations. Conner adds, "Because the user organization was behind this project (and the business case was strong) we were able to push on and get the job done."

Scope, budgets, deadlines, and solution design: As might be expected with a project that came in fundamentally as promised, no significant problems arose due to these areas. The scope, budget, and deadlines were fundamentally in balance. The solution design was objectively evaluated, despite some internal pushing and pulling concerning standards and future direction.

Experience. All of the TI people on this project—the user executive sponsor, the information systems executive sponsor, the user managers and representatives, the information systems managers and team members, and the purchasing personnel—had significant experience with technology projects. As might be expected, the entire supplier staff also had extensive experience. Most importantly, TI's entire culture is geared toward doing technology projects effectively.

However, the project team had limited client/server experience. None of the TI team had any material imaging experience. The application of sound information systems and project management disciplines allowed TI to partner with a new technology supplier and produce a positive project outcome. Because of team members' collective experience, the project team chose to emphasize certain issues within the project that are often overlooked by project teams with less experience. Following are some highlights.

For first-time efforts with new technology, keep it simple! As Sigle observes, "The project stayed very close to the base product from ViewStar. We made almost no deviations from the initially delivered system and we began with a fairly simple application." Conner adds, "We chose to start our learning curve with imaging technology on a non-mission critical application. This reduced the risk of the project."

Use of professional techniques: Both the client and supplier were accustomed to working with methodologies. A blend of the methods and procedures necessary for both sides resulted in strong cooperation and minimal surprises during the project. Sigle describes a project problem that was well handled: "As with many large companies, we are somewhat in a state of flux on internal standards. This created some risk and confusion. The only way to deal with this risk was to plan it into the project and manage it on a daily basis."

Milestones and deliverables that were enforced: Fowler provides an interesting perspective regarding contracts and milestones: "The ViewStar contract required us, as the internal project team, to complete our milestones on schedule. In the past, other distractions and priorities have come up during projects, which delay the completion of milestones. Having a tightly defined consulting contract prevented our normal 'death march' at the end of the project."

User involvement: "Due to geographic reasons, user involvement was less than optimum," Conner observes. "We were somewhat lucky, however, because we had reasonable users. This has not always been the case in the past." Due to the decentralized nature of the user group, TI's information system and services (IS&S) department took the internal lead on the project but stayed in close contact with the user groups.

A user requirements document was prepared that defined, in plain language and in less than fifteen pages, what the user wanted to see. After user review and acceptance of this requirements document, the technical (functional) specifications were

Making the Change from *Build* to *Buy*:
Texas Instruments Takes on a Large-Scale Client/Server Project

The accompanying article details a success story involving the addition of new technology onto existing accounting systems, but TI has far more ambitious goals for its core accounting and manufacturing systems. The company is in the early stages of a project to replace significant TI-developed internal systems with purchased products. Winston Baker, program director, Open Business Systems, provides some insight into this immense undertaking: "This will include the full range of accounting and manufacturing systems that can be purchased. As yet, we have not formally decided on the primary software package we will use."

The Business Case. "TI wants to enable our customers to reduce the cycle time associated with developing and changing business systems," Baker says. "Once we identified the need to do something in this area, the next decision was whether to develop the systems internally or buy them from an outside source. In the past, Texas Instruments has, for the most part, developed its systems internally."

Build versus Buy. In 1966, according to Baker, TI first began addressing the issue of whether to buy or build information systems. Until recently, the company believed that the cost/time/functionality tradeoff favored internal development. However, with the advent of products that are very strong, the cost/benefit tradeoffs are beginning to favor the buy approach. Additionally, he notes, TI is now focusing very heavily on understanding its areas of core competence and applying its resources in those strategic directions.

Baker explains: "When we are considering buy versus build, we think through (a) whether the needed item or service is outside of our strategic core competence, (b) whether outsourcing would compromise our competitive advantage, and (c) whether we can buy it effectively. This thought process resulted in the decision to purchase as much of the systems for this project as possible."

Startup Strategy. Several things have helped TI get off to the right start, Baker says. "We selected sixty-two people from across all functions and organizational boundaries of TI and brought them to Dallas so they can work in close physical proximity. Their initial charter was to do process analysis for the affected business units (rather than functional analysis).

"We targeted a very modest initial implementation for the fall of 1995. This involved installation of all modules from the accounting and manufacturing areas. We chose this particular business unit because it is in a startup mode and we can move down the learning curve rapidly without being encumbered by some of the constraints of a large existing operation. We plan to follow this on with larger business units and ultimately our largest business unit, the Semiconductor Group."

Concerns. "Some of the issues that I am watching very carefully," Baker notes, "include getting the network infrastructure right and delivering a system to our users that is high caliber. Our customers have come to expect very high quality systems that are reliable and stable. If either of these conditions are not met, it could seriously jeopardize the future of the project. Beyond those two major items, we need to do the basic 'blocking and tackling' well. It would be nice to be able to do all we are hoping to do within the projected budget, but time will tell."

Project Team. The project team will be a mix of TI internal personnel and professional services from outside firms, with TI maintaining responsibility for all project management activities.

Authority/Responsibility Match Necessary to Execute the Project. "I had the responsibility of developing the project budget and schedule and continue to work closely with senior management," Baker says, "so I am not concerned about having unreasonable targets imposed upon me and my team from above. Part of the ongoing work with senior management is the definition to scope, which presently includes implementation of financial systems, order management systems, and the supply chain process. We will start small, building to enterprisewide and ultimately worldwide implementation. This scope will be refined as we go along, and, as one might expect, we have had requests for scope increases already."

developed to enable the various technical experts to accomplish their tasks. The user group members were fundamentally insulated from *techno-speak* and were able to focus on clearly articulating their requirements in plain language.

Cooperative, problem-solving attitude: The chemistry between client and supplier was strong from the outset. The corporate culture of both firms promoted a win-win attitude for resolving problems. The few problems that did arise were resolved quickly by compromise on both sides.

Authority to Match Responsibility. This issue is most readily understood when it is clearly absent. Unfortunately, most project managers are held responsible for delivering a clearly impossible set of deliverables on a fixed deadline with a limited budget. When that project manager cannot affect the scope, budget, or deadline, he clearly does not have an authority/responsibility match. Not only is this extremely stressful for the project manager, but the project is headed for certain disaster. The TI project team provides additional observations.

User group authority: "The user management group provided the budget for this project and held final authority," Conner explains. "We had a joint user/information systems team, pushed by the user's organization. Their authority and drive strongly helped the project stay on track and moving forward."

Authority to enforce objective decisions: TI's organization and project approval process forced every decision in the project to stand up to objective scrutiny. Questions such as payback, design, and supplier selection had to be justified without bias.

Standards organization authority: "The standards group's management was actively involved in the project, and this added some constraints," observes Conner. "We did manage to get through it without severe impact to the project and stay within the standards desired by TI corporatewide."

Accountability. Accountability is often missing from information systems projects. The right accountability needs to include the person who originally sold the project to management, the original estimator, sales people, consultants, the information systems team, and the user team. As a high-technology defense contractor, TI's infrastructure was accustomed to holding suppliers accountable for performing as promised. Some key items were:

Strong supplier contracts: TI's procurement procedures can certainly be credited with assisting the project. Detailed acceptance tests were required in order for the supplier to be paid on both the base system software and the consulting deliverables. TI's contracts were researched and detailed thoroughly in the initial stages (to the chagrin of some). This diligence paid off when a slight conflict arose over a software option that was not included in the original bid. Because the supplier could not pass the acceptance criteria without this software, the software was ultimately provided to Texas Instruments at no charge.

Internal accountability: Sigle observes that "the financial systems department and the information systems part of our team were the most visible and accountable. Because the project was only six months in duration, the accountability remained firm and was not diluted by personnel turnover." It should also be noted that quality assurance was a formal aspect of the project.

Things That Could Have Gone Better

Consulting Services Estimate. More diligence could have been applied up-front on the consulting services estimate provided by the supplier. The sales negotiation process resulted in a fixed dollar figure for consulting services. The work done was somewhat forced into these budgetary constraints. It worked well in this case because TI dedicated two full-time information systems professionals to the project. They were able to become self-sufficient very quickly, allowing the consulting services to be deployed on the more difficult tasks. Other projects have attempted to accomplish similar goals with less than 50 percent of this assigned labor. Predictably, those projects have overrun their budgets and have not been able to deliver everything promised. Caution and a realistic assessment of the skill level and availability of internal personnel are called for.

Technical Design. Considering the *bleeding edge* factor of the technology involved, most people would consider the minor difficulties encountered in this project as acceptable. Conner describes the situation regarding an objective solution design: "Our hands were somewhat tied because we were required to use the Microsoft NT operating system for our servers. This created some risk because it was a new platform for TI. Fortunately, we got through it with minimal consequences." Two additional items might have been handled more effectively, however:

1. *Pre-sales design*: The technology involved was difficult to configure, and an important software option was overlooked during the pre-sales process. Fortunately, a site readiness review conducted immediately after the contracts were signed identified this oversight. To its credit, ViewStar acknowledged the error and gave the software option to TI at no charge. Because the error was identified early on in the process, no project downtime was incurred.

2. *Worldwide network design and response times*: Image files place a heavy burden on any communications system, especially a global wide area network. The project was undertaken with the identified risk that response times might be too slow for use in some parts of the world. This did prove to be the case, and the next phase of the project will involve network and database redesign to work around this constraint. This was a good example of accepting a technical risk and proactively managing the resolution of the risk. No one was surprised.

Key Technical Resource Availability. Sigle describes one of his "heartburn" issues: "We had a couple of close calls on key technical resource availability. I would like to have managed this risk area better, but in the final analysis, ViewStar and its people came through and the project was not impacted."

Amount of Effort Exerted in Hardware Area. The project team underestimated the amount of work necessary by TI's internal people on both hardware architecture and physical infrastructure to support the system. While this did not delay the project or generate a budget overrun, it did produce some fairly high levels of stress among TI's project team members.

Some Additional Recommendations

Up-Front Training. The TI team members agreed that they should have sent technical team members to training prior to making the final purchase decision. "We should have sent at least one person to the system administration/architecture class of the top two supplier choices *before* the decision was made," Conner explains. "We actually implemented the project with Version 3.1 of ViewStar. If we had done the training first, we might have waited for the release of 4.0 in the summer of 1995."

"Up-front training would have eliminated another problem," Fowler adds. "When we got into the press of the project, schedule conflicts prevented us from getting all the training we should have had. It would have been very helpful to have done the training before the purchase decision was finalized."

Estimate. Sigle recommends that "you scrutinize and re-scrutinize your estimates of internal effort and external consulting services. Our internal time spent on the project was 50 percent greater than we originally estimated."

Internal Challenges. The internal procurement process presented some significant challenges. TI's structure, controls, checks, balances, and methodologies provided many benefits to the project. One downside was the length of procurement time, even in emergency circumstances. The TI team agreed that a realistic assessment of procurement cycles would have prevented many late nights and long hours. Conner concedes that "we had some difficulty in this area."

Conclusion

TI benefited from a culture and project team that supported *objectivity, experienced people, authority/responsibility matching,* and *accountability.* The result was a very successful new technology experience and a project that came in on time and on budget.

Client/Server, Imaging, and Earned Value:
A Success Story
Part II: The Consultant's Perspective

Tom Ingram, PMP

Questions: "My project budget is 75 percent spent. How can I be certain that 75 percent of the work is done? How can I make sure we are on track for completion on budget?"

Answer: Work breakdown structure and earned value!

Most project managers and executive sponsors have found themselves in this position. Midway through a project, the activity level is furious, and your spreadsheet tells you that you have spent 75 percent of your budget (see Figure 1). On the surface things look good, but the hair on the back of your neck tells you that the work is not 75 percent done. The scary part is that you don't know for sure.

Earned value key benefits include:

* allowing us to hold people accountable to their estimates
* dealing with scope changes in a smooth, controlled fashion that does not disrupt accountability
* *knowing* that the planned work is done (rather than hoping or guessing).

To illustrate one approach to *knowing for sure*, let's look at a real example of earned value and work breakdown structure for a client/server imaging project.

The project began in the fall of 1994. In this case I was the project manager for the imaging system supplier (ViewStar Corporation) and Texas Instruments was the client. Figure 2, in which the earned value curve has been added to the data shown in Figure 1, shows that as of January 28, 1995, less than half of the *value* to be produced by this project was actually *earned*.

Basically, this meant that only half of the originally planned work was actually completed. Knowing this early allowed everyone to focus on completion of deliverables, make up the lost ground, and finish on time and on budget. This case study uses a simple example to illustrate how you can use the earned value concept to improve your chances of bringing projects in on time, on budget, and as promised.

Let me mention that most of the concepts presented here were learned through my association with the Project Management Institute (PMI) and the project management professional (PMP) certification that PMI offers. Also, the numbers quoted have been slightly altered to protect TI and ViewStar confidential information.

Project Overview

This project involved approximately thirty users in the United States and another fifty around the world. Figure 1 shows the general architecture. The application was for TI's accounts receivable department, using imaging technology to improve collection efforts and service to both internal and external customers. The technology was client/server based, with eight servers and a significant interface to the mainframe accounts receivable system. Some *bleeding edge* technology was desired by TI, so the project contained some material risks.

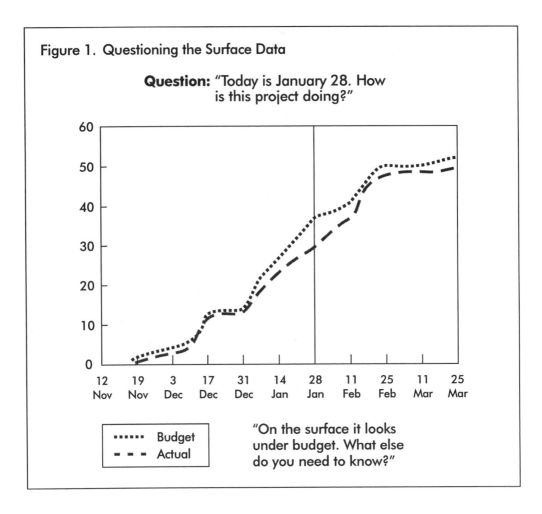

Figure 1. Questioning the Surface Data

Question: "Today is January 28. How is this project doing?"

Budget ······
Actual ‐ ‐ ‐

"On the surface it looks under budget. What else do you need to know?"

Illustrating the Key Concepts. To illustrate earned value and work break-down structures, I will walk you through the major events and deliverables of the project. The drawings and tables in the figures are from the actual project. Be aware that these numbers only represent external consulting costs. This works well for illustration, but remember that you may need to account for product costs and internal labor in your own projects. The original data was recorded based on con-sulting days but is converted to approximate dollars here for clarity.

Work Breakdown Structure Definition. Simply put, a work breakdown structure (WBS) is a project plan or task list that breaks down the tasks of a project under the key deliverables. Table 1 shows the WBS used in this project. Two key items differentiate this from a traditional information systems project plan:

1. Level of detail: If you break each deliverable down to four-hour segments (called work packets), you will be hopelessly mired in detail and data entry time. If you use 200-hour work packets, you will only be managing at a high level, and it might be a month or more before you discover that a task is not getting done. PMI's standard recommendation is to break down work packets so that they are no longer than your standard reporting period. In most cases this will be forty hours, based on having a weekly project status report. In twenty-twenty hindsight, I should have

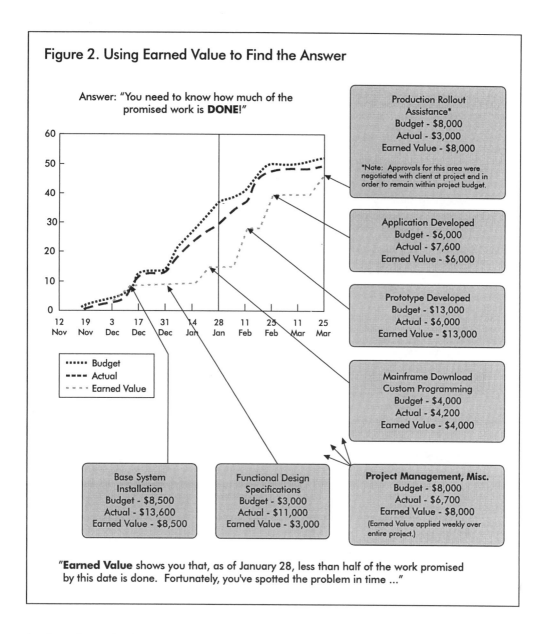

Figure 2. Using Earned Value to Find the Answer

broken the tasks down somewhat further in this project. It might have prevented our getting behind.

2. Accounting codes: Stay with me. This is important. Look at the column titled WBS ID# in Table 1. Note that the deliverables have high-level numbers and the tasks are broken down underneath them so that an accounting roll-up can occur. Note that we have a budget (or estimate) and an actual for each work packet. Earned value cannot be tracked unless you adhere to this discipline and capture the actuals in a timely manner.

Earned Value Definition. When the customer signs off that a work packet is complete (see WBS definition above) you are entitled to claim the amount budgeted for that task as earned value. In Figure 2, the earned value line shows the accumulated

Table 1. WBS and Budget-to-Actual Comparison

	WBS ID#	Total Budget[1]	Actual Spent[1]	Earned Value[1]
Base System Installation	10000	0	0	0
Site Readiness Workshop and Preparation Assistance	10100	3.5	2.9	3.5
SST Team Installs Software	10200	5	9.7	5
AST Workstation Testing	10300	0	0	0
Cache Utility Install/Training	10400	0	1	0
Subtotal		8.5	13.6	8.5
Functional Design Spec.	11000	0	0	0
Implementation Workshop	11100	1	1	1
Functional Design Spec. and User Requirements	11200	2	10	2
Subtotal		3	11	3
Mainframe Download Custom Programming	12000	4	4.2	4
Subtotal		4	4.2	4
Prototype Defined and Developed	13000	0	4	0
Definition	13100	5	1.7	5
Development	13200	5	0.25	5
User Review	13300	3	0	3
Subtotal		13	5.95	13
Application Developed		0	0	0
Development	14100	5	7.1	5
Application Testing	14200	0.5	0.5	0.5
Application Acceptance Testing	14300	0.5	0	0.5
Subtotal		6	7.6	6
Production Rollout Assistance	15000	0	0	0
System Stress Testing	15100	1.5	1	1.5
Problem Resolution	15200	6.5	1.5	6.5
Documentation	15300	0	0	0
Subtotal		8	2.5[2]	8
Post-Production Review	16000	0	0	0
Review (Sixty Day)	16100	0.5	0	0.5
Project Closeout	16200	0.5	.5	0.5
Subtotal		1	.5[2]	1
Project Management	17000	5.5	6.65	5.5
Miscellaneous	18000	2.5	0	2.5
Project Totals[1]		51.5	52	51.5

[1] In thousands of dollars

[2] Item adjusted by agreement with client

total of signed-off, completed tasks. In summary, earned value is the dollar value of completed work based on budget estimates. It is critical to remember that earned value is based on proposed or budgeted estimates, not on actual money spent. One overriding benefit of earned value is to hold suppliers, consultants, and internal people accountable for their estimates and proposals.

Walking Through the Project

I'd like to take you through the major deliverables of the project to illustrate some of these concepts. It is important to note that Texas Instruments' contract with ViewStar only permitted payment for services when the deliverable was signed off as complete. As we walk through the project, keep in mind the high degree of control that Texas Instruments is maintaining. The major deliverables were:

Base System Installation. This is the initial installation of the basic *out of the box* system. The contract budgeted $8,500 in consulting time. Due to some underestimation and some of the *bleeding edge* issues, we actually spent $13,600. Note that our earned value was only $8,500 (our proposed, budgeted amount). The overrun was our problem, not TI's.

Functional Design Specifications. Here is where we developed the specifications for customizing of the base product. ViewStar is more of a *toolkit* than a finished application, so this is an expected expense. Our proposal budgeted $3,000 for this work packet. I was required to *force fit* the services proposal to a $52,000 total. I knew $3,000 was severely inadequate, but ViewStar wanted Texas Instrument's business, so we went ahead with the force-fit budget. (Sound familiar?)

The actual cost for the functional design specification was $11,000 but the earned value was only $3,000. At this point, ViewStar had actually spent $24,600 but only *earned* $11,500. Clearly, we had to regain control, or we were going to have a disaster on our hands. It is interesting to point out that, due to the *earned value* concept, ViewStar was fully responsible for this overage and had no basis for asking Texas Instruments for more money. Because the *earned value* graphic was produced for each weekly status meeting, TI knew the exact status and could see we were having some difficulty. The company chose to act in a *win-win* manner and negotiated several items in good faith that helped us return to a mutual *win* outcome.

Project Management and Miscellaneous Items. Earned value for these items were taken each week. They did not necessarily produce measurable milestone deliverables, but they were necessary and consumed time and cost. We budgeted $8,000 and actually used only $6,700. Remember the key concept: The provider receives the budgeted amount when the deliverable is completed, no matter what was actually spent. Here we received more earned value than our cost, so we made up some of the ground lost on previous deliverables.

Mainframe Download Custom Programming. In this deliverable we worked with the client to create a custom program for downloading data from the mainframe. This involved considerable technical risk and our budget of $4,000 could have been severely inadequate. Fortunately, Texas Instruments had assigned two full-time, capable people to this project. Paul Conner and Chris Fowler were able to accomplish the custom programming with only limited help from ViewStar, resulting in $4,200 of consulting time actually spent. We received earned value of $4,000 for completion of this deliverable.

Prototype Developed. We budgeted $13,000 for the prototype, which was about average for a project of this nature. I had seen many prototypes exceed their budgets substantially, so I was concerned about this area of the project. Because we were meeting weekly and reviewing the status of our earned value, the entire team remained focused on completing only the key user requirements in the prototype. Actual consulting dollars spent were $6,000, with an earned value of $13,000. We had made up $7,000 in lost ground, and the project was looking much healthier from the consultant's point of view.

Application Developed. If you recall, the functional design specification was underestimated and we overspent considerably on it. The upside of this overage showed up in (a) a prototype completed for less than half of its budget; (b) a prototype that was easily developed into the final application; (c) a negligible overage on the final application development; and (d) relatively easy user sign-off on the final application.

We budgeted $6,000 and actually spent $7,600. Our earned value received was $6,000. Refer again to Figure 2. After completion of the application development milestone we had *earned* approximately $40,000 worth of the $52,000 *value* of this project. Note how the curves are coming together toward on-time, on-budget completion. The major technical risks were behind us, and it was beginning to look like this was going to be a successful project for both supplier and client.

Production Rollout. At this point we had a happy client but had overspent somewhat. Texas Instruments had a few minor items that it wanted to add to the project that were not strictly within our scope or responsibility. Again operating in a win-win mode, we negotiated an agreement to provide these extras in exchange for the client taking over most of the production rollout responsibilities. This was possible because Texas Instruments had adequately staffed the project with strong people. Production rollout support was budgeted for $8,000. We actually spent only $3,000 and received earned value of $8,000. Our total earned value for the project was within a few dollars of the originally budgeted $52,000.

Some Observations

Our contract allowed us to shift dollars between the deliverables to help compensate for being over in one area and under in another. I strongly encourage you to add this provision to your contracts. If you don't, the project can quickly become unfair to the supplier.

Priorities change in most projects over time. In this case, we did not encounter material scope changes. If we had, they could have easily been handled by making sure the scope change and attendant cost was signed off by all parties; creating a new WBS line item and ID number; and adding the dollar value to the budget line in the graphic. This way the scope change simply becomes one more deliverable that is managed through earned value.

When the project is in trouble in a certain area, remember that the client's priorities are probably changing somewhat. We had an opportunity at the end of the project to do a few small favors for the client in exchange for an agreement that let us finish on budget. You may find similar opportunities as well.

Conclusion

Going through the discipline of work breakdown structures, earned value tracking, and scope change management can yield strong benefits. It will allow you to hold internal and external people accountable for their promises. You will be able to deal with scope changes in a controlled fashion that maintains accountability. You will be confident that the planned work is actually getting done. By tracking earned value weekly you will help keep the project team focused and prevent procrastination.

If you are an experienced project manager, you can probably apply these concepts immediately. Please take into account that this example has been simplified and that the real world has a habit of throwing curve balls. To fully understand the concepts you will probably want to pursue project management professional (PMP) certification.

If you are new to project management, I would suggest that you begin studying for the PMP certification and pursue this goal. Along the way you will learn these concepts and many more that will improve your projects. If you need immediate application of this technique but are unsure about how to proceed, I suggest that you retain a PMP-certified consultant.

I encourage you to continue improving your project management skills. Prior to studying for the PMP certification I had managed some sixty projects and believed that I knew what project management was all about. I am delighted (and humbled) to report that PMI has opened a whole new world of professionalism to me. PMI and the PMP certification have helped me believe that it is possible to consistently deliver client/server projects on time, on budget, and as promised. My hope is that you will come to the same belief.

Acknowledgments

A special word of thanks for the help I received in passing the PMP exam and for TI's support in the use of these techniques. I was studying for the exam at the time, and the backdrop of this project allowed me to see the benefits of the earned value concept firsthand.

Ben Settle of Infotech Management, president of the Fort Worth PMI Chapter, tutored me in preparation for the exam. I had encountered the earned value concept before but did not see any real applicability to information systems projects. Ben helped me through the PMP test and helped me learn the benefit of these techniques.

Stan Sigle, the project manager for TI and a PMI member, was also instrumental in the success of this project. Stan supported the use of PMI techniques and provided valuable feedback. He negotiated in good faith when things got tough on the project.

The assistance and cooperative spirit of Ben, Stan, and the TI project team were of great benefit to me. I hope that this case study will be of benefit to you as well.

6.2.2 A Business Process Reengineering Success Story at Texas Instruments

A 400 Percent Improvement In Customer Service
Some Lessons in Business Process Design, Perseverance, and Reengineering

by Tom Ingram, PMP

In the fall of 1994 Texas Instruments (TI) initiated two client/server imaging projects simultaneously. The project for accounts receivable was described in *PM Network* magazine, December 1995. The accounts receivable case study deals primarily with the management of root issues and the earned value method of project accounting and management.

This case study discusses the other project, which was for TI's accounts payable department. The point of view expressed here is from the business perspective of that department. (The accounts receivable article is written from the point of view of the information systems department and an outside consultant). If you are interested in the technical approach used, refer to the accounts receivable success story. Technically, the two systems were very similar.

Original Project Objectives. The purpose of this accounts payable project was to increase the number of accounts payable transactions per person while simultaneously reducing the cost per transaction and improving service to external and internal customers. TI chose to use a client/server imaging system as the technology base.

Customer service for the TI accounts payable department is defined as quickly and accurately retrieving the documentation surrounding an invoice, an expense report, a purchase order, or any other accounts payable transaction. The Dallas-based accounts payable department services the entire $11 billion worldwide operations of TI. Accounts payable also acts as a central repository to ensure that accurate documentation is maintained.

Author's Note—"It's Not the Technology!" I was a participant in this project as an outside consultant. Because this project involved the introduction of a flashy, sexy, relatively expensive new technology, it is tempting to conclude that the system is responsible for all of these improvements. *This is most certainly not the case.* I have implemented this exact same system at other major corporations and seen nothing approaching these types of benefits. The introduction of the system caused the TI accounts payable department to substantially redesign its work processes. This is where the real benefit comes from. In twenty/twenty hindsight, it is possible that the TI accounts payable department could have accomplished 60 to 80 percent of these benefits with a significantly less expensive system (though no one could have predicted that with certainty up-front).

Hal Finley, manager of the accounts payable department, was interviewed in March of 1996 regarding his thoughts on what went right, what went wrong, and what might be done differently the next time.

What Went Right. Finley tells us about some of the positives:

- Uncharted waters: "We chose to press ahead of TI's internal group chartered to explore imaging and workflow systems. We did manage to get the system completed and into production (with some pain). If we had not pressed ahead, we would still be waiting for them."
- Get the basics working first: "The Accounts Payable team chose to implement the basics, first broadening the scope of capabilities, reporting, and measurement as the process evolved and smoothed out. This proved to be a very successful decision because some significant problems were encountered along the way. If TI had tried to do too much at first, the project may not have survived."
- Physical proximity: "Keeping the servers and other equipment in physical proximity to the project team was essential. Because we were doing this on our own, we had to grow our own expertise within the department. This was a much better solution than relying on a third party or other internal organization."
- Deployment approach: "We took a phased approach, rather than a *big bang effort*. Had we gone ahead with a big bang approach, the project quite likely would have collapsed."
- Customization: "The custom interface to our mainframe accounts payable system worked out fine. It was even ready on time!"
- User training: "We developed our own eight-hour training session. We even required that our people pass a Microsoft Windows certification test before they could take the training. We developed our own procedure book, and our people had to complete homework in that book prior to the class."

What Might Have Gone Better. Moving on to the decisions that didn't work out too well, Finley shares the following:

- Purchasing: "We tried to purchase and set up all of the hardware ourselves through our own departmental labor. In the future, I would recommend using a third party instead. Using our own people did not save any money in this area."
- Internal resources: "There was no way to know how much labor would be required from us to do this project. Some things went well because we knew the business. In some areas we didn't have access to the expertise that we needed and our project suffered. Windows NT and SyBase SQL Server were two examples where Texas Instruments had expertise, but we were not able to bring it to bear for our department. Those resources were committed elsewhere."

The Crunch of Implementation. Finley describes what it was like to actually bring the new system online: "Our backlog of work to be done actually got worse during the first few months of implementation. We had to cope with the new system, Texas Instruments, at an extremely fast growth rate and the physical relocation of our department."

"We initially thought the system was causing our increased backlog. By using some of the measurements within the new system, our team members were able to show us that the system was not at fault. *This forced other process problems to the surface that we were not aware of.* This is part of the *plateau challenge* of continuous improvement."

Benefits. When we turned to the topic of benefits, Finley was able to point out many specifics:

- Thirty percent increase in productivity: "We expected a productivity increase, and we got it. We were able to handle a 30 percent increase in our volume of accounts payable transactions without incremental headcount." Finley notes that prior to the new system, the accounts payable team was overworked. The ability to handle the increase in volume was certainly directly due to the system and the business process redesign efforts that were precipitated by the implementation of the system.

- Four hundred percent improvement in customer response time: Finley describes the before and after:

  > Before the new system, we would normally have to research a request for information and call our internal or external customer back. This would take an average of five to ten minutes. We now average thirty seconds or less and *are able to answer the request while the customer is still on the phone!*

  > This improvement was based on approximately 80,000 customer requests per year. By saving an average of five minutes per inquiry, the TI accounts payable team has saved approximately 400,000 *customer minutes* per year. The accounts payable department serves a total of about 5000 internal and external customers.

- The ultimate customer service improvement: "We were even able to give some of our internal customers their own search capability. We reduced our workload and at the same time gave them the ultimate improvement in customer service. They now control their own inquiries."

- Work processes closely measured: One of the benefits touted for *workflow* systems is the ability to have specific measurements of where business processes are working well and where they have bottlenecks. The TI accounts payable team certainly found this to be true. They are now able to accurately measure:
  — the time from mail delivery of a document to when it is scanned into the new system
  — the number of invoices that are waiting to be processed in each *work queue*: (TI groups the incoming documents into various queues to await specific types of processing. Examples include new documents, documents on hold, documents with exceptions, documents with invalid purchase orders, documents over a week old, and so on.) Finley notes: "We had chosen to measure and incent teamwork rather than individual performance. Grouping the work to be done by these types of teams and being able to accurately measure the performance has been very helpful."
  — the reporting of process bottlenecks: Finley comments: "The initial system had some capabilities for reporting, but we've gotten so much benefit from monitoring these processes that we are planning to buy a better reporting tool." Some of the specific items that the accounts payable team wants to measure include: tracking exceptions and *holds* by supplier (watching for problem suppliers), individual team member performance metrics (e.g., invoices processed per hour, average invoice processing time, and so forth), and cycle time from input to completion in all categories of documents and sub-processes.

- Capturing vendor discounts: Many vendors offer a discount for paying early. Finley describes improvements in this area: "Initially we got behind in capturing these discounts due to the problems we've already discussed. The upside is that our new process forces a much higher level of attention to available discounts (and makes it easier to capture these discounts). A new technical capability of the system also allows fax input of critical documents, which further speeds up the process in critical situations."

- Quality of life for accounts payable team members:

> Before, the workload was too high and people were stressed. After the new system and process changes, the workload is still too high and our people did experience some additional stress for the initial seven months of the project. After that time, things started to settle down. Now they like the new system and wouldn't give it up.

> We now find out earlier when we are getting behind. Before these changes, it could have been a week before we recognized that we had a significant backlog. Now we know within twenty-four hours when we are getting behind. This allows people a much greater capacity to prevent high stress situations.

- Continuous improvement: Finley observes: "We now have in place what we need for our next round of continuous improvement."

Summary. This project has dramatically improved customer service and simultaneously reduced the *cost per invoice* by enabling a fixed team of people to handle 30 percent more work. It took time, perseverance, technology, and business process redesign. As an outside observer, I want to personally commend the TI accounts payable team and Hal Finley. Although Finley is actually in charge, he made it clear through this entire process and this interview that he was only part of the solution. This project would not have been successful without the cooperation, perseverance, and contribution of everyone on the accounts payable team.

6.2.3 Other Success Stories
(All are located in the United States, unless otherwise noted.)

Success Story Cases

CASE PROFILE: AETNA		
Case ID: 501	**Industry: Insurance**	**Data Source:** Some items reported in *Resource Magazine* (August 1994), some in vendor's internal publications.
Type of Project: Client/server imaging, insurance back office processing.		**Project Outcome:** Generally successful, though longer and more difficult than hoped for. Included innovative use of real-time feedback and constructive competition.

SOME PROJECT HIGHLIGHTS:

Claims preparation and forward to processors: reduced average time per claim from nine days to eight hours.

Scanning and document coding: Original target was eighty-seven pages/hour per person. Actually achieved 300 pages/hour.

Work flow tracking and process improvement: Aetna was able to determine that 95–98 percent of incoming claim inquiry calls happened within six months of the claim. It was able to adjust its processes accordingly, moving excess optical storage units off the system after six months, producing a large system overhead savings. Bottleneck was identified by *average number of access requests graphed over time.*

CASE PROFILE: (NAME NOT DISCLOSED) TEWKSBURY, MASSACHUSETTS		
Case ID: 502	**Industry: Unknown**	**Data Source:** (from vendor's internal write-up)
Type of Project: Client/server imaging.		**Project Outcome:**

BENEFITS:

In 1992, employed 200 people and processed 1,000,000 transactions annually. Today uses 250 people to process 1,600,000 transactions.

CASE PROFILE: FEDERAL EDUCATION DEPARTMENT, FINANCE SECTION

Case ID: 503	Industry: Government	Data Source: *Federal Computer Week.*

Type of Project:	Project Outcome:
Client/server imaging, done by system integrator.	$400,000 project, kept project simple.

BENEFITS:

Strong gain derived from the simple elimination of manual sorting.

CASE PROFILE: FINANCIAL INSURANCE GROUP

Case ID: 504	Industry: Insurance	Data Source: Vendor annual conference presentation.

Type of Project:	Project Outcome:
Client/server imaging, insurance back end claims processing.	Results not yet verified.

BENEFITS:

Before: Sixty-six percent of claim processor's time spent in document preparation and validation. Thirty-three percent spent in execution.

Target: Seventy-five percent spent in document preparation and validation. Twenty-five percent spent in execution.

CASE PROFILE: LA INSURANCE COMPANY

Case ID: 505	Industry: Insurance	Data Source: Vendor's internal publications.
Type of Project: Client/server imaging, insurance claims back end processing.		**Project Outcome:**

BENEFITS:

Before: Processed 2,000 transactions per day with 234 people.

After: Processes 5,000 transactions per day with forty-seven people.

CASE PROFILE: PLAZA HOME FUNDING

Case ID: 506	Industry: Financial	Data Source: 1995 interview with project participant.
Type of Project: Client/server imaging, loan processing.		**Project Outcome:** $2,000,000; three-year project.

BENEFITS:

Before: Loan turnaround time from application to secondary financing: twenty days.

After: Ten days, resulting in a strong competitive advantage.

CASE PROFILE: TEXAS COMMERCE BANK

Case ID: 507	Industry: Financial	Data Source: Presented in vendor's videotape. Verified with project team member.
Type of Project: Client/server imaging, loan processing.		**Project Outcome:**

BENEFITS:

Before: Two-week loan turnaround.

After: Three hours.

Before: Average collection contacts per person: thirty per day.

After: Two hundred and fifty per day.

CASE PROFILE: ORYX

Case ID: 508	Industry: Energy	Data Source: Verified with CIO.
Type of Project: Client/server major reengineering initiative.		**Project Outcome:** Consolidated five separate oil and gas subsystems into single system.

BENEFITS:

Now able to run the business with 40 percent less headcount.

CASE PROFILE: RAYMOND JAMES CORP.

Case ID: 509	Industry: Financial	Data Source: Presentation by client at vendor annual conference.
Type of Project: Client/server imaging, reengineering.		**Project Outcome:** Able to consolidate four new account forms into one.

BENEFITS:
Before: New account processing backlog of thirty days.

After: No backlog.

CASE PROFILE: HALLMARK CARDS

Case ID: 510	Industry: Retail	Data Source: Michael Hammer and James Champy, *Reengineering the Corporation.*
Type of Project: Client/server reengineering, Point-of-Sale system.		**Project Outcome:** Proactive, not crisis driven. Went to case teams solution.

BENEFITS:
Before: Average concept-to-market time 2.5 years, with approximately eighty handoffs.

After: Average concept-to-market time 1.8 years, with approximately fifty-five handoffs.

Comments:
Higher retail operating costs and fragmented niches created an imperative to increase inventory turns and kill slow products quickly. Operating committee truly supported the effort.

CASE PROFILE: TACO BELL

Case ID: 511	Industry: Restaurant	Data Source: Michael Hammer and James Champy, *Reengineering the Corporation*.

Type of Project:	Project Outcome:
Client/server.	- Changed kitchen assumption. - Customer focus change and strategy. - Empowered store managers. - Stretch goal: giant among all food sellers. - Focused on non-direct costs.

BENEFITS:
Before: Troubled $500MM regional chain.

After: Successful $3BB national chain.

Before: Peak capacity per store $400/hour.

After: $1,500/hour.

CASE PROFILE: BELL ATLANTIC

Case ID: 512	Industry: Phone Service	Data Source: Michael Hammer and James Champy, *Reengineering the Corporation*.

Type of Project:	Project Outcome:
Client/server reengineering.	- Deregulation demanded order-of-magnitude change. - Zero cycle time stretch goal would force change. - Used core team and field team.

BENEFITS:
Before: Long distance sign-up time ranging from fifteen to thirty days.

After: Near zero cycle time.

Before: Long distance sign-up labor cost $88MM per year.

After: $6MM per year.

CASE PROFILE: WORLD CORP.

Case ID: 513	Industry: Transportation	Data Source: Meghan O'Leary, The Upshot of Downsizing, *CIO Magazine* (June 1, 1993).

Type of Project:	Project Outcome:
Downsize mainframe to client/server to avoid significant mainframe upgrade costs and improve overall cost benefit performance.	

BENEFITS:

Software maintenance fees reduced from $120,000 per year to $18,000 per year.

$1MM in mainframe hardware leasing costs saved.

Users have become substantially autonomous and able to do significant things on their own.

Reduced time required for month-end accounting close.

Now able to do applications that were not possible on mainframe. Examples include crew scheduling, flight and cargo tracking, and airplane/parts maintenance.

Comments:

World Corp. is a $400MM air transportation company.

Note: Many companies have failed miserably in justifying the switch from mainframe to client/server based on mainframe cost savings alone. This appears to be an exception. Note that several important benefits were gained besides the cost reduction, and the decision was precipitated by the need for a costly mainframe upgrade.

CASE PROFILE: COMCAR INDUSTRIES, INC.

Case ID: 514	Industry: Trucking	Data Source: Meghan O'Leary, The Upshot of Downsizing, *CIO Magazine* (June 1, 1993).

Type of Project:	Project Outcome:
Downsizing from mainframe to client/server (Unix) network and minicomputers.	

BENEFITS:

The operating ratio for the firm (expenses divided by revenue) has improved by five percentage points (a significant accomplishment in a low margin service business such as trucking).

New system has improved customer service with significantly fewer miles driven.

Accounts receivable collection time has been reduced by three days.

Corporate financial staff has been reduced from thirty-six to thirty with the extra employees deployed to other important areas such as an improved, twenty-four-hour-a-day customer service function.

Month-end accounting close reduced from three weeks to one week.

Comments:

Comcar is a trucking company located in Auburndale, Florida.

CASE PROFILE: PUBLIC SERVICE ELECTRIC & GAS (PSE&G), NEWARK, NEW JERSEY		
Case ID: 515	**Industry: Energy**	**Data Source:** *AIIM '95 Daily* (Association of Information and Imaging Managers) (April 12, 1995).
Type of Project: Client/server imaging of engineering drawings, procedures, vendor manuals, and other items required for nuclear regulatory commission requirements.		**Project Outcome:** Total investment: $5.2MM over three years.

BENEFITS:

Documented cost reductions of $1.1MM per year (for three years).

Substantially improved accuracy of all documentation supporting engineering and maintenance.

Easier access to accurate information for maintenance and engineering personnel.

CASE PROFILE: TEXAS INSTRUMENTS, CREDIT AND COLLECTIONS		
Case ID: 516	**Industry: Manufacturing**	**Data Source:** *PMNET* (Project Management International's monthly magazine) (December 1995).
Type of Project: Client/server imaging, eighty plus worldwide sites, accounts receivable, direct mainframe-to-image (COLD) process.		**Project Outcome:** - On time! - On budget! - As expected! (Some response time issues yet to be resolved, but this was a known risk.)

BENEFITS:

Expected reduction in outstanding day's receivable on a worldwide basis and improved customer service.

CASE PROFILE: TEXAS INSTRUMENTS, ACCOUNTS PAYABLE

Case ID: 517	Industry: Manufacturing	Data Source: Author's 1994–95 participation in project.

Type of Project:	Project Outcome:
Client/server imaging, accounts payable, custom mainframe interface, twenty-five plus users.	- Substantially on time. - Slightly over budget. - Substantially as expected.

BENEFITS:

Improving cashflow and discount management, improving vendor partnerships, operating cost reductions.

CASE PROFILE: MCI, AP DOCUMENT RETENTION

Case ID: 518	Industry: Phone Service	Data Source: Author's 1994 participation in project.

Type of Project:	Project Outcome:
Client/server imaging, accounts payable storage and retrieval, two sites.	Generally within budget and on time, but with many frustrations.

BENEFITS:

Learning curve accomplishments:

- First install took six weeks. Second one took three days.

- Now understand the need for *very strong* technical skills within the user department or effectively provided by the information systems department.

Improve customer service, audit response, cost reductions, learn imaging technology.

Comments:

Strong disappointment in vendor's technical support. Somewhat attributable to expectations not corrected during the pre-sales effort.

CASE PROFILE: FRITO LAY, ACCOUNTS PAYABLE

Case ID: 519	Industry: Manufacturing	Data Source: Author's 1994 participation in project.

Type of Project:	Project Outcome:
Client/server imaging, accounts payable.	Project was kept fairly simple and completed substantially on time, on budget, and as expected.

BENEFITS:

Improve vendor relations, cash management, and discount taking. Learn about imaging technology.

Comments:

Project was tough on project team technician. Amount of work and complexity was underestimated.

CASE PROFILE: NORTHERN TRUST, FINANCIAL TRADES

Case ID: 520	Industry: Financial	Data Source: Author's 1994 participation in project.

Type of Project:	Project Outcome:
Client/server imaging, workflow for financial instrument trades, twenty plus users.	On time, on budget, as expected!

BENEFITS:

Improved cycle time, improved customer service, some benefit from improved float management.

Project benefited greatly from client project manager that had sufficient authority to contain scope expansion demands by users. Project was kept relatively simple and did not involve dramatic business process changes. Vendor provided a strong lead technician and, secondarily, a capable project manager.

CASE PROFILE: Deutschebank Singapore

Case ID: 521	Industry: Financial	Data Source: *Computerworld* (May 8, 1995).

Type of Project: Client/server trade finance system.	Project Outcome: Not disclosed.

BENEFITS:

Twenty percent productivity improvement.

Big six success story.

CASE PROFILE: WPS SAS, Argentina State-Owned Oil and Gas Company

Case ID: 522	Industry: Energy	Data Source: *Computerworld* (May 8, 1995).

Type of Project: Client/server financial reporting system.	Project Outcome: Not disclosed.

BENEFITS:

Reduced monthly financial reporting time by 80 percent.

Big six success story.

CASE PROFILE: Banco Itamarati (Privately Held Brazilian Bank)

Case ID: 523	Industry: Financial	Data Source: Jim Johnson, Chaos, *Application Development Trends* (January 1995).

Type of Project:	Project Outcome:
Client/server technology materially assisting in strategic redirection of the firm.	Moved from forty-seventh to fifteenth place in the Brazilian banking industry, including annual net profit growth of 51 percent.

BENEFITS:

Project successfully contributed to the strategic redirection of the bank. It had three components of success:

1. A clear vision with documented, specific objectives.
2. Top-down level of involvement.
3. Producing incremental, measurable results throughout the planning and implementation period.

CASE PROFILE: St. Vincent's Hospital, Birmingham, Alabama

Case ID: 524	Industry: Medical Services	Data Source: *Computerworld* (August 7, 1995), p. 59.

Type of Project:	Project Outcome:
Client/server imaging system for patient registration, claims processing, and accounts receivable collection.	

BENEFITS:

Patient registration time reduced from ten to 2.6 minutes (on average).

Insurance verification time reduced by 66 percent.

Patient registrations increased by 40 percent even though office staff has been reduced by 20 percent.

Average outstanding receivables has been reduced from thirty-five days to twenty-eight days.

CASE PROFILE: HYATT HOTELS		
Case ID: 525	**Industry:** Hotel	**Data Source:** Published in *Trade* magazine (circa 1994; exact citation lost).
Type of Project: Client/server registration system.		**Project Outcome:** Completed ahead of schedule and under budget. $15MM total price tag.

BENEFITS:

Substantially improved customer service during registration process.

Note: This project was successfully accomplished during the same time period that Hyatt's competitors were failing miserably. See Horror Story #101, American Airlines (The Confirm Project).

CASE PROFILE: GLOBAL MARINE, HOUSTON, TEXAS		
Case ID: 526	**Industry:** Energy	**Data Source:** Personal interview in 1996 with project manager and executive sponsor.
Type of Project: Client/server imaging for accounts payable department.		**Project Outcome:**

BENEFITS:

Global Marine's business in 1994 exploded from the projected $50MM to $150MM.

The purchasing and payable aspects of oil and gas exploration are critical control factors. Without the new system this business growth would have occurred at a substantially increased risk.

The imaging system now provides a central database to access job and project cost records. It is the most readily available and accurate information for how much it costs to do a previous project. The explosion of business in 1994 was caused by a shift from time and materials bidding to fixed price bidding. Access to this information has been a critical assistance in dealing with the risks of large fixed-price projects.

Comments:

Global Marine is a worldwide oil and gas exploration firm.

6.3 Study Methodology and Cautions

This research was personally funded and conducted primarily by me and my wife, Jeanette Ingram, doing business as FAOSP Group of Dallas, a sole proprietorship. We were greatly aided by input, critique, and contributions from the practitioners, academicians, and journalists listed in Appendix H.

Purpose. As is seen throughout the book, our purpose in conducting this research is to aid project professionals, executives, and shareholders in recognizing the client/server threat and turning it to competitive advantage.

You may note an intentional attempt to speak to the business person in language, formatting, and detail levels that he will find comfortable. We have attempted to avoid the *academic* voice or the overly detailed data analysis that often accompanies major research papers. While the academic perspective has much value, and many of the reviewers in Appendix H are academic, we are striving for clarity and simplicity.

Given the purpose of the book and limits of the data, I believe that simple averages will suffice.

Data Sources. The sixty Horror Story cases shown in Section 6.1 were developed from either project participant interviews or publicly available information sources. The interviews and research took place between 1992 and 1996.

Survey Technique. In general, I used the questionnaire in Appendix E as an interview tool and in developing the analysis for each case. In the cases where a data item was not available, n/a is indicated.

Survey Caution. Please be aware that this was a pioneering effort and that the set of questions tended to evolve over time. Many of the initial interviews were based on very open-ended questions such as "What went wrong?" and "What would you do differently next time?" Somewhere in the middle of the research a pattern of root issue problems began to emerge. After that pattern was identified, it was a simple matter to construct the standard set of questions shown in Appendix E. In several cases I had to return to the original interviewees for further information.

Development of Conclusions. Section 2.2 provides the general trail of logic for developing each major conclusion.

Cost Definitions. Section 2.2.2 explains how the various cost categories are defined. This includes direct project costs, original budgets, total costs, waste, the cost of unrealized objectives, and the total cost of quality.

Remember that *our intent is to quantify the cost of not doing things right the first time,* which is the definition of the cost of quality. Additional definitions can be found in Appendix B.

Uses Of Data. Section 2.2 describes the Horror Stories that were used to draw each conclusion. In most cases this was some subset of the total sixty Horror Stories. You may also note that some of the Horror Stories do not include much hard data. They were included in the hope that the information that is available will provide some useful insights for the reader.

Random Sample Cautions. These Horror Stories are *not* a random sample of all client/server projects. The study team specifically sought problem projects, so the reader is cautioned against assuming that all client/server projects will average $2.5 million in direct project costs and $25 million in total cost of quality. It is, however, reasonably accurate to say that *given,* if a client/server project exceeds its original budget by approximately double (or more) it is considered a Horror Story for purposes of this study, then:

1. Based on the research summarized in Appendix A, which includes a sample set of hundreds of projects, there is at least a 50 percent chance that a given client/server project will result in a Horror Story.

2. As seen in Section 2.2.3, based on a sample set of between nineteen and twenty-six projects (depending on your preference), the subject client/server Horror Story will tend to have an ultimate total cost of quality of between eight and ten times the original project budget.

The probability of a project becoming a Horror Story is fairly well identified by Appendix A. The area of caution is in assuming that all Horror Stories will have a cost of quality between eight and ten times the original project budget. Until we have further research, we must acknowledge that the total cost of quality for the average Horror Story could be lower, or higher, than these averages indicate. The reader is again reminded that the intent of this book is to motivate executives, project managers, and shareholders to investigate these issues within their own firms.

Factors Which May Have Tended to Reduce or Inflate Cost of Quality Figures. Corporations actively work to suppress this type of bad news, so the study team recommends caution. Experience has shown that the true cost of quality for a bad project is rarely ever known and that the information that we do get is usually conservative. When interpreting the cost of quality data, keep in mind that:

- The cost of quality represents the cost of not doing things right the first time. *This assumes that the promises made to receive funding for a project were valid.* We know that this is not always the case, but measuring cost of quality in this manner tends to help keep everyone focused on performing as promised.
- Cost of quality figures may represent costs incurred in a single year or over a three-to-five year project life span.
- If a project was completed and delivered its promised benefits, the original project budget was not considered wasted or a part of the cost of not doing things right.
- In the area of the costs of unrealized objectives, many of the cost figures had to be estimated based on the size and scope of the project and the nature of the business environment. You will note that these costs often reflect multiples of the original project budget. This is due to prevailing industry practices. Projects of this type are usually funded to improve revenues and reduce costs. Projects usually must promise at least a 300 percent payback in order to get funded. Most of the time, these payback promises are more on the order of 500 percent to 1000 percent. If you do the math, you will see that the estimated costs of unrealized objectives are actually extremely conservative.

Miscellaneous Items. Consultants and involved vendor personnel are generally considered part of the *project team*. Their attributes contribute to right people/right motives/right actions rating.

A Summary of Current Research on Client/Server Project Outcomes

---

Client/Server (Open Systems) versus
Mainframe Project Research Key Findings

Research Conducted by:	KPMG Peat Marwick, London.	FAOSP Group, Carrollton, Texas.
Sample Size and Type:	252 organizations reporting on mainframe projects.	Sixty-two mission-critical client/server projects (open systems, UNIX, networks, etc.).
Study Purpose:	Identify causes, implications, and frequency of runaway projects.	Determine causes of client/server project problems and identify best solutions.

Key Findings

Percentage of Projects Materially Over Budget	33%	57%
Percentage of Projects Significantly Missing Deadlines	48%	72%
Percentage of Projects Falling Materially Short of User Expectations	56%	88%

Conclusion: "Roughly 70 percent of Client/Server projects will come in materially late, materially over budget or will fail to meet significant user expectations. Roughly 40 percent of Mainframe projects will come in materially late, materially over budget or will fail to meet significant user expectations."

IBM Consulting Group Study:
Twenty-Four Major United States Organizations, Results of Client/Server Projects

Research Conducted by: IBM Consulting Group.

Sample Size and Type: Twenty-four large United States organizations, client/server projects.

Study Purpose: Understand impact of new technology on project outcomes.

Key Findings

Percentage of Projects Materially Over Budget	55%
Percentage of Projects Significantly Missing Deadlines	68%
Percentage of Projects Requiring Material Redesign	88%

Software Productivity Research

United States and United Kingdom Client/Server Projects Study: Relationship Between Project Size and Outcome

Research Conducted by: Software Productivity Research (SPR), Burlington, Massachusetts, United States, as described in Management Meltdown by Rochelle Gardner, *Open Computing*, January 1995.

Sample Size and Type: Approximately 100 client/server projects in the United States and United Kingdom. Included small, medium, large, and very large projects.

Study Purpose: Objectively define project size via function points and correlate size to project outcome.

Key Findings

Percentage of Projects Materially Over Budget and/or Materially Late	66% of the projects actually finished exceeded cost and time estimates by approximately 100%.
Overall Percentage of Projects Abandoned	35% to 50%
Large Project Probability of Cancellation	24%
Very Large Project Probability of Cancellation	50%

(Note: Sample size for this study was not included in the *Open Computing* article.)

Software Engineering Institute, Carnegie-Mellon University: Study and Military Joint Venture Yields

Project and Software Capability Maturity Model

Research Conducted by: Software Engineering Institute, Carnegie-Mellon University, with support from more than 900 private and public organizations (including the military).

Sample Size and Type: 260 Organizations (*Open Computing,* January 1995).

Study Purpose: To identify organizational maturity level at managing software projects and identify overall trends.

Key Findings

Organizations at Stage 1 of Project Maturity	Approximately 195
Organizations at Stage 2 or 3 of Project Maturity	Approximately 64
Organizations at Stage 4 of Project Maturity	None
Organizations at Stage 5 of Project Maturity	One

Al Lederer, University of Oakland, Rochester, Michigan: Study on Root Causes of Bad Estimates

Research Conducted by: Al Lederer and Jayesh Prasad, University of Oakland, Rochester, Michigan, United States, study published in *The Journal of the ACM,* February 1992, Nine Management Guidelines for Better Cost Estimating.

Sample Size and Type: 115 randomly selected United States organizations.

Study Purpose: Regarding all types of information systems projects, how often are the estimates materially off and what are the root causes?

Key Findings

Percentage of Projects Materially Over Budget	63% of projects in excess of $50,000.
Root Cause(s)	We are taught that projects proceed according to a *rational* model. They, in fact, proceed according to a *political* model.
What to do about it	Study produced nine key recommendations. The primary thrust surrounded *accountability* for all parties.

Standish Group International Study:
High Number of Projects Failing and *It's Getting Worse!*

Research Conducted by: Standish Group International, Dennis, Massachusetts, United States.

Sample Size and Type: Large-scale projects by United States companies and government agencies covering 8,380 projects.*

Study Purpose: Assess how bad the situation really is.*

Key Findings

Percentage of application development projects canceled before getting started	31.1%
Percentage of Projects Materially Over Budget	52.7% will exceed their budgets by 89%
Percentage of Projects Completed on Time and on Budget	16.2%
Percentage of Originally Proposed Features Actually Delivered	42%
Percentage of Information Technology Executives Polled That Believe That More Projects Fail Currently Than Five Years Ago	48%

*Study synopsis published in *Application Development Trends,* January 1995, Chaos: The Dollar Drain of IT Project Failures, by Jim Johnson.

IDC Report on Client/Server Application Growth

Research Conducted by: Clare M. Gillan et al., International Data Corporation, Framingham, Massachusetts, United States.

Sample Size and Type: IDC's revenues database for over 500 software vendors worldwide.

Study Purpose: Identify the growth areas in application software and overall trends.

Key Findings

1994 Client/Server Application Growth	69%
1994 Non-Client/Server Application Growth	4%

Michael Hammer Comments on Reengineering Success/Failure Rate

Research Conducted by: Michael Hammer, author of *Reengineering the Corporation*, Cambridge, Massachusetts, United States.

Sample Size and Type: General observations of reengineering initiatives.

Study Purpose: Success/failure rate.

Key Findings

Amount That Will Be Spent by United States Businesses in 1994 on Reengineering	Approximately $32 billion.
Project Failure Rate	Approximately 66%, Revised to 50–60%, *Computerworld*, May 8, 1995.

A Study of the Recommendations of Sixty Reengineering Practitioners

Study by Lynne Markus, et al., of the Claremont Graduate School, Claremont, California 91711-6190 (909) 621-8555 ext. 3151

Study presents an in-depth look at recommendations and cautions offered by sixty reengineering practitioners covering hundreds of projects.

Glossary of Terms and Definitions

Client/Server generally refers to the new realm of technology that is based on a personal computer (PC) or other intelligent workstation rather than the traditional *dumb* terminal. The *client* does most of its own processing and is provided data from various servers (larger computers) on the network. The largest single difference between client/server computing and previous minicomputer or mainframe systems is the *non-proprietary* nature of the hardware and software. Prior to client/server, which rose to prominence in the late eighties and early nineties, most mainframe and minicomputer systems were based on proprietary hardware and software. This meant that the buyer was limited only to the products provided by a particular manufacturer. Personal computers, client/server systems, and systems based on the Unix operating system generally will work with a wide range of hardware and software products and are considered *non-proprietary*.

Commercial computer projects are defined as those projects that produce the type of systems that run major entities, normally tracking large volumes of people, dollars, and things. Examples would include accounting, manufacturing, distribution, and customer service systems. These projects are several orders of magnitude more difficult than the installation of simpler systems such as word processing, spreadsheets, or electronic mail. They may also be referred to as *guts of the business* systems.

Cost of Quality: Philip Crosby first defined this term in his 1979 book, *Quality Is Free,* published by McGraw-Hill. Crosby is regarded by many as one of the founding fathers of the quality movement in American business. In this book we use Crosby's definition of the cost of quality, which is *the cost of not doing things right the first time.*

Data processing (DP), information systems (IS), and information technology (IT) are all terms that may be used interchangeably to describe the internal department in most corporations that provides computer services.

Deliverable is a contractual term describing the tangible work product to be produced by a given amount of labor. For example, a working computerized reservations system would be the primary deliverable produced by the project described in Horror Story #101.

Earned value method of project accounting and management: The earned value project accounting and management concept is a method of converting work planned and work actually done into dollars so that measurement and control can reliably take place.

This addresses the primary problem of project accounting, which is to accurately *know* how much of the planned work is actually done. Some additional benefits of earned value include:

- Vendors and consultants get paid only what they budgeted for a deliverable—not what they spent. This protects the customer from overruns.

- Provides a clear measurement of the week-to-week progress on actual work done and completed to specifications; when progress is not forthcoming it is immediately visible and known by all.
- Forces project definition diligence prior to approving funds for further work.
- Forces a definition of internal resources required and a vehicle for holding people accountable for commitments.
- Provides a reliable way to predict unacceptable overruns before the project is 20 percent complete. (This conclusion and a further explanation of earned value is available in a book by Quentin W. Fleming and Joel M. Koppelman titled *Earned Value Project Management*, 1996, Project Management Institute.)
- Provides a proven method for managing complex technology projects.

Earned value traces its history back to the United States Department of Defense's efforts to build the first nuclear submarine. A case study using earned value may be found in section 6.2.1. Additional insights are available in Fleming and Koppelman's book.

Horror Story was generally defined by the study team as a project where the direct project costs were ultimately more than twice the original budget.

LAN is an acronym for local area network. This was one of the early buzzwords used to describe what we now call client/server. LAN generally refers to a network within a single physical building.

Open systems is a general designation for *non-proprietary* computer systems. See the definition of client/server.

PM Network and *Project Management Journal* are both published by the Project Management Institute.

Project Management Institute (PMI) is a cross-industry professional association that promotes project management effectiveness. PMI now has over 33,000 members, over 5,000 certified project management professionals (PMPs), and local chapters in most major cities in the world. For more information on PMI or PMP certification, contact PMI at the Central Administration Office, Project Management Institute Headquarters, Four Campus Boulevard, Newtown Square, Pennsylvania 19073-3299 USA (610) 356-4600.

Project management professional (PMP) certification is provided and administered by the Project Management Institute. The certification requires significant professional experience, exposure beyond a single industry or job role, and completion of a course of study that culminates in passing a rigorous written exam.

Resource is a generic term that normally means people, internal employees, full-time equivalents (FTEs), and so on, which can be deployed on projects.

System integrators generally are firms that help customers implement computer systems by selling services and possibly some products. They generally do not manufacture or develop their own products.

WAN (see LAN definition) stands for wide area network and normally refers to a network that includes multiple physical buildings.

Work breakdown structure (WBS) and work packages. WBS is a discipline advocated by PMI and an integral part of the earned value method of project accounting and management. The concept is to *break down* the work necessary for a project in a structured, controlled fashion. This breakdown process results in *chunks* of work called work packages. Note that the WBS and work package standards advocated by PMI require that the project be understood and defined to the point where the work packages are no larger than forty hours. This is a significantly greater degree of definition than is usually practiced and is critical to implementing the controls necessary for preventing Horror Stories.

APPENDIX C

A Study of Symptoms

The following study by the author was originally published in the June 1994 issue of *Project Management Journal*. It is reprinted here with the permission of the Project Management Institute.

What Is Important.

1. In hindsight, I must admit that this study was directed at symptoms rather than root issues.

2. While the study contains many useful recommendations, they cannot be fully implemented until the root issues are dealt with.

3. The failure of this study to materially improve project outcomes was a primary motivating factor behind my further research and efforts to deal with root issues, culminating in this book.

As you skim this study, think through the efforts to improve project management that you have seen in your own organization. *Are those efforts directed at root issues, or are they missing the mark and addressing symptoms?*

Managing Client/Server and Open Systems Projects: A Ten-Year Study of Sixty-Two Mission-Critical Projects

Tom Ingram, FAOSP Group, Carrollton, Texas

Overview

On May 19, 1993, *The Wall Street Journal* ran a feature story describing the *perils and glitches* of downsizing[1] mainframe applications to open systems[2] platforms. On June 1, 1993, *CIO Magazine* published a cover story describing several downsizing success stories. The organizations involved realized dramatic cost savings, functional improvements, and productivity gains. This study was initiated, in part, due to the seeming contradiction in the outcome of open systems and downsizing projects. The study team for this research project consisted of Tom Ingram, Jeanette Ingram, and various contributions made by the several individuals mentioned in note 9. The team sought to address two key questions:

1. Why do some open systems projects yield strongly positive results while others produce marginal or negative outcomes?

2. What are the common attributes of the successful projects?

The research covers sixty-two open systems projects that were considered vital or *mission critical* to their respective organizations. These projects usually involved financial, accounting, production, or human resource applications. Figure 2 shows the primary conclusions of the study, called Project Outcome Correlation Ratings. This figure describes the sixteen project attributes that were common to the successful projects and their relative frequency of occurrence. Other trends and items of note can be found in the Additional Observations portion of this article.

The Problem

An important finding emerged early in the research[3] and is generally described by the study team: "Roughly 70 percent of open systems projects will come in materially late, materially over budget, or will fail to meet significant user expectations." Is this problem specific to open systems? The London office of KPMG Peat Marwick conducted a similar study[4] of mainframe projects in the late 1980s and early 1990s. Our study team derived a similar statement regarding mainframe projects from Peat Marwick's data: "Roughly 40 percent of mainframe projects will come in materially late, materially over budget, or will fail to meet significant user expectations." *Based on this data, an open systems project is almost twice as likely to run into serious project problems as a mainframe project.*

Isn't this new open technology supposed to make things easier? What could possibly account for such poor performance in terms of bringing projects in on time, on budget, and as expected? What can be done to prevent these problems? Many would argue that these types of project problems are simply a fact of life. Others would claim that the productivity and qualitative improvements of open systems outweigh these hazards. The study team dismisses these

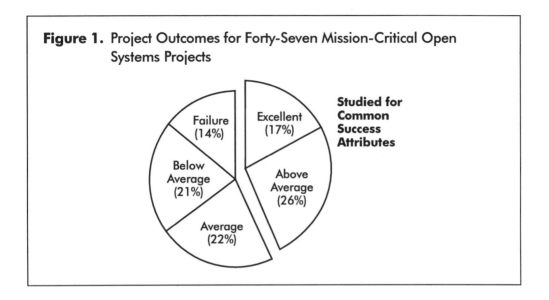

Figure 1. Project Outcomes for Forty-Seven Mission-Critical Open Systems Projects

assertions as lazy and self-serving. We believe that it is possible to conduct effective open systems projects, and we offer as evidence the many projects in this study that came in on time, on budget, and with performance results as expected. This research and subsequent recommendations are intended to address these key issues and provide specific direction for improving open systems project outcomes.

Defining Open Systems

Since the widespread acceptance of the personal computer in the early 1980s, a new area of information technology has gained critical mass. Collectively called *open systems*, this new technology provides many advantages over single-vendor, proprietary systems. For purposes of this article, *open systems* includes client/server,[5] Unix,[6] local area network (LAN)[7] and downsizing projects. A common thread that emerged during the study was a practical definition of open systems based on organizational purchasing behavior. The organizations studied wanted applications that were hardware-independent, which provided two key benefits:

1. Competition for hardware dollars.
2. A large variety of available application software and tools that could be easily moved to new hardware platforms as technology and price/performance improved.

Study Methodology

The study team developed a set of sixty-nine project attributes to measure the effectiveness of open systems projects. These attributes evolved from:

1. The author's eleven years of experience implementing open systems projects, including the development of an open systems project methodology.

2. Project management training provided to the author by Dun & Bradstreet software and subsequent efforts to adapt that training to the specific needs of open systems projects.

3. Contribution and review from a Project Management Institute chapter president.[8]

4. Professional critique and review by eight information systems professionals,[9] totaling over seventy-five years of project experience.

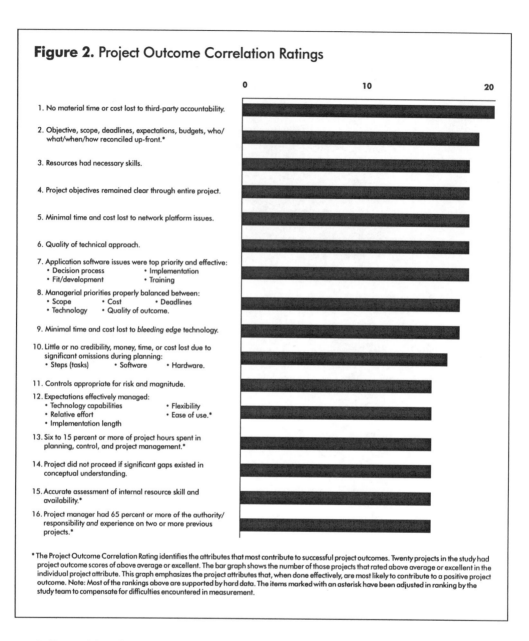

Figure 2. Project Outcome Correlation Ratings

The bar graph shows, on a scale from 0 to 20, the following attributes:

1. No material time or cost lost to third-party accountability.
2. Objective, scope, deadlines, expectations, budgets, who/what/when/how reconciled up-front.*
3. Resources had necessary skills.
4. Project objectives remained clear through entire project.
5. Minimal time and cost lost to network platform issues.
6. Quality of technical approach.
7. Application software issues were top priority and effective:
   • Decision process   • Implementation
   • Fit/development   • Training
8. Managerial priorities properly balanced between:
   • Scope   • Cost   • Deadlines
   • Technology   • Quality of outcome.
9. Minimal time and cost lost to *bleeding edge* technology.
10. Little or no credibility, money, time, or cost lost due to significant omissions during planning:
   • Steps (tasks)   • Software   • Hardware.
11. Controls appropriate for risk and magnitude.
12. Expectations effectively managed:
   • Technology capabilities   • Flexibility
   • Relative effort   • Ease of use.*
   • Implementation length
13. Six to 15 percent or more of project hours spent in planning, control, and project management.*
14. Project did not proceed if significant gaps existed in conceptual understanding.
15. Accurate assessment of internal resource skill and availability.*
16. Project manager had 65 percent or more of the authority/responsibility *and* experience on two or more previous projects.*

* The Project Outcome Correlation Rating identifies the attributes that most contribute to successful project outcomes. Twenty projects in the study had project outcome scores of above average or excellent. The bar graph shows the number of those projects that rated above average or excellent in the individual project attribute. This graph emphasizes the project attributes that, when done effectively, are most likely to contribute to a positive project outcome. Note: Most of the rankings above are supported by hard data. The items marked with an asterisk have been adjusted in ranking by the study team to compensate for difficulties encountered in measurement.

5. Recognition that open systems represents a significant change in project management issues and priorities. The study team attempted to be as specific and directly applicable to open systems as possible. Traditional mainframe and proprietary project management assumptions were challenged, modified, and discarded if not directly relevant to open systems. We were motivated to challenge the status quo by the wholly inadequate treatment of these issues in the current management literature (see Literature Search below). An additional factor suggesting the need for research is the large percentage of open systems projects that run into trouble.

The questionnaire developed from these project attributes was used to study sixty-two mission-critical projects implemented on open systems computing platforms between 1982 and 1992. Project attributes were generally measured on a scale of 1 to 5 with 5 representing an excellent rating and 1 representing a poor rating.

The projects studied in detail began with sixty-two projects but were reduced to forty-seven. These forty-seven had project records complete enough to make analysis meaningful. Observations from the other fifteen projects are used to support the conclusions of the base forty-seven. These projects ranged from a high of 8,000 personal computers (PCs) connected via wide area network[10] supporting a government welfare payments application to a two-workstation LAN running accounting applications for a pest control firm. Between were many accounting and manufacturing applications running on a variety of open systems platforms including client/server, LANs, and Unix. The primary criteria for project selection were that:

1. The application had to be mission-critical.

2. The implementing organization chose to use an open systems solution over a proprietary mainframe or minicomputer.

3. Sufficient project records and information were available to produce a complete assessment of the project.

Figure 1 summarizes the results of project outcomes.

Project Outcomes

The Project Outcome sidebar discusses the basis upon which the overall project outcomes were measured. Of a total possible score of 25, the project outcome scores ranged from a high of 25 to a low of 5. By graphing the project outcome score ranges, all projects were rated excellent, above average, average, below average, or failure. The excellent projects scored from 23 to 25, and the above average projects scored between 20 and 22. This article focuses on the attributes common among the above average and excellent projects (hereafter collectively referred to as the *successful* projects).

Project Success Attributes

A major goal of this study was to identify a small set of priorities for improving the outcome of open systems projects. The study team examined the successful projects to:

1. Determine which project attributes consistently appeared in the above average and excellent projects.

2. Measure how well the individual project teams managed that particular attribute. (Managing an attribute well was defined as scoring 4 or 5 out of a possible 5.)

3. Consolidate and reduce project management attributes to a handful that, when done well, will significantly improve open systems project outcomes. The number of attributes was further reduced in order to compensate for any potential error inherent in the study (see Study Qualifications below).

As a result, the study team agreed that if a project attribute was well managed (scoring a 4 or 5) in fifteen or more of the twenty successful projects, that attribute should be considered a project success *attribute*. The result was that the study team identified sixteen project success attributes.

Project Outcome Correlation Ratings (POC Rating)

Figure 2 shows the frequency at which the project success attributes occurred within the twenty successful projects. If a project attribute occurred in fifteen or more of the twenty successful projects, the study team concluded that it correlated positively with project outcome.

Example: Consider the project attribute "No material time or cost lost to third-party accountability." According to Figure 2, this attribute shows a Project Outcome Correlation Rating of 20. This means that of the twenty successful projects, twenty of them measured either a 4 or a 5 in the area of "No time or cost lost to third-party accountability." In plain terms, all of the successful project teams did well at controlling third parties, and their projects

Project Outcomes

Project outcomes were determined by rating the following five key questions on a scale from 1 to 5:

1. **Based on project outcome, would the executive sponsor do the project again**? End points of the scale were: 5 ("Yes, I would do the project again with little or no changes.") and 1 ("No, I absolutely would not do the project again.").

2. **Number and severity of surprises**. Respondents were given the opportunity to list up to three major surprises, rating the impact of each. End points of the scale were: 5 ("This surprise had little or no impact on the project.") and 1 ("This surprise had a very severe negative impact on the project.").

3. **Impact of any missed deadlines**. Respondents were given the opportunity to list up to three missed deadlines, rating the impact of each. End points of the scale were: 5 ("This missed deadline had little or no impact on the project.") and 1 ("This missed deadline had a very severe negative impact on the project.").

4. **Degree and impact of cost overruns**. Respondents were given the opportunity to list up to three cost overruns, rating the impact of each. End points of the scale were: 5 ("This cost overrun had little or no impact on the project.") and 1 ("This cost overrun had a very severe negative impact on the project.").

5. **Was the project ever put into production?**[11] End points of the scale were: 5 ("Yes, the project was fully put into production usage.") and 1 ("No, no portion of the project was put into production usage.").

suffered no material time lost or expense due to third-party performance problems. This project attribute is, therefore, given a Project Outcome Correlation Rating of 20. A further explanation of each attribute is provided in the Study Results section of this article.

Literature Search

In February 1993 the study team initiated a literature search to determine if others had researched these issues. The database searched was a complete listing of 77,584 computer industry trade journal articles provided by *Computer Select*. The search results were distressing to say the least. Only four articles contained any substantive instruction on project management. The balance were on technology, products, corporate events, and so on.

In December 1993 we initiated a second literature search in the *Magazine Index Plus* database published by Infotrack. The search included 400 titles of business, technical, and general publications from 1990 to December 1993, covering over 647,000 citations. The results were much the same as the first search, yielding only a handful of articles addressing the topic of open systems project management. None of the articles presented significant depth or referred to more than five case studies from which conclusions were drawn. We are, in general, critical of the current treatment of this topic in the management literature. Conclusions based on questionable *industry experts* and anecdotal evidence were rampant.

Project management gets very little media attention. It seems that journalists are more interested in writing about technology than basic managerial issues such as project management. The media's poor treatment of open systems project management was a significant motivating factor behind the completion of this study.

Study Qualificctions

The study team presents this information as generally valid and reliable but less than perfect in a true scientific/statistical sense. The reader is offered the following cautions:

- To our knowledge, this is the first open systems project management study of any depth or substance. Projects are, by their very nature, unique, and this study is a pioneering effort in a very subjective discipline. Due to the limited resources of a privately funded study, the study team decided to forge ahead and try to produce something meaningful, if less than perfect. It is hoped that time and resources will permit a more scientific treatment of the subject in the future.

- The questionnaires were completed individually by the study team rather than handled on a mail or telephone basis. The survey forms were based on project records and the direct personal involvement of the author with each individual project. Of the sixty-two projects, the author had direct managerial responsibilities in sixty and peripheral responsibilities in two. Every effort was made to remove subjectivity, but the common factor of a single person cannot be ignored. On the positive side, each measurement recorded in the study was subjected to the personal scrutiny of the author. This yielded a consistent measurement of project attributes and the opinion of a practicing professional regarding any areas of ambiguity. The result is probably more accurate than a mail-in study or telephone study conducted by non-professionals.

- While every effort was made to reduce project issues to tangible measures, it should be pointed out that some difficulties were encountered. The POC Ratings noted with an asterisk were combined or clarified by the study team to reflect their relative importance within the context of other results. While this introduces some subjectivity, the study team felt that clarity and succinctness were of greater value.

- A greater sample set would have been preferred, but the emerging nature of open systems and the nature of privately funded research limited the practical scope.

- The results of these projects probably have an optimistic bias. The author was materially involved in the project management of all but two of these projects. Less experienced project managers would not achieve the same results.

- A control group was not possible.

The project team chose to limit the conclusions to sixteen project success attributes. These attributes were demonstrated as common among fifteen or more successful projects. Many trends and observations were omitted from the study due to absence of definitive data but are referenced in the Additional Observations section of this article.

Study Results

Project Success Attributes and Project Outcome Correlation

Following is a description of some of the relevant observations surrounding each POC Rating.

1. Third party accountability (POC Rating: 20). The successful project teams kept a tight reign on third parties. They recognized that open systems projects tend to involve multiple parties and insisted on clear, measurable commitments. The measurements applied to third-party performance tended to be broken down into finite, understandable milestones (commonly called a work breakdown structure).[12]

The successful project teams recognized that third parties have a profit motive that acts as a double-edged sword. On the positive side, third parties are motivated and often fiercely competitive. On the negative side, the project manager must remember that third parties have a profit motive to keep labor costs down. In the unsuccessful projects, third parties often skipped tasks and requirements. If the project manager only planned and managed at a high level, she had little basis for monitoring and controlling third-party performance. The successful project teams exerted the effort necessary to verify that the third party had both the capacity and commitment to perform as promised. Further information on third-party defaults is presented in the Additional Observations section of this article.

2. Up-front reconciliation of objectives, scope, deadlines, expectations, budgets, and who will do what, when, and how (POC Rating: 19*). This issue emerged so frequently that the study team combined several questions and ranked this attribute according to its overall importance. The primary mistake made by the unsuccessful project teams was to *charge ahead* with a new technology or concept without reconciling these key issues. This would result in projects that appear to start well but quickly suffer from some of the following symptomatic problems. Midway through, the project team would often find that:

- Overall project objective seems unclear or is changing frequently.
- The project's scope is way beyond anything realistically attainable.
- Deadlines have been arbitrarily set and represent no basis in reality.
- User and management expectations are so high that *Star Trek* Commander Data couldn't meet them on a good day.
- Project budgets are exhausted with no chance of completing the project.
- It is unclear *who* is responsible for individual tasks and objectives, so work progress is spotty and uncontrolled, particularly regarding third parties.
- Regarding *what* will be done, project delays and problems have caused the project team and management to reduce the scope of what will be delivered by the project.
- Regarding *when*, schedules have been delayed several times, and actual completion appears as a distant fog on the horizon.
- Regarding *how*, it is discovered that a key technology component is unable to do what it was expected to do, and the entire project is jeopardized. (See Bleeding Edge Technology project attribute for more information.)

All of these common open systems project problems are *symptoms* of failing to balance and reconcile these key issues before the organization is committed to the project. Nearly every negative outcome in the entire study can be attributed to shortcuts or omissions in this area. The successful project teams consistently showed the discipline to effectively manage these issues up-front.

3. Resource[13] skills (POC Rating: 18). Having highly skilled people on the project team may seem obvious, but the best project teams put reliability and the ability to make progress on objectives ahead of technical brilliance. The successful project teams consistently planned for the technical skills needed and resisted having a person assigned to the project simply because he was available. Many of the successful project teams were composed of solid *worker bees*, with the technical *gurus* brought in from outside as needed. Effective project management tended to reduce the need for gurus because fewer crises were encountered.

4. Clarity of objectives through the entire project (POC Rating: 18). It is easy to start a project with a clear vision. To hold to those objectives when half of the project team has turned over and the company just laid off 20 percent of its employees is another matter entirely.

The successful projects tended to be based on strong business cases showing large paybacks. Because these projects were vital to the organization, they tended to survive the many challenges and obstacles encountered. There is a case to be made for not doing projects that have less dramatic paybacks. Adversity will come with open systems projects, and those projects without solid paybacks risk falling victim.

There is a school of thought that claims that open systems are *enabling* technologies. Its adherents believe that management should deploy client/server and Unix systems based on the assumption that productivity and functional gains will be enabled by the new technology. We strongly resist this concept and suspect that the concept is rooted in vendor rhetoric and personal agendas. While it is possible to cite isolated exceptions, the successful projects put significant effort into defining the *right* objectives for projects and sticking with them.

5. Network platform issues managed closely enough to prevent material time and cost loss (POC Rating: 18). Most of the *misery of choice*[14] and *exponential complexity*[15] of open systems projects can be attributed to the newness of the network platform. The successful projects turned a skeptical eye to vendor claims and, instead, compartmentalized risks by means of pilot projects. The top projects exhibited a common attribute of being able to discern which

elements of the computing platform could create delays and incur costs. These issues were then managed very closely. The technical breakdown structure (TBS)[16] thought process was used beforehand to think through *which* technical component will accomplish *what* technical tasks and *how* those assumptions can be validated.

6. Quality of technical approach (POC Rating: 18). Strong technical solutions were common to the top projects, but the emphasis remained on how the technology benefits the business. An objective of this study was to weigh the relative importance of technology against other management priorities. The study team concluded that projects that prioritize business benefits and effective management also tend to exhibit strong technology. It appeared that vendor motivations and the personal agendas of those associated with the project[17] were sufficient to ensure an emphasis on using the latest and best technology. Please refer to the section, Technology Focus versus Project Management Focus, in the Additional Observations portion of this study for more information.

Technical considerations that were prioritized by the top project teams included compatibility with present and future standards, absence of proprietary traps, stability, performance under load, and verifiability of vendor claims.

7. Application software issues carried top priority throughout the project and were effectively managed (POC Rating: 18). The top projects operated on the basis that "application software meeting business needs is all that really counts." Top application issues consistently performed well in these projects included:

- Quality of decision process: Was the choice of software based on solid thinking and due consideration of all key issues? Or was it the *path of least resistance*? Did personal or political agendas negatively affect the quality of decision-making? Did the decision makers have adequate experience?
- Development effort: Was the development effort planned and directed by experienced people? Was it based on solid tools and environments? Did it include the key elements of user involvement, process definition, design, coding, user feedback, and full testing?
- Application package fit: Did the choice of software package reflect the complete needs of the business processes affected? Were the users materially involved? Was there sufficient reason to believe that the software would work as promised?
- Implementation: Was the implementation part of a logical progression of steps based on solid methodology and experienced people? Did the implementation address all key risk areas and result in a smooth transition into production usage?
- Training: Was the training planned and provided for proactively? Did it provide both system and application training? Were the users able to use the system effectively after the training?

The top projects maintained the application focus throughout the project, even though compromises, tradeoffs, and adjustments were common.

8. Managerial priorities balanced between scope, deadlines, quality of outcome, cost, and technology (POC Rating: 18). The media, vendor rhetoric, and a shortage of time often combine to skew management's priority balance. The top projects consistently showed a balanced (if painful) recognition that trying to do "too much, too quickly, for too little money" puts the entire project at risk. A frequently observed problem among the unsuccessful projects was an overemphasis on technology and the low cost of technology. A project would gain momentum from vendor or individual rhetoric. Management would become interested because of the apparent low cost and high capabilities. Management would then allocate some monetary figure and assign a deadline. Scope, expectations, and qualitative issues would only be addressed in the later stages of the project when they became problems. The result was often disastrous. The successful project teams consistently showed a balance in these key areas throughout the project.

9. *Bleeding edge* technology contained, resulting in minimal time and cost loss (POC Rating: 17). A general rule emerged regarding new technology among the top projects. The project teams would resist using any new product or release of software unless it had been in the field six months and reference checks could be made. If a new technology was absolutely vital to the project, it would be put into a pilot test environment and thoroughly checked. Management was

kept informed that a potential risk existed and was given the opportunity to weigh the risks and rewards. The unsuccessful projects frequently blamed delays and increased costs on technology problems that would have been prevented had the recommendations of this study been available and followed.

10. Planning process identified all of the key steps, hardware, and software such that no material credibility, time, or cost was lost (POC Rating: 16). This was the acid test of effective planning. Some argue that open systems projects are so volatile that it is not possible to effectively plan. The top projects demonstrated that it is possible to identify all of the key steps and major hardware/software cost factors during planning. It should be noted that the top project teams did not plan the projects down to the micro-level of detail but used the WBS and TBS concepts to plan down to an effective level. Effectiveness was measured by the absence of material omissions.

11. Controls appropriate for risk and magnitude of project (POC Rating: 15). The successful projects consistently exhibited effective control mechanisms. The unsuccessful projects largely avoided controls (either through ignorance or apathy). Some effective controls included:

- using project managers with sufficient experience to know the difference between controls that are too loose and too tight
- identifying specific tasks to be completed by team members and holding them accountable for progress on those tasks
- contracts with third parties requiring specific performance by specific dates
- material involvement from executive sponsor with weekly reporting structure.

It must be remembered that people and vendors generally dislike controls being placed on them, yet the absence of these controls is clearly linked to major project problems. The successful project teams exhibited a proactive approach to designing and instituting control methods because it is often difficult or impossible to insert controls once a project is under way. A significant barometer of adequate authority for the project team is whether or not the team can enforce its agreed-upon controls. See the project success attribute Project Manager Responsibility/Authority Mix and Experience Level for more information.

12. Expectations managed effectively, including technology capabilities, relative effort, flexibility, implementation length, and ease of use (POC Rating: 15*). The successful project teams recognized that a variety of factors conspire to create an environment where people hear what they want to hear about a new technology or concept. These factors include the media, advertising, vendor rhetoric, and personal agendas.[17] Additionally, many people are under the illusion that mission-critical applications involving many people can be implemented as easily as personal computer (PC) productivity tools. The top project teams diligently worked to contain expectations with both the users and management. This issue requires proactive attention early in the project because it is very difficult to modify expectations after agreements have been reached by senior people. A common trap is for senior management to consider these expectation issues to be *delegatable details*. The result would often be projects that could not possibly meet the expectations of the senior managers who had funded them.

The successful project teams insisted on material involvement from the executive sponsor, and one of his primary roles was the management of the expectations of other senior managers in the organization. Absence of this executive sponsor involvement was often linked to negative project outcomes.

13. Project hours devoted to project management (POC Rating: 15*). Most of the successful projects devoted between 6 and 15 percent of the total project hours to planning, project management, and control. Many devoted significantly more than 15 percent. At less than 6 percent, a significant correlation is seen with negative project outcomes.

Where is all this time spent? If the reader will think through the activity level needed to act on the recommendations in this study, the answer becomes obvious. A commonly observed pitfall of the unsuccessful projects was the assumption that technologists were the only ones who really contribute, whereas project managers are simply *overhead*. Many organizations in the study paid a large price for that point of view, and one of our main goals in pursuing this research is to develop statistically sound data to refute this erroneous assumption.

14. Conceptual gaps (POC Rating: 15*). The successful projects did not permit significant conceptual gaps in the technical solution. They consistently exhibited the discipline and patience necessary to validate the conceptual approach *before* committing to the project. The technical breakdown structure (TBS) concept is intended to force the project team to think through the technical concepts and identify missing or undervalidated technical components.

One of the unsuccessful projects found out about a conceptual gap the hard way. The project required daily downloads of large amounts of data. Two-thirds of the way through the project it was discovered that these downloads would require forty hours each and every day! Since the technology chosen could not operate within a normal twenty-four-hour workday, the project stalled and ultimately produced little benefit.

15. Internal resource skills and availability (POC Rating: 15*). The top projects exhibited an accurate assessment of internal resources' skills and availability. They recognized that organizations often exhibit irrational assumptions about internal resources because they are perceived to be free. The successful projects resisted the temptation to settle for these resources. They defended their decisions by breaking the project down into *who* will do *what*, *when*, and *how*. The *when* and *what* questions address the actual workload, and the *how* question asks if the resource has the skills to do the tasks. Again, the work breakdown structure (WBS) efforts aided in lobbying for the right resources because the amount of work and skills needed are clearly defined.

16. Project manager responsibility/authority mix and experience level (POC Rating: 15*). This item is most difficult to measure but may rank among the most important. It was observed that the top project managers consistently demonstrated two key items in common:

1. They had experience managing two or more open systems projects of progressively increasing magnitude.

2. They were *empowered* to control the course, nature, and priorities of the project. The study team attempted to quantify authority and responsibility with 100 percent representing complete responsibility/authority and 0 percent representing none. Sixty-five percent became the study team's choice to represent a breakpoint. Recognizing that this is somewhat arbitrary, we request that the reader internalize this general concept: "If a project manager held substantially more than half of the authority and personal responsibility for a project, that project tended to perform significantly better than projects where this was not the case."

Some tests that determine the true level of authority include whether the project manager can:

- stop the project
- affect expectations, scope, and budgets
- choose or dismiss team members
- make decisions and operate openly for the good of the project without fear of recrimination.

This issue is most clearly identified by the symptoms shown by projects with an inadequate authority/responsibility mix for the project manager. In these cases it is common to find that the project manager is midway through the project, knows what needs to be done, and simply cannot exercise sufficient authority to do it. Frequently the project manager will become the scapegoat for all project problems when the real fault lies with her management for ignoring the issues presented in this study. The overall recommendation from this project success attribute is to use experienced open systems project managers, vest them with sufficient authority, and see that they remain personally responsible for the project.

Additional Observations

A number of other observations evolved from the study. These are not necessarily based on hard data but, rather, consistently appeared as important issues across multiple projects. They include:

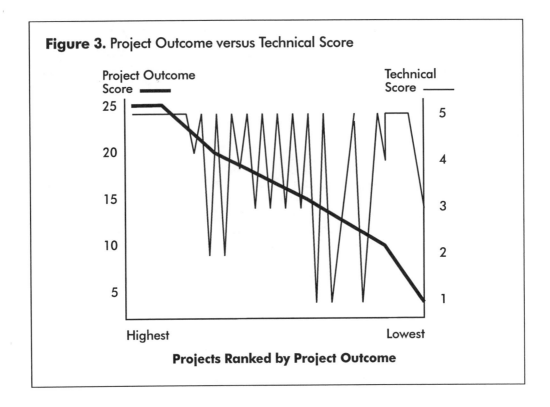

Figure 3. Project Outcome versus Technical Score

Technology Focus versus Project Management Focus. Which is the greater contributor to positive project outcomes? Figure 3 shows the correlation between overall project outcome score and the project's technical score. Note that many projects had excellent technical scores yet produced average or poor project outcome ratings. Note also that several projects had poor technical ratings but produced average or above average project outcomes. It is most distressing to note the large number of projects with very poor project outcomes and excellent technical scores. This may be attributable to a false sense of security generated by the excellent technology.

Figure 4 shows a very close relationship between project management score and positive project outcomes. The relationship appears strong, even considering the imprecision of this study.

In contrasting technical excellence and project management, the study team makes the firm conclusion that effective project management is directly linked to positive project outcomes while technical elegance shows only a minor correlation. *The overwhelming recommendation is for managers to downplay the technical aspect and focus on identifying and executing the correct project management tasks.*

Misery of Choice. A major strength of open systems is great flexibility with a multitude of choices. We estimate that a typical 100-workstation local area network (LAN) running a mission-critical application will:

1. Require over 180 material decisions.
2. Force choices among sixty-eight products.
3. Require management of nearly 300 major variables.

This will tend to force the project team into a pattern of *exponential complexity* and *misery of choice*. The consistently successful projects investigated these major issues early, made solid decisions, and strongly resisted changing those decisions without material reason.

Bias from the Vendors, the Media, and the Personal Computer's Ease of Use. Advertising and the media have created many misperceptions about success with open systems.

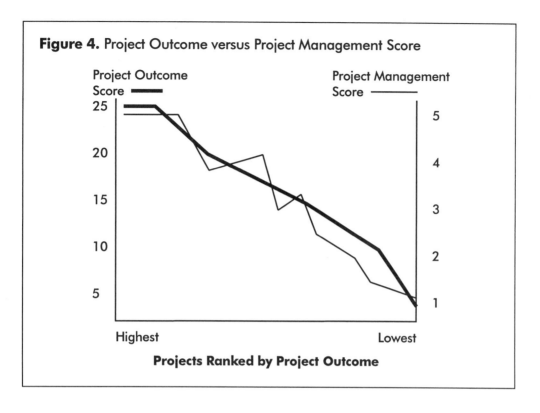

Figure 4. Project Outcome versus Project Management Score

Projects Ranked by Project Outcome

One reason this study was conducted was to generate quantitatively valid information to combat those misperceptions. The reader is encouraged to recognize the possible biases behind the media's articles and especially of advertisements.

Essential Minimums of Project Management. Many information systems (IS) professionals will recognize most of the sixteen project success attributes as issues addressed in traditional host-based projects. A key observation of the study was the need to manage open systems projects without the *perceived* bureaucracy and lethargy of traditional IS projects. The study team advocates reducing the normal overhead of project management to the key items mentioned herein *but remaining absolutely firm on requiring these essential minimums.*

Blinding Flash of the Obvious. As Tom Peters (co-author of *In Search of Excellence*) would observe, much of this material appears obvious and has been heard before. The real question is *can the project manager and executive sponsor sustain these priorities throughout the project?* Maintaining focus and requiring these essential minimums through the project conclusion is a consistent differentiator between positive and negative outcomes.

Third-Party Defaults. A large number of projects reported significant problems with third parties performing as promised. The shortfall was generally not attributed to deception or negative intent but rather the capacity to perform as promised. Key issues to verify regarding the capacity to perform include:

- Financial wherewithal: Has the third party's financial status been validated? Are any key exposures looming (such as litigation, major changes in technology, or the loss of a key customer)?
- Skills (technical and managerial): What basis exists for believing that the third party is technically capable of taking on the project? Is he strong in the areas of management seasoning and maturity, as well as technical areas? Is there a track record for bringing projects in on time, on budget, and performing as expected?
- Backlog of existing commitments: Could other customer commitments keep the third party from having the resources or attention span necessary to make promised deliveries?

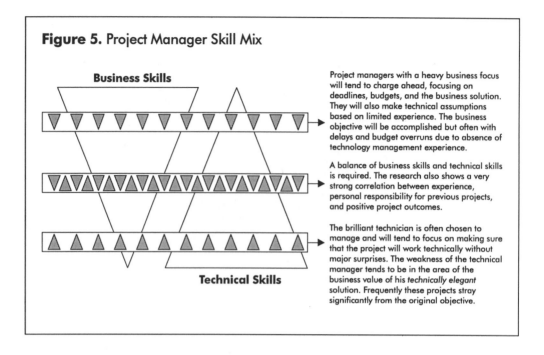

Figure 5. Project Manager Skill Mix

Business Skills

Project managers with a heavy business focus will tend to charge ahead, focusing on deadlines, budgets, and the business solution. They will also make technical assumptions based on limited experience. The business objective will be accomplished but often with delays and budget overruns due to absence of technology management experience.

A balance of business skills and technical skills is required. The research also shows a very strong correlation between experience, personal responsibility for previous projects, and positive project outcomes.

The brilliant technician is often chosen to manage and will tend to focus on making sure that the project will work technically without major surprises. The weakness of the technical manager tends to be in the area of the business value of his *technically elegant* solution. Frequently these projects stray significantly from the original objective.

Technical Skills

- Substance behind appearances: Sales efforts often focus on appearances and images. Have the depth and validity of third-party commitments been investigated? Is the project team being unduly swayed by images and *comfortable feelings*?

Industry-Specific Software Packages. Many projects reported that a narrowly defined, industry-specific application software package greatly contributed to successful outcomes. This is largely attributable to a good software fit, but an interesting side observation is the reduction in complexity and *misery of choice*. The application software limited the number of other options and variables because only specific configurations were supported. This allowed the organization to better focus on business and application priorities.

Just Do It. The *just do it* school of project management was frequently observed. Its adherents claim that PCs and open systems are so flexible and inexpensive that any barriers encountered downstream can be easily overcome. Study observations disagree and contend that these project managers are lazy and unwilling to put due diligence into the planning and management process. Watch for vague assurances that "we can do it" or "it will work." Open systems are dynamic and do experience change, but the successful projects consistently exhibited extensive up-front managerial effort before committing to the project.

Project Manager Qualifications. Figure 5 describes the balance needed between technical skills and business skills. Many projects in the study suffered from the *bright young person* (BYP) problem. The pattern is that a candidate for project manager demonstrates a technical aptitude in one or two areas and also projects a team spirit, enthusiasm, presentability, and so on. Remember the 180 material decisions affecting 300 variables? The senior manager has no background with which to appreciate the breadth of skills necessary to deal with this complexity. The sad outcome for many projects was that an executive pressed for time made a quick decision to put a BYP in charge, only to find that the project floundered in areas outside the direct experience of the BYP.

Prediction: more runaway projects will occur with open systems technologies than have generally been experienced with proprietary systems. The study points to the conclusion that project management is more critical in open systems projects than in traditional proprietary host projects. The standard for traditional projects is generally to have 10 to 15 percent of the

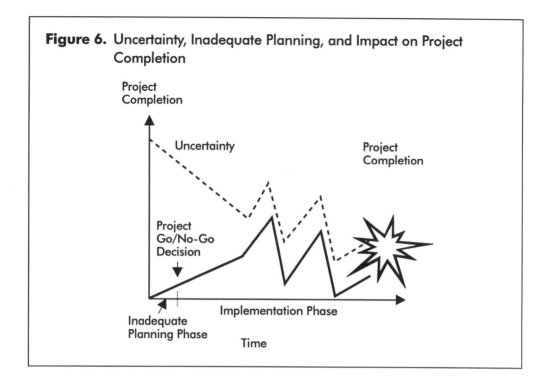

Figure 6. Uncertainty, Inadequate Planning, and Impact on Project Completion

project's resource budget devoted to project management. In practice, it has been rare to get more than 7 percent. We believe that the nature of open systems projects requires *even more project management*, but management and end-user expectations for open systems projects are almost universally counter to that reality. We predict that more projects will be initiated with insufficient project management than during the days of proprietary systems. This will result in substantial negative outcomes, runaway projects, and the need for project intervention.

Take the Time to Plan Effectively Before the Go/No-Go Decision. Many pressures exist that tend to force projects to move ahead quickly. The result is often an inadequate treatment of the issues described in this study, which are primarily planning issues. Figures 6 and 7 show the relationship between planning, uncertainty, and project completion. The primary value of planning is reducing uncertainty, and the research shows a direct link between reduced uncertainty and positive project outcomes.

Conclusion

Positive outcomes can be realized from open systems projects by learning from the experiences of others. The recommendations contained herein are the product of a large sample set and meaningful correlations. The reader is encouraged to resist anecdotal or biased recommendations while looking closely at the true motivations of those advocating certain technologies or solutions.

It is important to remember to keep technology in its proper place. By prioritizing the sixteen project success attributes and the other issues mentioned above, the reader has taken a major step forward in producing substantially improved open systems project outcomes.

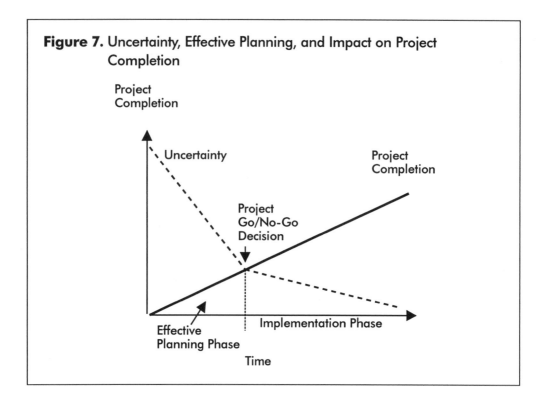

Figure 7. Uncertainty, Effective Planning, and Impact on Project Completion

Notes

1. Downsizing generally refers to moving software applications from big, proprietary computers *down* to smaller open systems computing environments.

2. Open systems generally refers to a series of new technologies including client/server, Unix, LANs, and personal computers. See the text section on Defining Open Systems or other notes for more information.

3. The research team came to this general conclusion very early in the study: "Roughly 70 percent of Open Systems projects will come in materially late, materially over budget or will fail to meet significant user expectations." The actual results regarding the sixty-two open systems projects in this study were (a) 57 percent of projects came in materially late, (b) 72 percent came in materially over budget, and (c) 88 percent failed to meet some significant user expectations. The study team's general statement is based on a blended, weighted average of these figures.

4. The study conducted by the London office of KPMG Peat Marwick regarding mainframe projects studied 252 organizations and found that (a) 33 percent of projects came in materially late, (b) 48 percent came in materially over budget, and (c) 56 percent failed to meet some significant user expectations. The study team derived a blended, weighted average general statement as follows: "Roughly 40 percent of Mainframe projects will come in materially late, materially over budget, or will fail to meet significant user expectations." This consolidation of Peat Marwick's data is intended for comparison purposes only.

5. Client/server generally refers to the new realm of technology that is based on a PC or other intelligent workstation rather than the traditional dumb terminal. The *client*, or intelligent workstation, does most of its own processing and is provided data from various servers (large computers) on the network.

6. Unix is the commonly used term for a set of operating system software originally developed by AT&T's Bell Labs. It is considered an *open* operating system because applications developed on one Unix machine can generally be transported to a different Unix machine with relatively little effort.

7. Local area networks (LANs) are computer communication networks that generally are contained in a single building and connect PCs or other intelligent workstations with other computers.

8. PMI feedback was provided by Dave Reinmuth, Dallas PMI Chapter president.

9. Study input provided by Greg Smith, State of Texas Board of Insurance; Mary Lou Blumenfeld, KPMG Peat Marwick; Jim Ingram, Marion Merrill Dow Corporation; Doug Brown, Computer Task Group; Tim Ingram, Federal Government Department of Justice; Jack Ledbetter, Novell Corporation; Jay VanDerLeest, Dun & Bradstreet Software; and Keith Farr, Dun & Bradstreet Software. A special thanks is due to each of these professionals for their input and support.

10. A wide area network (WAN) is generally defined as a computer communications network that spans buildings, cities, or countries.

11. *Production* usage of an information systems project refers to usage of the completed project in the mainstream of the business rather than in a test or development mode.

12. Work breakdown structure (WBS) is a concept championed by the Project Management Institute. The WBS concept advocates breaking down large projects and subprojects into discreet, measurable work components. WBS requires effort during planning stages but yields significant payoffs in cost estimating, scheduling, quality management, on-time completion, accountability, and actual cost measurement.

13. *Resources* refers to personnel assigned to the project.

14. *Misery of choice* refers to the overwhelming number of choices available for each component of an open systems project. The task of choosing between all these options is both wonderful and burdensome.

15. *Exponential complexity* refers to the complexity generated by the large number of variables in an open systems project. Details regarding the magnitude of these variables can be found in the *Misery of Choice* section under Additional Observations.

16. Technical breakdown structures (TBS) are similar to work breakdown structures (see note 12) in that the objective is to break high-level issues into manageable subunits. TBS facilitates the process of planning through *which* technical component will accomplish *what* technical tasks and *how* those assumptions can be validated. TBS involves significant effort and diligence but produces enormous paybacks by preventing serious project technical problems. Absence of a TBS thought process was consistently observed in the projects that failed or were significantly delayed due to technical reasons.

17. Nine Management Guidelines for Better Cost Estimating, Al Lederer, et al.; *Communications of the ACM*, February 1992. In this article, Lederer describes his conclusions regarding personal agendas and their implications for projects and project estimating. He concludes that nearly everyone in the organization has some vested interest in being associated with new technology initiatives. These motivations run the spectrum from résumé building for technologists to personal prestige and visibility for user managers. Lederer introduces a *political motivation model* for examining why projects and estimates so frequently go awry. The study team agrees with his conclusions and urges the reader to closely examine the motivations of those advocating technology solutions.

APPENDIX D

Literature Search Results

The literature search for the original study is described in Appendix C. From 1994 through 1996 several additional literature searches were conducted. Following is a list of all sources consulted for the literature search.

- *Whitaker's Books in Print* (1993)
- *World Cat* catalog of books and magazines, online service provided by Online Computer Library Center, Inc., Dublin, Ohio, United States (1994 edition), featuring thirty million worldwide citations
- *Subject Guide to Books in Print, 1993–94,* R. R. Bowker, Reed Reference Publishing
- *Computer Select* online database, 77,7584 citations (1994 edition)
- *Magazine Index Plus* online database published by Infotrack, 647,000 citations (1994 edition)
- *The 1995 Proceedings for the Annual Seminar/Symposium of the Project Management Institute*
- *Compact Disclosure* online database (1996 edition)

The Literature Search Results.
- Over 11,000 project management citations
- Seventy-nine project management books
- Eleven project management books specifically for information systems
- One book on the management of client/server and open systems projects

Conclusions from the Literature Search.

1. Literature for the early stages of the client/server and open systems revolution has focused on technology and products, just as the mainframe and minicomputer markets did in the early years.

2. The information that has been published on client/server project management has generally been:
- too technical to be of use to executives and shareholders seeking to solve root problems
- generally written by journalists rather than practitioners
- drawing conclusions and recommendations from anecdotal information.

3. The general information published on project management tends to be of little use to the shareholder or executive. It tends to focus on the technical aspects of advanced project management techniques and loses the shareholder/executive audience in the process.

(Note: Several exceptions to the above generalities were identified and were typically of great value in developing this book. The reader will note references to these items throughout the text.)

Generally speaking, it appears that no other significant body of literature has been published that addresses the need of shareholders and executives to identify and solve the root problems of client/server projects.

A Cost of Quality Questionnaire

Cost of Quality Root Issue Questionnaire

Case ID: _____   Organization Name: _____

Industry: _____   Data Source: _____

Project Type: _____

Original Project Objectives (which justified funding) _____

_____

Project Outcome: _____

_____

Original Project Budget: $_____ (including hardware, software, and internal and external labor)

Project Final Total Cost: $_____ (either actual total cost, if known, or best estimate, including hardware, software, and internal and external labor)

Estimate of Wasted Project Costs: $_____ (The difference between original budget and final budget is considered waste because the project objectives were originally promised for the original budget. Also, include other wasted costs, if known. If the project was canceled, the entire total cost spent is considered waste.)

Describe Any Unrealized Project Objectives: (primarily lost incremental revenues or unrealized cost savings)

_____

_____

Estimated Costs of Unrealized Project Objectives: $_____

Total Estimated Cost of Quality: $_____ (add wasted project costs to the cost of unrealized objectives)

Project Root Issue Checklist

Check Any of the Following Problems That Were Present
(Attach Explanation Separately)

Objectivity:

- ❏ Will the business case for doing the project stand objective cost/benefit scrutiny?
- ❏ Scope, deliverable, and objective definition: Were scope and deliverables broken into controllable, defined work packages (less than forty hours each) prior to approval for the execution phase?
- ❏ Were budgets objectively set based on scope, available resources, and timeline?
- ❏ Were schedules and deadlines objectively set?
- ❏ Did objective, solid thinking that will stand third party review lead to the solution design?
- ❏ Were the resource requirements, availability, and assignment developed objectively?

Right People/Right Motives/Right Actions:

Regarding the executives (top executive, initial sponsor, subsequent sponsor(s), peer executives):
- ❏ Were they the right people for the project?
- ❏ Did they appear to have the right motives?
- ❏ Were their actions correct?

Regarding middle managers (business unit, information systems):
- ❏ Were they the right people for the project?
- ❏ Did they appear to have the right motives?
- ❏ Were their actions correct?

Regarding the front-line people (business process and requirements people, estimators/designers, users, technical people):
- ❏ Were they the right people for the project?
- ❏ Did they appear to have the right motives?
- ❏ Were their actions correct?

Externals (consultants, contractors, hardware/software suppliers):
- ❏ Were they the right people for the project?
- ❏ Did they appear to have the right motives?
- ❏ Were their actions correct?

Authority/Responsibility Match (for Project Manager) Root Issue Problems:

Was the project manager's sign-off required for:
- ❏ initial scope/deliverables
- ❏ deadlines
- ❏ budget
- ❏ scope changes (even from powerful people)
- ❏ stopping the project?

Did the project manager have the following direct project team authorities:
- ❑ hire/fire
- ❑ assignments
- ❑ incentive compensation control
- ❑ capacity to deal with resisters or detractors
- ❑ ability to hold employees/contractors/outsiders from other functional areas accountable for the commitments given by their respective executives?

❑ Was the project manager's authority and support from upper management visible (e.g., reporting level, face time with executives, the ability to correct erroneous expectations, and so on)?

❑ Did the project manager's chain of command compromise his ability to conduct the project in the best interests of the shareholders?

❑ Could the project manager be arbitrarily removed from the project if she stood up for the good of the project when a powerful person wanted something different?

❑ Did the project manager's responsibilities outside the project compromise his effectiveness?

❑ Did the organization reward or penalize the project manager fairly for doing the right things? (Did the project manager believe it?)

Accountability Root Issue Problems:

❑ Did general safeguards exist to ensure that people were held to their responsibilities in the areas of:
- ❑ objectivity
- ❑ right people/right motives/right actions
- ❑ authority/responsibility for the project manager?

❑ Did a *safety valve* exist to escalate significant project problems high enough to ensure that no agenda other than the good of the shareholder prevailed?

❑ Could a project team member initiate that safety valve without fear of short- or long-term reprisal?

❑ Did the executive sponsor(s) truly have accountability for the parts of the project under their control? Could they avoid responsibility if things went wrong? Would the organization truly reward them for doing the right things and penalize them for doing the wrong things?

Issues for Field Testing and Further Research

Will Department of Defense earned value predictors for projects hold in the client/server commercial sector? In reengineering projects? In product development projects?

Can we implement the controls called for with an acceptable overhead and without constraining innovation?

A hypothetical business case for implementing these recommendations is provided in Section 4.4. Can this be validated?

What are the best organization models for supporting effective client/server, reengineering, and product development projects?

A pivotal component of these recommendations includes the intervention of shareholders and third party monitoring. Is this really necessary? What are the project cost-of-quality patterns for organizations with and without these attributes?

What are the best sustainable results for reduced project cost of quality?

Is a fast-track approach possible, or will this type of change require long-term investments similar to other quality initiatives?

Can we demonstrate a link between reduced project cost of quality and improved shareholder returns and stock price?

Do client/server projects attract a certain executive profile (both on customer and vendor/consultant sides)? Is this type of person attracted to jobs where image and impressions are highly valued but accountability is limited?

What are the measurable criteria that will predict whether leaders will tend to put their self-interest above the good of the shareholder?

What are the best available techniques (consistent with the above recommendations) for delivering business results in six months or less?

An Overview of the Differences between Mainframe and Client/Server Computer Systems

To understand these differences, let's take another look at the first research summary in Appendix A. This summary is a deliberate attempt to contrast the effectiveness of client/server projects against the more mature, stable technology of mainframes. To restate the bottom line:

- Roughly 70 percent of client/server projects will come in materially late, materially over budget, or will fail to meet significant user expectations.
- Roughly 40 percent of mainframe projects will come in materially late, materially over budget, or will fail to meet significant user expectations.

It is not surprising to find that a new technology area such as client/server is more risky than a mature technology such as mainframe computers. It is surprising to see a 40 percent failure rate in a supposedly stable technology area. The real questions that we need to ask are:

- Why do mainframe projects still fail 40 percent of the time when we've had thirty years to learn how to do them?
- Thirty years from now, will client/server projects still be failing 40 percent of the time?
- Could it be that the technology is not the root problem?

We will quite likely find that the technical differences between client/server and mainframes are smaller than the similarities. Nevertheless, following are areas where some differences between the two can be identified.

Expectations. The media, the vendors, and the ease of doing certain tasks with personal computers have combined to create a general set of expectations that Superman with a Cray computer could not meet on a good day. From front-line users to chief executives and board members, these expectations frequently run tenfold ahead of reality. The research identified six key areas where these expectations tend to run dramatically higher than the traditional mainframe environment: 1) technology capabilities; 2) ease of use; 3) flexibility; 4) relative effort; 5) time to implement; and 6) cost of expert services (either internal or external) is expected to be as relatively low as the cost of hardware and software

If we can check to make sure that our expectations are grounded in reality in these areas, everyone will benefit.

Executive Distance. Most senior managers have a working understanding of mainframe systems. They have a reasonably accurate understanding of what is *doable* and roughly how long it will take. The client/server environment is an altogether different matter.

As discussed in Sections 2.3 and 2.4, many factors combine to keep managers from really understanding client/server project issues. Due to staff reductions and downsizing, senior managers have more responsibilities than ever and less time for technical details. The personal

---

Table 11. Misery of Choice and Exponential Complexity

One Hundred Workstation Mainframe Project versus One Hundred Workstation Client/Server Project

Research Conducted by: FAOSP Group, Carrollton, Texas.

Sample Size and Type: Compare theoretical one hundred workstation mainframe accounting system project to theoretical one hundred workstation client/server accounting system project.

Study Purpose: Understand key differences.

Key Findings

	Mainframe	Client/Server
Major Decisions Required	110	145
Major Variables	147	296
Number of Major Products to Evaluate and Choose between	24	68

---

learning curve required to bring an executive to the same level of knowledge in client/server that she possessed in mainframes is staggering and, for all but a few, completely unattainable. The research team observed that some executives actively distanced themselves from any attempt at learning the new systems. They placed project managers or other scapegoats between themselves and responsibility.

Misery of Choice and Exponential Complexity. Table 11 is an attempt to show the large number of choices and decisions that must be considered with client/server. We can see that, as a practical matter, the client/server system has approximately twice the complexity.

User Involvement/Ownership. In the eighties it became clearly evident that users need to be involved in the project process. In practice, however, this involvement was often cursory. Client/server projects not only tend toward substantially more user involvement, the users frequently own the project! They also tend to choose their own personal computer tools and take a great deal of responsibility for report development and screen design and development. If information systems professionals are not sufficiently responsive, the users frequently can get the authority to proceed on their own.

Mission-critical projects tend to be cross departmental. Client/server projects accelerate that trend and bring several additional considerations into play. Information systems must now cope with the (real or imagined) departmental expert. Because this expert is looking out for the interests of the user department, user department executives now have much better information on alternatives, options, and controls. Client/server has prospered partly due to this increased sense of control for line executives.

Due to the consistently poor results of information systems (IS) departments completing projects on time and within budget, many progressive organizations are insisting that the user department *own* the project. The user department is then responsible for project management and strategy, drawing on the IS department and contractors for technical resources. Although the jury is still out on this concept, early results are promising. Active user ownership seems to cut through many of the hidden problems encountered during projects.

Inexperienced User Executives Are Often Driving the Project. Unfortunately, there is a downside to the trend toward business units driving projects. Those in charge are often not very experienced in project issues, particularly on larger scale endeavors. This may be a factor in the leadership integrity issue discussed in Section 2.2.7. It may be that these inexperienced managers put their own interests ahead of the corporation's, and this is at least partly due to ignorance. Whatever the cause, it is clear that the trend toward business unit-driven projects carries a risk of inexperienced leadership.

Competition for Information Services. Client/server has created competition for internal information systems departments. The user departments were formerly at the mercy of the information systems department's monopoly. Client/server creates a very real possibility that the user department may be able to do the application substantially on its own. Internal information systems (IS) departments have responded just the same as any other monopoly has responded to increased competition. When the shock, horror, and denial have worn off, information systems departments have recognized the need to improve services to users and reduce cost structure. Just as, in the long run, competition is healthy for monopolies, competition created by client/server and user department initiatives will ultimately bring benefit to the corporation.

Vendor Activities. Now that the vendors are generally free to make their cases to individual user departments, the opportunity for bias and unattainable expectations has increased dramatically. Having been on the vendor side, I would emphasize that the pressures involved in multi-hundred-thousand and multi-million dollar procurements are unbelievable. Project managers and executive project sponsors should not be surprised at any legal or illegal tactic that a vendor might attempt.

The primary focus of most vendor efforts will be a top-down effort to sell their solutions to user department executives. Their credibility and resources are often formidable. They can often bring to bear expertise in functional areas that in-house personnel are hard pressed to match. Nonetheless, the project manager and executive sponsor must be continually watching for vendor influence that can skew the effective project balance.

The Traditional Information Systems Department *View* of Projects. For those who have built their careers in mainframe-driven information systems departments, 99 percent of the work involved in new projects comes from the software effort (analysis, software development, and/or package implementation). These mainframe projects take place in a stable environment with known tools. *Client/server* projects are an entirely different mix of issues. Approximately 50 percent of the effort goes to the software issues while the balance of the project work is directed at platform design, compatibility issues, interfaces to other open technologies, learning a host of new tools, learning about the new platforms, and getting the environment stabilized.

For IS professionals, this results in an extreme departure from comfortable known territory. Results can range from arrogance and presumption to fear and a lethargic response to user needs due to perceived risks.

Current Climate of Understaffing. Again, as described in Sections 2.3 and 2.4, downsizing, rightsizing, layoffs, and reengineering have created a climate where most people have more to do and less time to do it in. One of the overwhelming conclusions from the research is that the root causes of client/server project problems are not visible and not readily preventable. The nature of this climate of understaffing substantially exacerbates the problems because they can only be prevented through experience, professionalism, due diligence, and attention to root issues.

Conclusion. While the technical differences between client/server and mainframe projects have some importance, the larger issues have more to do with the changing business climate and the underlying root issues of project management. This summary of differences is intended as one more way to help the reader understand the necessity of the recommendations and principles described in Section 5.

List of Reviewers and Contributors

Al Leder, University of Oakland, Rochester, Michigan, United States
Ben Settle, Infotech Management
Bert Canella, Texas A&M, Department of Management
Bill Redmond, formerly of ARCO
Brad Bass, Hewlett-Packard
Charlie Jones, Robbins Gioia
Dan Williams, Williams Investigations, formerly with the Texas Department of Public Safety
Dick Woodman, Texas A&M, Department of Management
Eric Jenett, formerly of Brown & Root
Erwin Martinez, formerly of Computer Sciences Corp.
Fran Webster, formerly of Project Management Institute
Garland Lawerence, formerly of Central Louisiana Electric
Hal Finley, Texas Instruments
Helen Cooke, Project Management Institute
Herb Stortz, Cambridge Technology Partners
Howard Chamberlain, Texas A&M, Department of Management
Jay VanDerLeest, formerly of Dun & Bradstreet Software
Jeff Pawlik
Jerry Rose, Hallelujah Designs
Jim Ingram, Celertis Technologies
Joe Christian, The Teamsters
Joe Miller, formerly of EDS
John Abernathy, Triton Energy
John Miller, John Miller Associates
Lew Ireland, Project Technologies Corp.
Lindsey Thomas, formerly of Frito Lay
Lynne Markus, Claremont Graduate School of Business, California, United States
Mary Lou Blumenfeld, formerly of Peat Marwick
Mike Korotka, formerly of Blue Cross/Blue Shield of Wisconsin, United States
Nathan Griffin
Paul Strauss, Ph.D., Human Resource Associates
Quentin Fleming, Fleming Associates
Stan Feighny, Database Consultants
Tim Ingram, National Animal Disease Center, United States Government
Wyatt Dunn, formerly of Deliotte Touche

APPENDIX I

About the Author

Tom Ingram, PMP

Tom Ingram has been a pioneer on the front-line of client/server project management since 1983. Since then he has held managerial responsibility for more than seventy client/server projects. He and his project teams have delivered over $16 million in project contracts substantially on time, on budget, and as promised. These projects have generated at least $60 million in measured benefits for Ingram's clients. Ingram is equally quick to point out that there have been many failures as well. His passion for root issues, best practices, and client results is a product of both success and failure.

Ingram's employers and clients include such notable firms as Xerox, Sperry Univac, United Telecom, Dun & Bradstreet, Texas Instruments, Frito Lay, MCI, Cleanese, the City of Fort Worth, and the State of Texas. Ingram has also worked with small and medium sized firms, including running his own firm for two-and-a-half years.

Some additional career highlights include multi-million dollar project turnarounds, significant reengineering successes, developing a technical risk management methodology, Year 2000 project management, and some twenty-five lectures to universities and professional associations.

Ingram has published two bodies of original research on client/server computer projects. He has published numerous articles and has served as the client/server feature editor for the publications of the Project Management Institute.

Ingram resides in Carrollton, Texas, USA (a suburb of Dallas), where he continues to promote the improvement of project outcomes through consulting, research, best practices, writing, and lecturing. He may be contacted at the address in the front of this book or through the Project Management Institute.

APPENDIX J

A Summary of
Projects Studied by Industry

Following is a summary of the Horror Stories by industry. In general, no industry-specific trends were identified, in part due to the relatively small sample size.

Project-Driven Industries. You may note that Horror Stories 129, 120, 111, 116, 117, 124, 133, and 153 all took place in industries that are considered project driven rather than operations driven (see Section 3.1 for more information). Although we have seen that project-driven industries tend to be substantially better at executing projects, clearly they are not immune to client/server Horror Stories. In the cases where I had personal knowledge, it was very clear that the general disciplines of the project-driven industries were not applied. The fault is not in the techniques but rather in a lack of effective application of those techniques.

Table 12. A Summary of Projects Studied by Industry

Organization Name	Case ID	Industry	Total Estimated Cost of Quality
American Airlines (The Confirm Project)	101	Airline	$460,000,000
American Management Systems	113	Computer Software & Services	$2,000,000
Rogers Group	129	Construction	n/a
Andersen Consulting Internal Project	149	Consulting Services	n/a
Lockheed	120	Defense Contractor	$525,000
FoxMeyer Corp. (Delta Project)	155	Distribution	$25,000,000
Diamond Shamrock	111	Energy	$3,000,000
South-Central United States Retail Energy Products Firm	116	Energy	$250,000
South-Central United States Oil and Gas Firm #2	117	Energy	$475,000
South-Central United States Oil and Gas Firm #3	124	Energy	$50,000
Very Large Central United States Bank	107	Financial Services	$6,200,000
Fidelity Investments	154	Financial Services	$110,000,000
Nations Bank	115	Financial Services	$750,000
West Coast Savings and Loan	134	Financial Services	$1,500,000
Associates Financial	150	Financial Services	n/a
Federal Reserve Bank of Dallas	103	Government	$50,000,000
DFW Airport Board	108	Government	$3,000,000
Quasi-Governmental Agency	136	Government	$28,000,000
Federal Agency, Austin, Texas	140	Government	$300,000
Dallas/Fort Worth Area City Government	143	Government	$50,000
California Department of Motor Vehicles	151	Government	$95,000,000
East Coast Health Care Firm	105	Health Care	$10,000,000
East Coast Medical Testing Firm	157	Health Care	$1,800,000
PPP (Largest Health Insurance Provider in United Kingdom)	161	Insurance	$10,750,000
CIGNA	112	Insurance	$4,000,000
Midwestern Insurance Carrier	104	Insurance	$40,000,000
Dallas-Based Insurance Agency	119	Insurance	$300,000
Reinsurance Firm	135	Insurance	$200,000
Midwestern Reinsurance Firm	139	Insurance	$12,000,000
Dallas-Based Insurance Firm	156	Insurance	n/a
South-Central United States Pharmaceutical Laboratory	127	Manufacturing	n/a
Dallas-Based Telecommunications Manufacturer	137	Manufacturing	$11,500,000
Central United States Building Products Manufacturer	160	Manufacturing	$100,000,000
Data General	121	Manufacturing	$125,000
The Envelope Man	123	Manufacturing	$150,000
East Coast-Based Telecommunications Firm (Name Not Disclosed)	102	Manufacturing	$130,000,000
Division of Dallas-Based Telecommunications Manufacturer	118	Manufacturing	$1,150,000

(Continued on next page)

Table 12—Continued

Organization Name	Case ID	Industry	Total Estimated Cost of Quality
East Coast Pharmaceutical Firm	132	Manufacturing	$200,000
ULP, Des Plaines, Illinois	144	Manufacturing	$100,000,000
Alcoa	148	Manufacturing	n/a
Central United States Pharmaceutical Manufacturer	152	Manufacturing	n/a
Upper Midwest Steel Manufacturer	158	Manufacturing	$160,000,000
East Coast Healthcare Products Provider	114	Medical Supply	$600,000
McGaw, Inc.	106	Medical Supply	$7,500,000
$500 Million Mega Project in Trouble (Name Not disclosed)	162	n/a	$250,000,000
Case Deleted as Not Relevant	126	n/a	
Case Deleted as Not Relevant	146	n/a	
A Subsidiary of Southland Corp. (Merrit Foods)	125	Public Warehouse	$75,000
French SNCF Railway	109	Railroad	$400,000,000
Midwestern Real Estate Services Firm	131	Real Estate Services	n/a
Boston Market (Boston Chicken)	145	Restaurant	$15,000,000
Burlington Coat Factory	128	Retail Clothing	n/a
Large United States Service Firm	159	Services	$106,000,000
Independent Telephone Company	141	Telecommunications	n/a
East Coast-Based Long Distance Carrier	142	Telecommunications	$400,000
Cellular Service Subsidiary of Former Bell Operating Company	147	Telecommunications	$208,000,000
Information Industries, Inc.	122	Temporary Services	$175,000
Greyhound	110	Transportation	$3,500,000
National Trucking Services	130	Transportation	$500,000
Accor SA (France)	138	Travel Agency	$10,000,000
Southeastern U.S. Electric Utility	133	Utility	$100,000
Duke Power	153	Utility	$87,000,000

Notes

Section 1: Some High-Level Conclusions

1. *Client/server* generally refers to the new realm of technology that is based on a personal computer (PC) or other intelligent workstation rather than the traditional *dumb* terminal. The PC, or *client*, does most of its own processing and is provided data from various servers (larger computers) on the network. The largest single difference between client/server computing and previous minicomputer or mainframe systems is the *nonproprietary* nature of the hardware and software. Prior to client/server, which rose to prominence in the late 1980s and 1990s, most mainframe and minicomputer systems were based on proprietary hardware and software. This meant that the buyer was limited only to the products provided by a particular manufacturer. Personal computers, client/server systems, and systems based on the Unix operating system generally will work with a wide range of hardware and software products and are considered non-proprietary.

2. *Cost of quality*: Philip Crosby first defined this term in his 1979 book, *Quality Is Free*, published by McGraw-Hill. Crosby is regarded by many as one of the founding fathers of the quality movement in American business. In this book, Crosby's definition of cost of quality, which is *the cost of not doing things right the first time*, is used.

3. *Best Practices of Project Management Groups in Large, Functional Organizations*, Frank Toney and Ray Powers, 1997, Project Management Institute.

4. Commercial computer projects are defined as those projects that produce the type of systems that run major entities, normally tracking large volumes of people, dollars, and things. Examples would include accounting, manufacturing, distribution, and customer service systems. These projects are several orders of magnitude more difficult than the installation of simpler systems such as word processing, spread sheets, or electronic mail. They may also be referred to as *guts of the business systems*.

5. United States Department of Defense project success rate data was compiled through interviews with Charlie Jones, a twenty-year Pentagon veteran, now with the consulting firm of Robbins Gioia; with Dr. Lew Ireland, Project Technologies Corp., long-time defense industry participant, and PMI Fellow; and the writings of Quentin Fleming, a noted author and lecturer on the adoption of defense department techniques to commercial projects.

Commercial computer project data has been compiled from the studies summarized in Appendix A.

Section 2: The Current and Future State of Client/Server Project Outcomes

1. See #2 for Section 1. Crosby pioneered many of the concepts used in this book to help quantify the costs of not doing things right and to motivate people to change.

2. This term (cost of unrealized project objectives) was coined in collaboration with Howard Chamberlain, Dick Woodman, and Bert Canella of Texas A&M, the Department of Management (United States).

3. Al Lederer and Jayesh Prasad, University of Oakland, Rochester, Michigan, study published in *The Journal of the ACM*, February 1992, Nine Management Guidelines for Better Cost Estimating.

4. Roger Lowenstein, Intrinsic Value Column, *The Wall Street Journal,* July 25, 1996.

Section 3: Key Lessons from Other Industries and the Project Management Institute

1. See Endnote #2 for Section 1 and Endnote #1 for Section 2.

2. Quentin W. Fleming and Joel M. Koppelman, The Earned Value Body of Knowledge, *PM Network,* May 1996.

Section 4: To Investors: Awareness and Warning

1. In his sixth book called *Investor Capitalism*, from Basic Books (1996), Michael Useem describes the changes in ownership and governance of corporations over the last twenty years. His conclusions are credible and frightening. His work leads the study team to believe that many large corporations have such fundamental flaws in executive accountability and integrity that the recommendations of this text could never be implemented.

Section 5: Eight Principles for Turning Weaknesses into Competitive Advantage

1. This story is related in the manual for *The Ancient Art of War*, a computer simulation of the strategies and tactics for war prepared by Broderbund Software, San Rafael, California, United States (1981), Dave and Barry Murray, authors.

2. Herbert Simon's Nobel Prize-winning research and its application to information systems is described in *The Journal of Systems Management* (March 1991), Avoiding Group Induced Errors in System Development, by Michael Kettlehut.

3. Reported by Louis Fried of SRI International, as quoted in his *Computerworld* column (Fall 1994).

4. Study of Canadian Department of National Defense (DND) projects published in *Project Management Journal* (December 1995), The Role of Project Risk in Determining Project Management Approach, by Jean Couillard, University of Ottawa, Ontario, Canada.

5. The business process *lab* concept was advocated in Michael Hammer's Advanced Reengineering class, 1994.

6. *Earned Value Project Management* by Fleming and Koppelman, 1996, Project Management Institute.

7. GE case linking executive compensation to quality, *The Wall Street Journal*, Jan. 13, 1997, page 1. *The Wall Street Journal*, Fri., Sept. 29, 1995, page B1, Panhandle Eastern's Gainsharing Program.

Index

KEYWORDS

Avoiding Group Induced Errors in System Development: 234

Chaos: The Dollar Drain of IT Project Failures: 190

Human Thought Processes: 54

Management Meltdown: 188

Nine Management Guidelines for Better Cost Estimating: 189, 211, 234

Reengineering the Corporation: 176–177, 191

Upshot of Downsizing, The: 178

Users Share Stories of Downsizing Pros, Cons: 113

$500 Million Mega Project in Trouble: 89, 231

A

Accor SA (France): 123, 231

accountability: 12, 17, 35, 64, 65, 74, 77, 160, 161, 167, 234
    and client/server projects: 219
    and information systems projects: 158
    and WBS: 211
    avoiding: 5

breakdown of: 7
for all parties: 20, 151, 189
increased: 50
in Horror Stories: 88–89, 93, 97–102, 105–108, 116–121, 123–125, 127, 132, 136, 139
lack of: 28–29, 31–32, 34, 43
root issue problems: 217
standards: 62–63
third party: 199, 201
traps: 73

Aetna: 172

AIIM: 179

Alcoa: 133, 231

American Airlines: 78, 82, 91–92, 184, 230

American Management Systems: 96, 230

analyzing earnings forecasts: 46, 76

Ancient Art of War, The: 234

Andersen Consulting: 129, 134, 144, 230

Application Development Trends: 136, 183, 190

Art of War, The: 53

Associates Financial: 135, 230

authority to match responsibility: 17, 31, 151, 158

authority/responsibility: 5, 13, 20, 28, 62, 157–158, 160, 205, 216–217
    in Horror Stories: 72–73, 105–108, 120

B

Baker, Winston: 153–154, 157

Banco Itamarati: 183

basic project structure: 36

Bell Atlantic: 177

benchmark: 8

best practices: 5, 11, 153–154, 227, 233

Big Deal About Thinking Small, The: 87, 95, 96, 103, 112

bleeding edge: 159, 161, 165, 202, 203

Boston Market (Boston Chicken): 130, 231

British Columbia Hydro: 9, 37

Brunner, McLeod, and LaLiberte: 9, 37

Bruno, Mark: 153, 154

Budget (the company): 78, 82

budget(s): 5, 17, 19, 28, 35, 46, 49, 51, 58, 60–62, 70, 72–74, 76, 78, 151, 155–156, 158–159, 161, 163, 166

    in Horror Stories: 85, 87–88, 90, 94–95, 97, 100, 103–105, 109, 111, 120, 132, 135, 138, 142, 144, 146

    See also original budget

    See also project budget

bull's-eye: 154, 155

Burlington Coat Factory: 112, 231

business case: 19, 51, 60–61, 66–68, 70, 72–75, 155–157, 202, 216, 219

    in Horror Stories: 87–88, 93, 97, 99, 100, 104, 111, 132, 136, 139, 141, 144, 146

business unit manager: 24, 57, 62, 67, 74

business unit(s): 27, 28, 70, 133, 153–154, 157, 223

C

California Department of Motor Vehicles: 136, 230

Canadian Department of National Defense (DND): 24, 55, 234

Cannella, Bert: 225, 234

Carnegie-Mellon University: 154, 189

Cellular Service Subsidiary of Former Bell Operating Company: 132, 231

Central United States Building Products Manufacturer: 146, 230

Central United States Pharmaceutical Manufacturer: 137, 231

Chamberlain, Howard: 225, 234

champion for the cause: 70

Champy, James: 176, 177

Choyce, Russ: 68

CIGNA: 95, 230

CIO Magazine: 178, 196

Claremont Graduate School: 192, 225

client/server: 1, 7, 15, 27–30, 32, 34, 40, 46–47, 58, 64–65, 70, 73, 151–153, 161

    beta project: 97, 100, 104

    computer system: 29, 46, 221

    cost of quality: 16, 48

    experience: 31, 156

    Horror Stories: 16, 18, 19, 32, 37, 40, 44, 186, 229

    imaging system: 155, 168, 183

        project(s): 161, 168

        in Horror Stories: 94, 99, 107, 116–118, 124–125, 127–128, 141, 147

        technology: 151

    in Horror Stories: 82–86, 88, 90–91, 95–96, 101–105, 111–114, 120–121

    platform: 84, 98, 106, 108

    project management: 55, 63, 213, 227

    project managers: 67

    project outcome(s): 15, 30, 34, 41, 53, 57–58, 187, 234

        in Horror Stories: 105, 106, 108

project(s): 15–16, 24, 26, 29–33, 35, 39, 44, 46–49, 57–58, 63, 66, 71, 76, 151, 155, 157, 167, 185–188, 213, 219, 221–223, 227

software: 75

system(s): 193, 222, 233
    in Horror Stories: 93, 95, 129–130, 133, 139, 144

technology: 15, 32, 183

threat(s): 46, 76, 185

Comcar Industries, Inc.: 178

commercial computer projects: 8, 9, 193, 233

compensation: 64
    control: 62, 217
    system: 13
    See also executive compensation; worker compensation

competence issue(s): 5, 16, 23, 24

Computerworld: 77, 113, 129, 130, 133, 138, 148, 182, 183, 191, 234

concept phase: 36, 60

Concept, Development, Execution, Finish (C/D/E/F): 36, 59

Conner, Paul: 152, 155–156, 158–160, 165

Construction Industry Institute (CII): 11

consulting firm(s): 46, 50, 51, 55, 76, 120, 123, 124, 233

Cooke, Helen: 54, 225

Cooper, Dr. Ken: 50

core competency: 28, 29, 30

corporate earnings: 1

cost of quality: 1, 2, 16, 17, 18, 19, 20, 26, 28, 48, 56, 81, 150, 185, 186, 193, 219, 233

cost of quality review: 17, 48, 51, 56, 57, 67, 69, 70, 71, 73, 126

cost of unrealized project objectives: 17, 18, 234

Couillard, Jean: 234

Crosby, Philip: 16, 48, 66, 69, 78, 193, 233–234

D

Dallas Morning News, The: 82, 91, 140

Dallas/Fort Worth Area City Government: 128, 230

Dallas-Based Insurance Agency: 102, 230

Dallas-Based Insurance Firm: 141, 230

Dallas-Based Telecommunications Manufacturer: 121, 230

Data General: 104, 230

data processing: 136, 193

Day, Maguy: 91

deadlines: 7, 19–20, 28, 61–62, 72–74, 151, 155–156, 187–188, 200, 202–203, 216
    in Horror Stories: 85, 87–88, 90, 94–95, 97, 100, 103–104, 109, 120–121, 132, 138–139, 142, 144, 146

decision process: 54, 203

deliverables: 35–36, 61–62, 68, 155–156, 158, 161–163, 165–166, 216
    in Horror Stories: 83, 94–95, 97, 100, 104, 129, 132, 135–137, 144

Deutschebank Singapore: 182

development phase: 36, 60, 61

DFW Airport Board: 90, 230

Diamond Shamrock: 94, 230

direct project costs: 1, 16–17, 19, 185, 194

dirty tricks: 75

Division of Dallas-Based Telecommunications Manufacturer: 101, 230

downsizing: 7, 29, 31, 75, 178, 196–197, 210, 221, 223
    in Horror Stories: 87, 95–96, 103, 112–113

Duke Power: 138, 231

Dundee, Angelo: 40

E

earned benefits: 65

earned value: 44, 59, 61, 63–66, 68, 78, 150, 161–163, 165–167, 193–194, 219

    concept: 40, 65, 161, 165, 167

        project accounting and management: 34, 37, 63, 68, 72, 193–194

    method: 37, 43, 63

    tracking: 65, 167

    See also earned benefits; earned value method of project accounting and management

earned value method of project accounting and management: 34, 37, 68, 72, 168, 193, 194

    See also earned value

Earned Value Project Management: 194, 234

East Coast Health Care Firm: 86, 230

East Coast Healthcare Products Provider: 97, 231

East Coast Medical Testing Firm: 142, 230

East Coast Pharmaceutical Firm: 116, 231

East Coast-Based Long Distance Carrier: 127, 231

East Coast-Based Telecommunications Firm: 83, 230

EDS: 43, 225

Envelope Man, The: 106, 230

execution phase: 36, 61, 216

executive compensation: 7, 13, 234

executive roundtable: 2

executive sponsor: 20, 24, 28, 59–60, 63, 72–73, 77, 156, 161, 184, 200, 204, 207, 217, 223

    in Horror Stories: 88–89, 90, 101–102, 108, 115, 121–122, 144–145

    See also information systems executive sponsor

expertise: 29, 31, 35, 37, 55, 57–58, 68, 70, 75, 105, 154, 169, 223

exposure: 43, 46, 70, 194, 207

F

fads: 74–75

    see also fads, traps, and dirty tricks to avoid

Fads, traps, and dirty tricks to avoid: 36, 71, 243

    in Horror Stories: 82–149

    see also fads

FAOSP Group: 185, 187, 196, 222

Federal Agency, Austin, Texas: 125, 230

Federal Computer Week: 173

Federal Education Department, Finance Section: 173

Federal Reserve Bank of Dallas: 84, 230

Fidelity Investments: 139, 230

Financial Insurance Group: 173

finish phase: 61

Finley, Hal: 31, 169, 170, 171, 225

Fleming, Quentin W.: 37, 194, 225, 233, 234

Forbes, ASAP: 87, 95, 96, 103, 112

Fowler, Chris: 152, 156, 160, 165

FoxMeyer Corp. (Delta Project): 140, 230

French SNCF Railway: 72, 91, 231

Frito Lay, Accounts Payable: 181

G

Gardner, Rochelle: 188

Gillan, Clare M.: 190

Global Marine, Houston, Texas: 184

Greyhound: 93, 231

H

Haddon Jackson Associates: 9, 37

Hallmark Cards: 176

Hammer, Dr. Michael: 60, 68, 176–177, 191, 234

Hirsch, James S.: 139

Hoffman, Thomas: 113

Horror Story (ies): 1–3, 5, 8, 15–17, 19–20, 24, 26, 28, 34, 36, 40–41, 43–45, 47–49, 54, 56, 58–59, 64–65, 67, 70–72, 74–79, 81–149, 151, 185–186, 193–194, 229

   See also client/server Horror Stories

Hyatt Hotel: 78, 79, 184

I

IBM: 16, 77, 84, 113, 140

IBM Consulting Group: 188

Imaging in Insurance: 147

independent telephone company, an: 24, 126, 231

independent third party verification: 55

Information Industries, Inc.: 105, 231

information systems (IS): 33, 35, 46, 70, 73, 152–153, 156–159, 193, 197, 207, 213, 216, 222, 234

   departments: 27, 28, 57, 222–223

   executive sponsor: 156

   in Horror Stories: 83, 88, 95, 98, 111, 122, 135, 138, 140, 144

   industry(ies): 33–34, 37

   IS-driven project trap: 73, 111, 119

   manager: 62, 156

   project management: 31, 54–55

   project(s): 1, 65, 158, 162, 167, 189, 211

Information Technology (IT): 190, 193

Infotech Management: 68, 167, 225

InfoWorld: 85, 86

International Data Corporation (IDC): 190

Investor Capitalism: 234

investors: 32, 43, 145, 234

Ireland, Dr. Lew: 225, 233

J

Jenett, Eric: 9, 225

Johnson, Jim: 183, 190

Jones, Charlie: 225, 233

Journal of Systems Management, The: 234

Journal of the ACM, The: 189, 234

K

Kerzner's Project Triangle: 35

Kettlehut, Michael: 234

Khan, Genghis: 40

King of Wu: 53–54, 78

Koppelman, Joel M.: 194, 234

KPMG Peat Marwick, London: 30, 187, 196, 210–211

L

LA Insurance Company: 174

LaPlante, Alice: 87, 95–96, 103, 112

Large United States Service Firm: 144, 231

Lawerence, Garland: 9, 225

leadership integrity: 5, 17, 23–24, 26, 43, 50, 54–55, 61, 70, 72–73, 223

Lederer, Al: 24, 26, 30–31, 189, 211, 234

local area network (LAN): 194, 197, 206, 210–211

Lockheed: 103, 230

Lowenstein, Roger: 32, 234

M

mainframe: 7, 27, 31, 73, 75, 161,
164–165, 169, 178–179, 180, 193,
196, 198–199, 213, 221–223, 233
  computer: 30, 221
  financial data: 97, 100, 104
  in Horror Stories: 84, 87, 90–91,
    95–96, 105, 112, 114, 122, 128,
    132, 140, 148
  project: 30, 44, 187, 196, 210,
    221–223
  system: 88, 126, 136, 193, 221, 233
  to client/server: 101, 103, 112–113,
    121, 148, 178
Award, Malcolm Baldrige Quality: 153
Markus, Lynne: 192, 225
McGaw, Inc.: 87, 231
MCI: 180, 227
Mercer Management: 29
Merrit Foods, a Subsidiary of Southland
  Corp.: 108, 231
Midwestern Insurance Carrier: 85, 230
Midwestern Real Estate Services Firm:
  115, 231
Midwestern Reinsurance Firm: 124, 230
milestones: 155, 156, 201
military model: 40
millennium: 32
Miller, Joe: 43, 44, 225
Misery of Choice and Exponential
  Complexity: 222
mission-critical: 151, 187, 196–199, 204,
  206, 222
Murray, Dave and Barry: 234
Murrow, Kirk: 9

N

Napoleon: 40
National Trucking Services: 114, 231
Nations Bank: 98, 230

non-proprietary: 193–194, 233
Northern Trust, Financial Trades: 181

O

O'Leary, Meghan: 178
objective definition: 61, 136, 216
objectivity: 17, 62, 84, 117, 119, 151,
  155, 160, 216–217
  safety valve: 70
  traps: 73
  standards: 61
Open Computing: 123, 188, 189
open systems: 153, 187, 194, 196–199,
  201–202, 205–206, 208, 210, 213
  project management: 200–201
  project(s): 151, 196–199, 201–202,
    204–205, 207–211, 213
  project outcomes: 197, 199, 209
operations-driven industries: 35
original budget(s): 1–2, 16–19, 32, 81,
  88, 96, 185, 194, 215
Oryx: 175
ownership involvement: 51, 53–54

P

Panhandle Eastern: 234
peer review: 66
pilot: 49, 58–59, 61, 66, 74, 78, 203
  in Horror Stories: 88–89, 94, 97, 100,
    104–105, 107, 118, 124, 127,
    129, 132, 147
  project: 57–59, 74, 147, 202
Plaza Home Funding: 174
PM Network: 68, 150, 168, 194, 234
Porter, Michael: 4
Powers, Ray: 2, 233
PPP (Largest Health Insurance Provider in
  United Kingdom): 147, 230
Prasad, Jayesh: 189, 234

process maps: 64, 148

process steps: 64

project accounting and management standards: 58–59, 70

project budget(s): 1, 16–17, 19, 48, 60–61, 157, 161, 186

project executive: 5

project foundation standards: 32

Project Management Body of Knowledge (PMBOK): 37, 40, 153

Project Management Institute (PMI): 8–9, 11, 24, 29, 31, 33–34, 36–37, 54–55, 58, 60, 67, 150–153, 161–162, 167, 194–195, 197, 211, 213, 225, 227, 233–234

Project Management Journal: 151, 194–195, 234

project management professional (PMP): 1, 37, 46, 58, 65, 194

project management professional (PMP) certification: 37, 161, 167, 194

project management software: 40, 68, 71

project management training: 24, 31, 40, 197

project manager (italic type): 20, 31, 38–39, 67, 72–73, 207

    in Horror Stories: 102, 105, 116–117, 120–121

    See also traps, mega-, project manager versus *project manager*

project manager (regular type): 5, 7, 12, 19–20, 24, 26, 28, 30–31, 35, 38–40, 55, 58, 60, 62–63, 67–68, 70–73, 75, 77–78, 153–155, 158, 161, 167, 181, 184, 186, 201, 204–205, 208, 216–217, 222–223

    in Horror Stories: 88, 90, 93–94, 100–102, 105, 108–109, 111, 115–117, 120–121, 126–128, 139, 141, 145

    See also traps, mega-, project manager versus *project manager*

project office: 12, 13, 31, 65, 70–72

project outcome correlation ratings: 196, 198, 199

Project Technologies Corp.: 225, 233

project-driven industries: 34, 35, 50, 51, 58, 68, 72, 76, 77, 229

prototype: 60–61, 74, 164, 166

prototype/pilot trap: 74

    in Horror Stories: 88–89, 94, 97, 100, 104–105, 107, 118, 124, 127, 129, 139, 145, 147

Public Service Electric & Gas (PSE&G), Newark, New Jersey: 179

Q

quality, cost of: *See* cost of quality

quality review, cost of: *See* cost of quality review

Quality Is Free: 16, 33, 48, 66, 69, 78, 193, 233

quantify(ing): 1, 17, 185, 205, 234

Quasi-Governmental Agency: 72, 120, 230

questionnaire: 20, 28, 47, 56, 185, 198, 201, 215

R

Raymond James Corp.: 176

reengineering: 15, 29, 33–35, 48, 57–59, 64, 66, 68, 70, 74, 88–89, 153, 168, 175–177, 191–192, 219, 223, 227, 234

Reinsurance Firm: 119, 230

Resource Magazine: 172

responsibility: 5, 13, 28, 34, 39, 41, 53–54, 63, 72–75, 78, 151, 157, 166, 205, 217, 222, 227

    in Horror Stories: 101, 107, 115, 124, 144–145

    See also authority to match responsibility

responsibility/authority: 204–205

    See also authority/responsibility

right people/right motives/right actions:
   in Horror Stories: 82–149
   traps: 186, 216–217, 243
Rogers Group: 113, 230
root issue scorecard: 19, 81
   See also root issues
root issues: 8, 16, 17, 19, 20, 21, 23, 26,
   31, 39, 40, 47, 81, 168, 195, 223,
   227
   in Horror Stories: 129, 130, 149
   See also root issue scorecard
root-of-all-evil: *See* traps, mega-, root-of-
   all-evil

S

safety valve: 51, 55, 58, 63, 67, 70–72,
   217
schedule(s): 61, 153, 156–157, 160, 184,
   202, 216
   in Horror Stories: 114, 119, 121,
   136–137
scope: 7, 19, 28, 36, 44, 61–62, 65, 68,
   72, 74, 151, 153, 155–158, 161,
   166–167, 169, 181, 186, 201–203,
   205, 216
   in Horror Stories: 82–83, 85, 87–88,
   90, 94–95, 97, 100, 103–106,
   109, 116, 121, 127–128, 132,
   134–139, 142, 144–146, 148,
self-interest: 24, 26, 72, 88, 219
Semiconductor Group: 153, 154, 155,
   157
Settle, Ben: 68, 167, 225
shareholder: 5, 15, 17, 19, 24, 26, 37,
   46, 50–51, 53–56, 59, 62–64, 66–67,
   70–72, 74, 76–79, 185–186, 213,
   217, 219
   in Horror Stories: 122, 144–145
shareholder interest
   See traps, mega-, putting self interest
   over shareholder interest
Sigle, Stan: 152, 155–156, 158–160, 167

Simon, Herbert: 54, 234
Software Engineering Institute (SEI): 16,
   153–154, 189
Software Productivity Research (SPR): 16,
   188
solution design: 19, 61, 146, 151,
   155–156, 159, 216
South-Central United States Oil and Gas
   Firm #2: 100, 230
South-Central United States Oil and Gas
   Firm #3: 107, 230
South-Central United States
   Pharmaceutical Laboratory: 111, 230
South-Central United States Retail Energy
   Products Firm: 99, 230
Southeastern United States Electric Utility:
   117, 231
specific interest group (SIG): 33, 58, 246
Sperry Univac: 77, 227
sponsor: 20, 57, 62, 90, 100, 111, 119,
   145, 216, 223
   See also executive sponsor(s)
St. Vincent's Hospital: 183
staff manager: 57
Stafford, Jean: 148–149
stand-alone output: 34
Standish Group International: 190
stock price: 26, 44–45, 79, 219
strategy: 4, 29, 40, 119, 157, 177, 222
success story(ies): 31, 34, 37, 63, 75,
   150–151, 157, 168, 182, 196
Success Story(ies: 15, 56, 78, 150, 161,
   171–184
Sugar Ray Leonard: 40
Sun Tzu: 40, 52–54, 57, 59, 78
Supporting output: 34
system integrator(s): 107, 125, 173, 194

T

Taco Bell: 177
tactics: 7, 30, 40, 234

Texas A&M: 225, 234

Texas Commerce Bank: 15, 175

Texas Instruments (TI): 31, 34, 37, 63, 150–161, 165–171, 179–180, 225, 227

third party: 47, 55, 56, 58, 61, 72, 77–78, 105–106, 169, 201, 207, 216

   independent: 40, 55–56, 58–59, 63, 65, 67, 70, 72, 77

   monitoring: 50–51, 53, 219

   See also independent third party verification

Toney, Dr. Frank: 2, 233

traps: 36, 67, 71–73, 75, 147, 203

   mega-traps: 72

      being forced to act: 72

      Project Manager versus *Project Manager:* 72, 73, 102, 116, 117, 120, 121

      putting self interest over shareholder interest: 72

      root-of-all-evil: 36, 59, 72

         in Horror Stories: 103, 109, 111–114, 116, 118, 120–121, 123–125, 127, 129

   See also objectivity traps; accountability traps; dirty tricks; right people/right motives/right actions traps; prototype/pilot trap; dirty tricks

true power: 55

U

ULP: 129, 231

United States Air Force: 37

United States Department of Defense (DOD): 55, 194, 233

University of Oakland: 24, 30–31, 189, 225, 234

unrealized project objectives, cost of: *See* cost of unrealized project objectives

Upper Midwest Steel Manufacturer: 143, 231

Useem, Michael: 234

user group: 156, 158

V

Very Large Central United States Bank: 88, 230

ViewStar: 151, 156, 159–161, 165

W

Wall Street Journal, The: 29, 48, 139, 196, 234

warm-fuzzy: 77

West Coast Savings and Loan: 118, 230

wide area network (WAN): 159, 194, 199, 211

Woodman, Dick: 225, 234

work authorization process: 65, 68

work breakdown structure (WBS): 55, 60, 68, 161–163, 167, 194, 201, 204–205, 211

work packages: 60–61, 72, 74, 194, 216

   in Horror Stories: 83, 85, 88, 94–95, 97, 100, 103–104, 136, 139, 142, 144, 148

worker compensation: 13

workflow: 115, 119, 128, 169, 170, 181

World Corp.: 178

WPS SAS, Argentina State-Owned Oil and Gas Company: 182

Y–Z

year 2000: 7, 32, 138, 227

Zells, Lois: 58

Upgrade Your Project Management Knowledge with First Class Publications from PMI

A Guide to the Project Management Body of Knowledge

The basic management reference for everyone who works on projects. Serves as a tool for learning about the generally accepted knowledge and practices of the profession. As "management by projects" becomes more and more a recommended business practice worldwide, the *PMBOK Guide* becomes an essential source of information that should be on every manager's bookshelf. Available in hardcover or paperback, the *PMBOK Guide* is an official standards document of the Project Management Institute.

ISBN: 1-880410-12-5 (paperback), 1-880410-13-3 (hardcover)

Interactive PMBOK Guide

This CD-ROM makes it easy for you to access the valuable information in PMI's *A Guide to the Project Management Body of Knowledge*. Features hypertext links for easy reference—simply click on underlined works in the text, and the software will take you to that particular section in the *PMBOK Guide*. Minimum system requirements: 486 PC, 8MB RAM, 10MB free disk space, CD-ROM drive, mouse or other pointing device, and Windows 3.1 or greater.

PMBOK Review Package

This "Box of Books" offers you a set of materials that supplements the *PMBOK Guide* in helping you develop a deeper understanding of the Project Management Body of Knowledge. These important and authoritative publications offer the depth and breadth you need to learn more about project integration, scope, time, cost, quality, human resources, communications, risk, and procurement management. Includes the following titles: *Project Management Casebook; Human Resource Skills for the Project Manager; Project and Program Risk Management; Quality Management for Projects & Programs; PMBOK Q&A; Managing the Project Team; Organizing Projects for Success;* and *Principles of Project Management*.

Managing Projects Step-by-Step™

Follow the steps, standards, and procedures used and proven by thousands of professional project managers and leading corporations. This interactive multimedia CD-ROM based on PMI's *A Guide to the Project Management Body of Knowledge* will enable you to customize, standardize, and distribute your project plan standards, procedures, and methodology across your entire organization. Multimedia illustrations using 3-D animations and audio make this perfect for both self-paced training or for use by a facilitator.

PMBOK Q&A

Use this handy pocket-sized question-and-answer study guide to learn more about the key themes and concepts presented in PMI's international standard, *A Guide to the Project Management Body of Knowledge*. More than 160 multiple-choice questions with answers (referenced to the *PMBOK Guide*) help you with the breadth of knowledge needed to understand key project management concepts.

ISBN: 1-880410-21-4

PMI Proceedings Library CD-ROM

This interactive guide to PMI's Annual Seminars & Symposium Proceedings offers a powerful new option to the traditional methods of document storage and retrieval, research, training, and technical writing. Contains complete paper presentations from PMI '91–PMI '97. Full text-search capability, convenient on-screen readability, and PC/Mac compatibility.

PMI Publications Library CD-ROM

Using state-of-the-art technology, PMI offers complete articles and information from its major publications on one CD-ROM, including *PM Network* (1991–97), *Project Management Journal* (1991–97), and *A Guide to the Project Management Body of Knowledge*. Offers full text-search capability and indexing by *PMBOK Guide* knowledge areas. Electronic indexing schemes and sophisticated search engines help to find and retrieve articles quickly that are relevant to your topic or research area.

Also Available from PMI

Achieving the Promise of Information Technology
Ralph Sackman
ISBN: 1-880410-03-6

Leadership Skills for Project Managers
Editors' Choice Series
Edited by Jeffrey Pinto and Jeffrey Trailer
ISBN: 1-880410-49-4

The Virtual Edge
Margery Mayer
ISBN: 1-880410-16-8

ABCs of DPC
PMI's Design-Procurement-Construction Specific Interest Group
ISBN: 1-880410-07-9

Project Management Casebook
Edited by David Cleland, Karen Bursic, Richard Puerzer, and A. Yaroslav Vlasak
ISBN: 1-880410-45-1

Project Management Casebook Instructor's Manual
Edited by David Cleland, Karen Bursic, Richard Puerzer, and A. Yaroslav Vlasak
ISBN: 1-880410-18-4

PMI Book of Project Management Forms
Spiral bound   Diskette version 1.0
ISBN: 1-880410-31-1   ISBN: 1-880410-50-8

Principles of Project Management
John Adams et al.
ISBN: 1-880410-30-3

Organizing Projects for Success
Human Aspects of Project Management Series, Volume 1
Vijay Verma
ISBN: 1-880410-40-0

Human Resource Skills for the Project Manager
Human Aspects of Project Management Series, Volume 2
Vijay Verma
ISBN: 1-880410-41-9

Managing the Project Team
Human Aspects of Project Management Series, Volume 3
Vijay Verma
ISBN: 1-880410-42-7

Earned Value Project Management
Quentin Fleming, Joel Koppelman
ISBN: 1-880410-38-9

Value Management Practice
Michel Thiry
ISBN: 1-880410-14-1

Decision Analysis in Projects
John Schuyler
ISBN: 1-880410-39-7

The World's Greatest Project
Russell Darnall
ISBN: 1-880410-46-X

Power & Politics in Project Management
Jeffrey Pinto
ISBN: 1-880410-43-5

Best Practices of Project Management Groups in Large Functional Organizations
Frank Toney, Ray Powers
ISBN: 1-880410-05-2

Project Management in Russia
Vladimir I. Voropajev
ISBN: 1-880410-02-8

Experience, Cooperation and the Future:
The Global Status of the Project Management Profession
ISBN: 1-880410-04-4

A Framework for Project and Program Management Integration
R. Max Wideman
ISBN: 1-880410-01-X

Quality Management for Projects & Programs
Lewis R. Ireland
ISBN: 1-880410-11-7

Project & Program Risk Management
R. Max Wideman
ISBN: 1-880410-06-0

Order online at www.pmibookstore.org

To order by mail:

PMI Headquarters
Four Campus Boulevard
Newtown Square, Pennsylvania 19073-3299 USA

Or call 610-356-4600 or fax 610-356-4647